YESTERDAY:
The Search Continues

By

DAVID TURNER

INKWATER
PRESS

PORTLAND • OREGON
INKWATERPRESS.COM

*Scan QR Code to learn
more about this title*

Publisher: Inkwater Press

Paperback
ISBN-13 978-1-62901-173-8 | ISBN-10 1-62901-173-8

Kindle
ISBN-13 978-1-62901-174-5 | ISBN-10 1-62901-174-6

All paper is acid free and meets all ANSI standards for archival quality paper.

1 3 5 7 9 10 8 6 4 2

This book is dedicated to all those who asked...
"When are you going to write a second book?"

Yesterday's ordinary happenings become today's treasured memories.

Contents

YESTERDAY: THE SEARCH CONTINUES

Coming of Age

THE CITY OF TORONTO CLAIMED BUT 150,000 RESIDENTS IN 1885, the year my grandfather William Carruthers was born. Just three years earlier his parents had landed on Canadian shores from their home in Scotland. Although my grandfather was an agriculturist at heart, often spending his summers working and vacationing at his uncle's farm in the Beaver Valley near Kimberley in Grey County, Toronto was home, and its growing stature guaranteed plenty to keep a lad Will's age occupied.

Union Station was a favourite hang-out, where he'd sit fascinated for hours watching the never-ending procession of freight and passengers trains arriving and departing from the giant rail terminal, dreaming of all the cities and towns across North America where the huge coal burners might be heading. In fact it was as recently as 1885, the year Will was born, that the last spike had been driven, thus bringing to reality Prime Minister John A. MacDonald's dream of uniting Canada by rail from Atlantic to Pacific.

One of the greatest events in young Will's life was the day Toronto changed over from gas lighting to electric power. Adam Beck, the pioneer of electricity in Ontario, had overseen construction of a huge hydro-electric facility at Niagara Falls capable of supplying the needs of Southwestern Ontario, and particularly the city of Toronto. Until this time, all streetlights were gas powered. Every evening at dusk, lamplighters complete with ladders would make their rounds, stopping at each lamp post to ignite the flame. Next morning at dawn their steps would be retraced and the lamps extinguished.

My grandfather recalled that summer evening in 1896, standing with his family among thousands of fellow Torontonians, when Adam Beck announced the city's entry into this new era of electricity. With the pull of a single switch, the city's downtown corridors were instantly illuminated. Compared to the yellow flickering flame of the gas lamps, these new electrically powered lights seemed a world apart.

An 1898 back page newspaper item that at the time probably caused little stir proclaimed that a Hamilton, Ontario man, John Moodie, had become Canada's first motorist by purchasing a new Winton automobile. In Europe the automobile had been gaining ground, albeit slowly, but in North America the contraption was little more than a curiosity.

The chief mode of transportation in Toronto as well as every other city across the Dominion in the 1890s was the bicycle. Everyone it seemed owned one of these two-wheeled wonders. On downtown streets on any given day, swarms of bicycles darted among the carriages and streetcars, and hundreds could be counted cruising High Park any summer Sunday afternoon.

On the subject of streetcars...this passenger transporter was a marvel in its own right, a vehicle having the capabilities of propelling itself on a pair of steel wheels while utilizing power from an overhead electrical system.

Up until this point, all Toronto trolleys had been powered by horses. My grandfather had seen plenty of these units operating on the city's gravel and dirt streets, which during periods of sustained rain became quagmires capable of sinking wagons to their axles. Toronto wasn't known as "Muddy York" for nothing! The area between the rails however was paved or bricked, at least providing solid footing for the horses drawing the trolleys.

Horses were relieved of duty every two hours and replaced by a fresh team, but the drivers probably could have used a reprieve as well. They were expected to stand for twelve to fourteen hours a day exposed to sleet, snow, rain, dust, and mud. This was before unions, so every issue raised by employees for better working conditions was a major and usually hopeless battle. Drivers pleaded for stools but management claimed they would be "lulled to sleep." When asked for glass partitions on the front of the coaches for a defense against the elements, they were informed the glass would become caked with mud, snow, and ice, resulting in drivers "driving blind."

With no shelter from environmental concerns, hence no heat inside the coach itself, a common practice was to spread straw along the floor of the coach to aid in keeping passengers' feet from freezing. Often the driver himself could be seen standing in a straw-filled box; that was as luxurious as it got.

Conductors fared little better. The coaches were open on both sides with seats extending across the entire width. A narrow plank stretched the length of the vehicle, on which the conductor maneuvered to collect fares and punch tickets. Because of the precarious footing it wasn't uncommon in especially wet or freezing weather for a conductor to slip from his plank walkway and fall headfirst into the street. But now this phenomenon known as electricity would scatter the horse-drawn streetcar to extinction, replaced by a vast network of wires, generators, controllers, conductors, and electric motors.

As with anything new, there were detractors. The *Toronto Telegram,* one of the city's two leading daily papers, feared some major malfunction would electrocute the entire city's population. Within a year, however, Toronto was totally electric and the last horse-drawn trolley headed west with the sun.

Ontario's capital was steadily moving towards the 20th century but there were still solid signs of the old ways, like the numerous water troughs placed strategically around the city to satisfy the thirst of the thousands of horses that continued to walk the streets. Actually the water was available for anyone or anything that happened by...people, horses, cats, and dogs all found the troughs convenient. There was nothing unusual about seeing a horse, dog, or human tanking up at the same time. In at least a stab at hygienic exercise, the general public were provided with a cup that hung on a chain above the wooden trough.

Another regular occurrence was the weekly parade of livestock making their way towards St. Lawrence Market. On market day it was a common sight along the city's corridors to witness a herd of cattle ambling along among the carriages, streetcars, and bicycles.

When Will Carruthers hit the 20-year milestone, he was still unclear as to future plans. He'd been spending his summers in the country labouring at his uncle's farm, whereas winters were spent in the city performing odd jobs, mostly carpentry oriented.

It was during this period that Will's father, after being employed for several years at Massey-Harris, decided it was time for a change of venue and purchased a general store in Dufferin County near Orangeville, Ontario.

My grandfather had been pondering the notion for some time to go west, as friends had settled near Weyburn, Saskatchewan, a few years earlier and promised employment if he chose to come. With the family relocating, Will figured it was time to act on his dream.

It was a long journey to the Canadian West in 1905. Initially the passengers discussed the romantic ruggedness and beauty of northern pine, crystal clear lakes, and sheer rock cuts. Soon, however, the fascination began to wane and the view simply became rocks, trees, and lakes, and more rocks, trees, and lakes.

When Will Carruthers first set eyes on Saskatchewan, all the books read plus his own expectations became reality. Hour after hour as the train rolled along, he gazed across the endless expanse of prairie flatland, mesmerized by miles of wheat just beginning to turn that brilliant shade of amber for which it was famous.

My grandfather spent four years in Saskatchewan and that four-year span proved a limitless educational exercise for the young man, witnessing the best and worst of the challenges of prairie life.

Nothing seemed certain in the West. The wheat and barley crops would show nothing but promise, only to be stripped clean by a hail storm in a matter of minutes or ravaged by a grasshopper infestation. Dry summers heightened the fear of prairie fires, where just a spark from a steam tractor's exhaust or cinder from the smokestack of a passing train could scorch hundreds of acres to blackness in minutes.

The frightening fury of a prairie blizzard that could last for days – when you would have to literally tie a rope between the house and barn for a guide, otherwise you could get completely disoriented, so severe were the storms. In one of his frequent letters home, Will had written, "I have nothing but respect and admiration for the tireless struggle of these prairie settlers. They are indeed the true pioneers of this great country."

A Changing World

WHEN MY GRANDFATHER WILL CARRUTHERS LEFT TORONTO to work at the wheat harvest in Saskatchewan in the summer of 1905, he had no firm commitment as to how long he'd stay. As it turned out he spent four years in the Canadian West, returning in the autumn of 1909.

Although many things had remained the same in his home city, change was coming. Bicycles and horse-drawn buggies were still the predominant transportation, but young Will was surprised at the number of automobiles travelling city streets. Formerly, horse manure was the predominant odour in the air, but now fumes from these new gasoline engines left a very different atmospheric aroma.

Most of these motorized vehicles were very expensive and out of reach for the average labourer but times were changing. An inventor by the name of Ransom Olds had built the first relatively inexpensive automobile several years earlier, and his Oldsmobile had become the most popular car to date. The previous autumn another inventive mind had introduced a low-priced auto which he claimed would put a car into the hands of every working man in North America. His name was Henry Ford.

Even Toronto's favourite department store, the T. Eaton Company, was now using a few Packard trucks for their expanding delivery service. As the city spread further abroad, the famous "Eaton Greys" had become less practical. Will had enjoyed passing the Yonge Street store in the early morning hours as the beautiful animals stood in a row stretching the length of the building, waiting to depart with their cargo-laden wagons. Eaton owned more than 200 horses, which took part in countless parades throughout the years transporting various dignitaries.

Standing out in particular in Will's mind was the time Canada's Governor-General visited the city and was to be drawn by carriage down Yonge Street to the Parliament Buildings. The assigned horse for the event, used to turning into the stables as it passed the Eaton store, did just that, giving the Governor-General an unscheduled tour of the building.

As the Packard truck passed by with the familiar name on the door, it was with a twinge of sadness Will realized this magnificent part of Toronto's history was slowly slipping away.

An item of a more personal nature captured Will's attention upon his return from the West. He discovered that a girl he'd met years ago while working at his uncle's farm in Grey County was now here in Toronto.

It was quite common in that era for unmarried women to hire themselves out as farm labourers during the busy haying and harvesting seasons, and it was under these circumstances Will had met Rebecca Turner. "Reba," as she preferred to be called, was now working as a sales clerk at Eaton's Department Store. Although not perfect, Eaton's had earned a reputation as a fair employer over the years. When 10- and 12-hour days, six days a week, were common, Timothy Eaton surprised the rest of the business community when he began closing his store at six, and noon on Saturdays. A quarter century would pass before many companies adopted similar schedules. And in an era when dark, dingy, smoked-stained factories were the norm, Eaton believed that bright, well-lit spacious work areas provided a more comfortable environment, hence better productivity.

Since his return from the West, Will had worked at a couple of part-time factory jobs and for a few weeks as a carpenter's assistant. Although he favoured agriculture, carpentry was a close second as a career choice. My grandfather had always maintained the desire, but honestly was never able to follow through with the actual talent needed to make carpentry his lifetime trade.

Will's father had begun at Massey-Harris...or Massey Manufacturing Co. as it was then known...in 1887; with the exceptionof a short stint operating a store he'd spent his working career there and suggested his son apply for a position.

The Massey-Harris building in 1910 covered an entire city block and right in the midst of all the red brick, a small white section stood out in contrast. During an interview, Will had been shown through the interior of this building and learned it contained nothing but cream separators in various degrees of manufacture. It would be from this department that my grandfather would earn his living for the next thirty years.

When Will Carruthers began his tenure with Massey-Harris, the company could best be described as in transition...between the ever expanding farm machinery market of the late 1800s and the troubling historical period that lay ahead. In the coming years, a world war, the agricultural recession of the 1920s, and a crippling depression in the 1930s would test Canada's premier company to the limit.

But these factors seemed far away in 1910. Generally things were still in an upward cycle. Toronto's population had doubled again in the past dozen years largely due to a heavy immigration flow. The automobile was now taken very seriously and for the first time, dealer franchises outnumbered livery stables. Names like Locomobile, Gasmobile, Winton, Ford, and Buick, as well as the Canadian-built Columbia, McLaughlin, and Russell, motored the arteries of Toronto, sometimes unbelievably with women at the controls!

An event that garnered plenty of publicity for Toronto, and particularly for the T. Eaton Company, was Canada's first escalator. This gadget provided Torontonians hours of entertainment as they lined up to look at the wondrous invention. That's mostly all they did...as the majority were too frightened to ride, figuring they would somehow become entangled and disappear into the machine's mechanism. To combat these fears, Timothy Eaton sent some of his braver employees to ride the escalator for sustained periods, impressing upon onlookers its safety. Another incentive was offering a free ice cream cone to anyone who did ride to the top. Before long, customers were actually shopping at the Eaton store just to ride the magic sliding staircase.

Now that my grandfather had found employment that seemingly might lead to a career, he figured he could support a wife, so in December 1910, Will Carruthers and Reba

Turner were married. Their wedding, like most in their day, had been simple, an attendant each for witness and a minister to solemnize the affair.

Following the ceremony the couple left on their honeymoon to Grey County, making stops at Will's relatives at Kimberley and Reba's at Eugenia. This area of Grey County, with its rolling hills and breathtaking view of the Beaver Valley, is a beautiful setting...three seasons of the year. In the middle of December, however, when the only mode of travel was horse and sleigh, I'd imagine it to be rather inhospitable.

Several factors far removed from everyday happenings were beginning to take shape across the Atlantic Ocean that would change the course of world history. What simply started as Eastern European squabbles over land claims accelerated until Germany, Austria-Hungary, and Turkey, known as the "Central Powers," declared war on Russia and some neighbouring countries in the summer of 1914; France and Belgium were allies of Russia, so when they became involved, England had no choice but to defend her neighbours across the English Channel. As Canada was a Dominion of Great Britain, we were in the fight as well.

My grandfather was as ready to join as the next man, despite a regular job and growing family. Will and Reba had a two-year-old daughter (my mother), and Reba was pregnant when the call-up was declared. However there'd be nothing wrong with a few months off, as that's all it would take to win this war.

According to attestation records, Will passed the army physical but was excluded from service. The fact that he had a young family might have had some bearing. My mother claimed the reason for denial was fallen arches. Will's malady, more frequently referred to as "flat feet," would not likely exclude anyone from service today, but in 1914, when marching was a major factor, it was a different story.

Whatever the judgment, Will Carruthers spent the duration of the war training troops. Before long he gained Sergeant-Major status and continued to ready recruits for the ever-expanding army in Europe. Canada's armed forces were pretty dismal in this period. Total army recruits in 1914 numbered 3100 while our navy countered with two ships! Three months after war was declared, thousands of Canadian enlisted men were still wearing civilian garb and substituting broomsticks for rifles. Another three months passed before the first contingent made its way across the Channel to France.

The struggle the Canadian regiments joined had already settled into a pattern that would last not months but years. Both the Central Powers and Allied Forces had built miles and miles of trenches, and in these flooded, mud-caked, disease-ridden ditches, tens of thousands of soldiers spent the next four years, separated by just a few hundred yards from their enemy in the area known as "no man's land."

Although some training was done at the Exhibition Grounds on Toronto's waterfront, most of my grandfather's recruits were trained at Camp Borden Armed Forces Base near Barrie, Ontario. In this period of our military history, soldiers practiced their marching abilities incessantly; as well many hours were filled with the labour of polishing leather and shining brass...especially the latter. The buttons that lined the front of their uniforms, the buttons that secured each pocket, the buttons on each sleeve, and the brass buckles on their boots and belt and hats all had to be polished until glowing, as inspections were frequent.

Puttees also claimed their share of labour...puttees, a long continuous strip of cloth about four inches wide that a soldier wrapped around his leg, starting at the ankle and spiralling upward to the knee. Thick wool socks overlapped the puttees and heavy regulation boots completed the dress code. The reasoning for the puttees was to hinder the entry of moisture and provide support for the calves on the lengthy marches that soldiers were expected to endure.

Not only did brass have to sparkle but puttees had to be wrapped just right, with every overlap of the cloth the exact same distance apart. When the soldiers were shipped overseas and became embroiled in combat on ground that was a constant quagmire, their perfectly wrapped puttees and shiny brass buttons, as well as all those endless hours spent honing their impeccable marching abilities, must have seemed beyond ridiculous.

Seventy thousand recruits marched off to war from the city of Toronto alone; 10,000 never returned. Sixty thousand Canadian soldiers died in that war. Another 170,000 would spend the rest of their lives in veterans hospitals across the country after being shipped home armless, legless, blind, poisoned by chemical gas, shell-shocked, or simply insane.

As my grandfather and hundreds like him continued to ready the thousands of recruits for duty overseas, they couldn't have imagined in their worst dreams the kind of hell into which these carefree young men were headed.

Weren't they the fine boys, you never saw the beat
of them
As they went marching off to battle with their
throats bronze bare.

They were fighting fit and mirth mad there was
    music in the steppin';
Singing down a long white road all the afternoon.
And it only seems like yesterday, that great glad
    sight of them
Singing on to battle as the sky grew black and black
Strangers in a strange land, miles and miles and
    miles of them;
Now you just whistle "Tipperary" and it all comes
    back.

From Robert Service, "Tipperary Days"

All in a Day's Work

To my father, who was a teenager in the 1920s, its pace may have appeared leisurely and unhurried…however, agricultural mechanization was indeed creeping down the concessions of Artemesia Township during the decade following World War One.

The sickle mower, dump rake, and hay loader had lessened considerably the time involved to get a crop to the barn. The hay loader had especially eased the burden of transporting hay from field to wagon. It was still no picnic, however, stacking and levelling a load, particularly on a windy day, especially for the person at the front of the wagon. The cascading hay from the loader showed no mercy, enveloping the operator in chaff, dust, leaves, and weed seeds.

At the barn a large steel two-pronged fork operated on a wooden track suspended from the barn peak. Powered by horses and guided by human hand through a series of ropes and pulleys, the fork was lowered into the loaded wagon. At that point, tines on the bottom of the fork pivoted at a right angle, allowing a "jag of hay" to be lifted and transported to the haymow, then released wherever desired by another simple pull of a rope...a giant stride forward from the previous generation when every wagon load was emptied and stacked in the haymow one single forkful at a time.

Harvest had seen great improvement as well in time and labour efficiency during the previous generation. A scythe in the hands of skilled personnel may have been impressive to watch, as the smooth strokes of the razor-sharp blade sliced the ripened grain. However, anyone familiar with back pain, try to imagine the aches our forefathers endured, standing in a slightly bent position for hours on end as they slowly inched their way across the field.

But then appeared that marvellous invention of Cyrus McCormick, the reaper; followed by an even greater invention...the binder, which not only cut the grain but bundled and tied the crop into convenient sized sheaves that could be transformed into a pyramid known as a "stook."

As a kid my father had looked forward to harvest season with great anticipation. Now that he was older and had to share in the daily labour, harvest had lost some of its bloom, but there was still something exciting about the day the threshing machine arrived on the scene.

Josh Dobson was the custom thresher for the immediate Artemesia Township area. What Josh didn't know about threshing machines simply wasn't worth knowing, although his knowledge had exacted a high price. Early in his career, he'd broken the most important rule of agricultural maintenance by adjusting a machine while it was operating. That mistake had cost him his right hand, replaced by a steel hook. A steel hook as a kid I found absolutely fascinating! So unique it had the strength to cut wire yet was sensitive enough to pick up the most delicate china cup.

Josh always brought a hired man to look after the tractor; keeping an eye on oil pressure, engine temperature, fuel level, etc., while he supervised the thresher. Checking chains and belts for tightness, monitoring bearings for excessive heat and regular lubrication of anything that moved kept Josh occupied. One of the most important jobs in keeping the thresher operating smoothly was a good "feeder"... someone who could satisfy the ravenous appetite of the machine with a steady flow of sheaves for hours on end.

Without a doubt, the person tramping the straw mow had the worst of all possible jobs. Straw by its very nature light and fluffy has to be tramped or the mow would fill up in no time. This ordeal generally fell to the owner of the farm...or his son. A straw mow while the thresher was in operation was an indescribably dirty place and my father had spent more hours than he cared to recall in the midst of these dust storms. Between dust and rust and smut and seemingly millions of weed seeds, the air was almost impossible to breathe.

Occasionally if the day was hot enough and the dust thick enough, the "feeder" might be overcome with compassion and while Josh wasn't looking, place a few sheaves in backwards, thus plugging up the machine. The fifteen or twenty minutes needed to clear the thresher would be sufficient to allow the dust to settle and the poor bastard in the mow to resume breathing.

Josh Dobson was committed to gasoline power by this time, but my father could easily recall the sight and sound of that steam outfit he knew as a kid: the monstrous engine puffing and wheezing up the steep incline that led to their place, black smoke belching from its stack. Hooked behind the engine was the thresher and behind it the water wagon. While the thresher was being manoeuvred into position and the huge flat drive belt aligned between it and the engine, the wagon was pulled to the swamp for filling. An hour's steady work, utilizing a hand pump, was needed to completely fill the tank. As the engine had a lusty appetite for water, this operation would be repeated often.

The steam tractor also consumed plenty of wood...good seasoned hardwood, supplied by the individual farmer. The better quality of wood, the more power was realized. It became quite competitive among local farmers to submit a superior product. With the advent of the gasoline tractor, this segment of harvesting became obsolete.

Although haying and harvest constituted the greatest input of time and labour, "everyday farming" in the 1920s was no easy ride. My grandfather Oliver Turner's farm, like most farms of that era, fell into the "mixed" category. A dozen Shorthorn cattle formed the backbone, a registered herd that had won its share of ribbons at local fairs over the years. During summer cows were milked outside; a rock roughly the shape of a huge armchair sat in the orchard making an ideal milking stand. It seemed as if Mother Nature had carved it for this express purpose. Cows stood untethered beside the rock as they were milked by hand, and as the pails were filled they were placed on the "stand," thereby preventing any upsets from kicking hooves. The milk was run through a cream separator, with the pigs and calves getting the skim and the household the cream. Most of the cream was utilized for baking but some churned for butter.

The cattle's summer diet consisted of grass foraged from a wide area. Neighbours weren't too concerned whose cattle pastured where. Provided they were kept out of the grain fields and garden, little effort was made for confinement; it wasn't uncommon to see cows pasturing along roadside ditches. Oliver let his bull mingle with the herd throughout the year offering free service. For "neighbourhood" service, a dollar fee was charged.

During winter, cattle were sent to the swamp each morning for a drink, a hole having to be chopped in the ice beforehand. Winter diet consisted of hay mixed with straw, chopped oats, and barley, and always a favourite...turnips. Horses received the pick of the hay crop as well as a large percentage of the oats. They were the mainstay of your operation and had to be maintained in peak condition.

Sheep were another enterprise. They pastured across the road but were housed in a shed next to the barn at night, necessitating a daily routine of herding back and forth. Then as now, wolves and wild dogs were a constant threat. Oliver had done an impressive job on the interior of this sheep shed, constructing pens and hay racks. Continuing to utilize his carpentry skills, he built a chicken house complete with roosts and nests. He built pig pens, plus a raised farrowing area where young pigs could sleep without getting squashed. And anyone who has ever fed pigs is familiar with the problem of getting feed into the trough without dumping it on top of their heads. This issue was eliminated when Oliver furnished hinged gates that locked behind the feed trough while filling.

My grandfather was a better than average carpenter who could construct most anything if he had a plan to follow. He therefore didn't have a lot of sympathy for mediocrity.

Like the time he hired someone to rebuild a shed wall and observing its crookedness, immediately brought it to the builder's attention. "I told you I was just a rough carpenter," he groused defensively. Oliver, a man of few words, merely answered, "yes...damn rough!"

When it came to sheep, spring was the busiest time of year: first, lambing season, then shearing. But before they could be sheared they had to be washed. The best method as far as Oliver was concerned was to pick the sheep up bodily then wade into the swamp. By vigorously massaging the wool, you could eliminate most foreign particles such as straw, manure, mud, and of course the ever-present ticks.

Although washing sheep was an exhausting and time-consuming ordeal, it was an absolute necessity. John Nuhn, operator of the Flesherton Woollen Mill, was very selective as to the quality of wool he processed. His enterprise manufactured yarn, woollen socks, underwear, and blankets that were shipped world-wide. Occasionally a fleece for whatever reason would miss getting washed, but seldom did the oversight go unnoticed. Nuhn would sift through the pile feeling the texture of each, and when his hands contacted the objectionable fleece he'd hesitate and growl, "not vashed" in his heavy German accent and throw the offender in the reject pile.

But all facets of livestock had their drawbacks. At least wool couldn't run away on its way to market, as livestock often did. The stockyards at Ceylon Station, eight miles from my grandfather's farm, were the gathering point for Artemesia Township. Oliver built a trailer for transporting pigs, but cattle were simply tied together and driven the entire route, although there were always instances of animals breaking loose for a last effort at freedom. Tuesday was market day at Ceylon and one could hear the squeal of hogs, bleating of sheep, and bawling of cattle a mile away. Each farmer's offering was tagged and held in holding pens until being loaded on box cars bound for the Ontario Stockyards in Toronto.

As time went by, individual truckers began picking up livestock at the farm, eliminating the long and often dangerous practice of driving cattle to market, as happened the day an area farmer was driving his bull to the train station. Normally a short solid pole between the ring in the bull's nose and the handler would keep any potential trouble at a safe distance. Perhaps this particular animal had a history of gentleness and the farmer figured no precautions were needed, but without warning and as quick as lightning the bull drove his horns into the back of the unsuspecting man. Blood shot from his ears and he fell like a cement block, dead practically before he hit the ground. The hired man who witnessed the gruesome spectacle suffered a complete mental breakdown from which, it was said, it took years to overcome.

Just as important as animal husbandry was the large garden and orchard that was part of every homestead of that era. A poor garden or orchard crop could constitute a lean and hungry winter. Almost any vegetable could and would be grown, but potatoes were the mainstay, often two or three acres being planted. Keeping them weed free with just the use of a hoe was a steady summer occupation for the entire family.

Whereas potatoes dominated the vegetable garden, apples did likewise in the orchard. To ensure a constant supply throughout the winter months, the Turners, like others in the neighbourhood, dried apples. After quartering, the individual apples were punched with a darning needle then strung on lengths of cord running over the entire upstairs of the house. To aid in the drying process, windows were kept open as much as possible. A negative side to all this fresh air was the flies that were continually drawn to the sweet smell. The apples were left hanging for an indefinite period until noticeably brown, then made into pie.

I recall asking my father his view on this type of apple pie; his answer was clear and to the point. "I almost choke just thinking about them. They were the most tasteless excuse for a dessert I ever encountered! Without something to drink to wash them down, those dried-up half-rotten apples would literally get stuck in your throat. The house stunk all fall with the odour of rotten apples and of course the flies were drawn to the smell...as if we didn't have enough problems concerning flies without welcoming hordes of them into the house.

Rustic Glance

DESPITE BEING TIED TO A LABOUR-INTENSIVE WAY OF LIFE, MY ancestors in the early part of the 20th century inevitably found themselves with a surprising amount of free time. Outside entertainment was a welcome distraction, encompassing a wide range of events...fall fairs, election campaigns, school board meetings, farm auctions, evangelistic "camp meetings," etc.

One form of rural entertainment expected with yearly regularity was the "gypsies" in their travelling caravan. These colourful men and women provided a broad array of talent. Singing, dancing, magic shows, comedy, all interspersed with "live" commercials as cast members pitched a variety of wares to anyone who showed up. The favourite was usually "Doctor" somebody or other's elixir...a cure for whatever affliction might ail you. The concoction varied from year to year and from show to show, but was usually no more than some formula high in alcohol and sweetened with honey or sugar.

Often the sales pitch ran in conjunction with a lottery or contest. The most familiar involved choosing a couple of the better looking girls of the neighbourhood and then "giving" you a ticket with your preferred girl's name upon it with each bottle of stimulant sold. The show would hang around for a week and a running tabulation of which girl was leading the race continually circulated. If your particular choice was losing ground, the situation could be easily rectified by simply buying another bottle of the wonder tonic.

For some entertainment one had to travel to a larger population centre like the circus in Owen Sound when my father was in his teens. This first-class show contained all the expected features: wild animals, trapeze artists, magic acts and clowns, amongst an atmosphere of candy apples, caramel corn, and cotton candy. A dozen barkers competed for a share of the public's change in as many sideshows.

The "sideshows" were always the main drawing card of the circus. The mystery of what was hidden in those tents was meant to play on the audience's curiosity. But what would it be? My father had only a few cents to gamble. The bearded lady?...The world's fattest man?...How about a half man/half woman? No...well, how about the wild man from Borneo who supposedly lived exclusively on raw meat?

Along with these human misfits were animal freaks as well, like the two-headed calf or the cow with its head where its tail should be. Dad couldn't resist that come-on and parted with a dime to see a cow merely turned around in its stall.

Skating and hockey were familiar pastimes for rural kids. The ice on "Cameron's pond" would be checked for thickness on the way home from school and if in reasonable shape, whoever was available would meet following supper. Somebody would bring a coal oil lantern and the kids would skate or play hockey until their hands and feet were sufficiently frozen. The lantern helped brighten up the "rink" but if playing hockey, one had to be careful an errant shot didn't extinguish the light permanently.

A shared characteristic among rural communities whether young or old was superstition, and that was certainly the case in our family. Many people entertain a few elements of superstition. Most are routine and well known...don't sit 13 at a table; don't meet on the stairs; always leave by the same door you enter.

Less familiar, perhaps, at least with my ancestors...don't sit near a wet dog in a thunderstorm as it attracts lightning or plant certain vegetables under a full moon. It's bad luck to see an owl in direct sunlight or leave your shoes upside down; however they believed if one caught a falling leaf on the first day of autumn they'd not catch a cold all winter.

Dad's cousin Isla was especially geared towards omens and supernatural beliefs. One particular incident concerned a friend of hers who was quite ill...in fact near death in her mind.

Apparently the only chance this sick friend had for survival involved hurling an egg over the roof of the house. Isla went out in the front yard to execute the ceremony, but not before my Dad intervened, stating "a girl" would never get it over the high peak and he'd perform the ritual. Through tears, Isla made it clear the only way the spell would work was if she did it.

Dad resigned himself to let her try and stood back to watch the show. A dramatic wind-up followed by a high velocity release. Splatt!...right against the side of the house, some four feet below the eaves. One can imagine the wailing as Isla realized she'd just signed her friend's death warrant, but I guess a higher authority than "eggs" intervened and her friend was spared.

A somewhat related practice to superstition was "tea reading." Josh Dobson, the custom thresher for the Arteme-sia Township area, among the women at least was renowned for his reading abilities. Whereas the men figured the ritual a complete waste of time better spent harvesting, my grand-mother and her sisters took great stock in having their futures foretold.

A certain procedure was in order, Josh always making a big production by turning the cup around a few times and turning the handle in a particular direction while he studied the leaves. The handle position depended upon the phase of the moon or something. Isla, especially, would sit almost in reverence as Josh predicted the tall, handsome, rich gentleman she was about to meet. How seriously Josh himself took these projections is debatable, but they were part of mealtime ceremony for years.

I suppose such diversions were needed as rural life was pretty quiet. While in their teens, both Dad and his sister Margaret undertook piano and violin lessons, their parents not wanting to miss a chance to nurture any talent lurking in the shadows. My father claimed he had "no talent" when it came to the keyboard; a switch to violin provided only marginal gain, torturing the family with his squawking and scraping until he at least learned the scales. Things went a little smoother at this point and he actually managed to learn a few songs, mostly hymns.

Music instruction was courtesy of a gentleman who showed up once a week and charged 50 cents for a half-hour lesson. These were very informal sessions. Whether you were forking manure in the stable, pitching hay from the mow, or cutting wood in the bush, you simply ceased what you were doing, headed for the house, picked up the violin, and the lesson began. Probably wondering if he was getting his money's worth, Dad's father after a length of time inquired as to his son's progress. "Average" was the instructor's answer.

No doubt the greatest form of entertainment in the rural outreaches was the telephone. Alexander Graham Bell's invention was the lifeline of the rural community. With as many as 20 families on some lines there was always somebody talking...or listening.

"Listening in," a nice phrase for eavesdropping, was almost universal practice. If you heard someone's ring which you thought might be of interest, you simply lifted the receiver and listened. If it happened to be a long distance call nearly everyone would be on the line. With so many "listening in," those old battery-operated phones could barely generate enough power to complete the call. Often one of the active parties would have to holler at the unwanted audience to get off the line so they could hear.

There were actually rules that governed telephone conduct. Calls were supposed to be limited to a five-minute span and quarrelling and profanity were supposedly monitored. Even "listening in" was an offence worthy a hefty fine though I doubt few were handed out. For most communities the telephone company would have had to charge nearly everyone on the line at some point.

Crime or not, some never hid the fact they eaves-dropped..."I heard on the phone this morning..." while others who didn't wish their habit known would explain how they just happened to lift the receiver and "heard someone telling someone…" Then there were those who stated how they mistakenly picked up the receiver thinking it was their ring and after five minutes learned it wasn't.

With so many utilizing the system, you always knew somebody was listening, so a catty game of phone-line gossip developed. The Turners' neighbour, Rita Magee, was a master. Her daily chats with her daughters always contained a barb or two.

"So what are you doing, Christena?"…"Well I just finished making some bran muffins…how about you?" "I got all my whites washed and hung…I notice Mrs. Turner hasn't a thing on the line yet…she must still be in bed." Anyone on the line could almost feel my grandmother's pulse skyrocket.

A form of "entertainment" my father enjoyed in his teen years, especially, was visiting the local blacksmith shop. This small one-storey building was the centre of the community, where farmers mostly would gather to socialize while waiting for their repair work to be done. Scattered around the drab interior of the building and darkened by years of fire and smoke, assorted wheel rims, axles, ploughs, coulters, and harrow teeth lay waiting repair.

Although the blacksmith repaired and welded machinery, his main talent of course was the care of horses' feet. The forge and anvil were the focal point of the shop and it was here the horseshoes were repaired, rebuilt, or replaced. While hand pumping the bellows to keep the forge hot, the blacksmith held the shoe with a pair of long-handled tongs over the fire until it literally glowed red. The shoe was then placed on the anvil and with repeated strikes of the hammer, shaped to his specifications. In my father's mind, that was a most wonderful sound, that steady ring as the hammer hit its target and sparks scattered across the floor. One could hear the clarity of the ring a half a block away. The blacksmith then lifted the horse's leg between his and placed the shoe against the hoof, holding it a few seconds. Because it was still hot, the shoe would burn any rough or high spots off the hoof, providing a perfect fit. Sixty years later my father could still recall the pungent odour emitted the moment the hot shoe came in contact with the foot. The shoe was then dropped into a vat of water, sizzling like a steak on a grill as it sank. The cooled shoe was now ready to nail to the hoof with nails especially fashioned for this purpose.

Nobody knew more about village happenings than the blacksmith, always keeping one ear cocked to the conversation of his customers. Likewise it was an excellent venue for a young lad to be educated in the interests of politics, world and current events, local gossip, sex, and the latest off-colour jokes.

My grandfather's farm, unlike many in the area, had the services of a full-time hired man. Fred Wilkinson had been around as long as my own father could recall, his family having been neighbours of the Turners in England, so when young Fred immigrated to Canada in the early 1900s, he looked up my great-grandfather Solomon Turner for a job. When World War One broke out, Fred enlisted with the army in France as an artillery hauler, but by the time he returned Solomon had passed away, so Fred continued on as hired help for his son Oliver, my grandfather.

Fred Wilkinson was a big man...a man slow to anger and slow to judge his fellowman. Gentleness, kindness, trust, patience, and loyalty were key factors of Fred's character.

This trait extended to animals as well, being a natural with a team, the horses seemingly an extension of Fred himself. He also held a great fondness for cats, forever stroking their fur and talking to them as he went about his business.

Fred received the average 1920s wage, $1.00 a day plus board. During winter when no field work existed, just board and tobacco; he performed many jobs but his main task throughout the autumn was ploughing. Beginning in September and not ending until early November, Fred steadily worked his way over the approximately 50 acres of ground. It was a long slow process with a single nine-inch furrow walking plough. Every acre turned constituted a walk of ten miles, so Fred covered a lot of ground without really going anywhere.

During ploughing season, Fred would be in the field by 7 a.m. At noon he'd head for the barn, where he'd water and feed the horses, giving them a full hour's rest while he had his own dinner. Then it was back to the field until 6 p.m. when the team would be retired for the day, but not before being watered, fed, unharnessed, and "rubbed down." Only then would Fred's day be complete.

Occasionally over the years, Fred would announce his attention to return "over 'ome." He'd book passage on a steamship carrying livestock, thus working his way across the Atlantic for the price of a ticket to his native Lincolnshire. Sometimes he'd stay for two or three months, working and visiting with family and friends before returning. My grandfather had to sign a document with the Department of Immigration each time upon his return.

Fred obviously missed his homeland, making several trips throughout his lifetime, and even when he was back in Canada, England was never far from his thoughts. Walking behind the plough, fetching cows, pitching sheaves, fixing fence...there was a song Fred often sang.

> *I saw the old homeland, the faces I love, I saw*
> *England's valleys and hills.*
> *I listened with joy as I did when a boy to the sound*
> *of the old village bells.*
> *The moon was shining brightly, it was a night that*
> *would banish all sin.*
> *The bells were ringing the old year out and the new*
> *year in.*

As the years advanced, my father gradually assumed the role of "main ploughman" and admitted that under the right conditions the task of turning sod and stubble was one of his favourites. As this was Grey County, this tranquil scene might be interrupted as the plough struck one of the numerous stones that lay hidden beneath the surface, but on level, stone-free ground on a crisp autumn afternoon, it was a satisfying experience to walk behind a well matched team.

In this pre-tractor era, one could hear the screaming of seagulls as they continuously landed and took flight behind the plough, gobbling up earthworms lying vulnerable on the surface. The rattling of dying leaves stirred by a soft breeze sifting through the sugar maples, the steady breathing of the horses as they made their way across the field, or that unmistakable odour of newly-turned fertile soil passing over a polished steel moldboard...

Together these elements orchestrated a singular and distinct environment most of us living today never knew... and with each advancing season the numbers of those who recall its existence at all decline.

One for Both and
Both for One

ON OCTOBER 8, 1942, MY MOTHER GAVE BIRTH TO A BABY boy...William Harold Oliver Turner...or "Billy." Perhaps my parents figured he might be their only son, so as not to offend any family members, loaded him with the Christian names of his father and both maternal and paternal grandfathers. Mom and Dad were now blessed with a boy and girl in less than a year, Vivien still 20 days short of her first birthday.

The "baby years" passed quickly, and by the autumn of 1947 it was time for Vivien to begin her tenure in the public school system, though certainly not without reluctance. "There's no use me going...I can't make '2s'!" My father actually thought it would be a good idea to delay Vivien's education one year and start the two together. Maybe he figured another year would buy enough time for

Vivien to master that pesky "2" digit. The suggestion went nowhere, with Vivien beginning school as planned and Billy a year later.

Although her grades were satisfactory (once she mastered her 2s) Vivien never cared much for school. Academics didn't come easily...nor did much else. Skating, skiing, swimming, or riding a bike all provided major challenges. Vivien and Billy received new bicycles at the same time, and although the change from three to two wheels proved relatively easy for my brother, it simply added one more item to the list of things in which my sister was inept.

Unable or unwilling to allow the principle of balance to govern, Vivien was perfectly content to simply "walk" her bike anywhere she went. Against her will, Dad took Vivien out to practice in an adjacent pasture field notorious for its steep hills. He reasoned the lush clover would provide a cushion for the inevitable spills, while the inclines would provide "natural momentum." Vivien was convinced Dad was simply trying to kill her.

Billy fared better at school than his sister...at least on the academic side. Socially he had more difficulty. The senior kids seemed to revel in bullying the younger set, and because Billy was overweight it made the exercise that much more enjoyable. Along with cruel rhymes, he had to endure the usual "fat" pseudonyms of the day as well. Wearing glasses at such a young age didn't help either; hide his glasses, hide his hat, hide his books...the fun was endless.

The Dutch children who formed a large contingent of the one-room school were also singled out. Making fun of their wooden shoes, how their parents talked, the food they ate, or any number of prejudices all helped to pass the time. But Billy did have one talent that never failed to bring a laugh. Even the big kids smiled on occasion. By rhythmically wiggling his ears, he could make his hat move up and down. It was probably one of the better local acts.

Billy's extra girth had always been problematic. Boys' clothes of that era never quite fit so Mom was forever altering men's clothing...usually Dad's, to suit. This practice generally comprised about two feet being lopped off a pair of trousers, making them as wide as they were long...stylish they weren't.

Occasionally Mom would locate a pair of "real" boys' pants. Never mind they were labelled "Husky," "Big Boy," or some other substantial adjective...they weren't Dad's trousers and that's all that mattered! This particular discovery sported a green plaid lining that looked especially appealing with the cuffs turned up six inches...now if he could just get them buttoned up! It wasn't an easy task by any stretch, but did manage to secure the fastener.

"How does that feel?" asked Mom. "Too tight?"..."No, they feel great!" In truth the pants were as uncomfortable as one could imagine, but no way was my brother going to allow this moment to escape.

A Sunday school picnic was being held that night at our place and Billy was looking forward to modelling his new wardrobe. Events progressed smoothly until some kid suggested they go play in the barn. Once in the haymow, the game chosen was "see who can jump the farthest."

Now Billy may have been a lot of things, but stupid he wasn't. Jumping was definitely out of the question. He could barely walk! Grabbing quickly for an excuse, he announced he had a sore leg and would act as scorekeeper. He realized even one leap in those skin-tight jeans would have resulted in an explosion of thread.

Getting to school each day entailed a mile and a half walk. About eight kids made the trek. As children tend to dawdle, 8:00 was the prescribed time of departure. One morning they lingered longer than usual and realizing time was against them, Billy got the bright idea to cut across a hay field as a shortcut. Anyone who has ventured through a thick stand of dew-laden alfalfa is aware what the kids were up against. All were soaked within minutes. However there was nothing to do but continue, the crop emitting a spray of water with every step.

Their teacher Mrs. Gould wasn't impressed..."And you with a new dress!" she scolded Vivien when the tardy group finally arrived. After the scolding came what was natural and normal discipline of that era...the strap. Following a taste of leather, she loaded the offenders into her car and drove them to their respective homes for dry clothes. The teacher then returned to school, leaving the individual parents to administer further authority, which usually consisted of another "reminder." For most households the rules were simple but unbending: a strapping at school...a strapping at home.

The passageway that beckoned the young scholars to school each day was known to the locals as the "green road," although it bore more resemblance to a nature trail than a road, being much too narrow to accept vehicular traffic. Thick rows of trees lined either side, and during autumn layers of leaves added a colourful dimension to the daily commute. Birds flitted from branch to branch over-head, while squirrels, chipmunks, rabbits, and groundhogs conducted their business on the ground.

And snakes: it wasn't uncommon to see two or three crawlers on any given day, all harmless garden variety...but startling enough for their appearance to generate a scream from the girls. The boys had no more fondness for reptiles, just assumed a braver front. Billy spied a dead snake on the road one afternoon and picked it up with the toe of his boot and fired it towards the girls. He waited for the screams, but the stunt backfired, the snake going straight up...and straight down. Guess who screamed?

The "green road" was strictly a fair-weather road. When the first snowstorm blocked travel, the students were chauffeured by car for the remainder of the winter. During this season, snowball fights, fort building, and tobogganing filled recess period.

Many kids scrap like cats and dogs, but Vivien and Billy rarely fought. However Vivien never missed a chance for a little fun if the occasion arose. Mom owned one of those old pedal-operated sewing machines. A large wooden cover protected the mechanism from dust, which Vivien noted when inverted looked very much like a boat. Realizing the potential she convinced her brother to climb in, whereupon she proceeded to push Billy and the "boat" down the stairs. A short bumpy ride culminated in a crash landing into the washing machine at the bottom of the stairs, where an amused Vivien would observe Billy suffer the wrath of Mom.

Stupidity reigned for this matter, for no matter how many times Billy received a scolding or even spanking, Vivien could somehow convince him to get back in for "just one more ride."

Bond Haven Farms at Bond Head, Ontario, where Dad was employed, boasted a large Holstein herd, in which my brother took special interest. By the time he was six, Billy knew all of the forty-plus cows' names and was becoming an enormous help to the outside operation of the farm as well. By the time he was nine he'd mastered driving the Jeep, often being called to deliver hay bales or a block of salt to a distant pasture or perhaps a couple bags of calf feed to another barn. Billy worked tirelessly one summer, driving wagons, raking hay and straw and performing countless other jobs, and for his labour received ten dollars. Billy felt he was a millionaire.

No way can one allow a windfall like that to lie dormant, so my brother was escorted to the Royal Bank in nearby Beeton to open a savings account. After the teller filled out the appropriate forms, she handed the paper to the bank's newest customer, whereby he carved "Billy Turner" on the dotted line. On the way home, Mom hinted he should've written "Bill" on the bank form, a suggestion I'm sure he thought strange…as no one in his lifetime had ever called him anything but "Billy."

In 1953 we moved about five miles northeast to our own farm near Bradford, where Vivien and Billy, now twelve and eleven respectively, acquired an even greater role. With Mom spending increasing time in the fields operating the tractor on the binder, hay loader, mower, etc.,…more household chores were delegated to Vivien.

Farming in the 1950s called for plenty of manual labour, and Dad counted on Billy for a large portion of that workload. Cows to milk, milk to carry, hay and grain to feed, straw to spread, manure to remove, and cattle to water.

On a work-related subject, there was one item Billy wanted more than anything but was refused…a simple pair of rubber boots. He had to wear galoshes…and the reason? Rubber boots were bad for the eyes, he was told. I'm unaware of any studies, scientific or otherwise, concerning rubber boots versus eye health, but Mom and Dad must have read it somewhere. Billy had poor eyesight anyway, so he probably figured...what's to lose!

Despite a full day of school work ahead each day, Billy rose shortly after six o'clock to help Dad with the milking, both arriving for breakfast shortly before eight, when we'd all eat together. We had the original "big breakfast": porridge, steaming hot; toasted homemade bread; fried eggs, fried bologna, and fried tomatoes when in season, were followed by honey, jam, peanut butter, and corn syrup. Pure unpasteurized milk for us kids, perked coffee for Mom and Dad.

Everybody would be talking while CJBC crackled from the speaker of our Stromberg-Carlson radio. During the sportscast, Billy would vainly try to shut the rest of us up so he could hear the results from the previous night's games. Baseball and hockey were his favourites...hockey especially, where he collected labels from Beehive Golden Corn Syrup tins by the score to cash in on hockey portraits of his favourite players. I think he had a full collection of all six NHL teams, so consequently we ate a lot of syrup! Breakfast was bedlam personified, with everyone talking, Mom constantly nagging us to hurry, making sure we all had our books, homework assignments, and lunches as we dashed off to school.

The autumn of 1955 brought a change in our educational routine when Vivien graduated to high school in Bradford. For her this meant catching the bus at 7:30 on the overpass at "400" highway, a quarter mile away. Vivien hated standing "on display" as she awaited the bus, like most teenagers figuring everyone driving by was looking at her. In her regulation uniform consisting of

short black tunic, long black stockings and white blouse...
maybe they were!

During winter, that highway overpass seemed like the coldest place on the face of the earth with the windswept snow drifting across the snow-encrusted fields. However there was really no other choice as under the bridge you simply couldn't see the bus. Days like this it was a joy to get inside that old Ford school bus. One perk of getting on first of which Vivien took full advantage...you could choose the seat under which the single solitary heater was positioned.

When my sister began high school she also joined Girl Guides. Then as now, selling cookies was part of the curriculum. From our place clear down to the next concession, Vivien pitched her product. Whatever techniques she employed were well received, for she sold a lot of cookies.

Now that he was in his eighth and final year of public school, Billy officially adopted "Bill" to better recognize this new role. Despite the name change, most friends, neighbours, relatives, and Dad himself would continue to call him "Billy" for another decade or two...some for life.

Billy...I mean "Bill's" new leadership status in school didn't mean much when he tangled with Patricia Barton, a classmate who lived across the road. The two were on their way home from school and for whatever reason...he obviously did something to deserve it...Pat retaliated by slugging him over the head with a Coke bottle...and they weren't plastic back then! By the time Bill stumbled home, blood was streaming from the laceration on his head.

A big deal ensued over that episode! A meeting was scheduled straightaway including all concerned...victim, attacker, parents of victim, parents of attacker, teacher, fellow students who witnessed the confrontation...no one was left out. I remember Dad was very angry. "You could kill someone hitting them like that!" I don't recall the rest of the exchange, but for the next several weeks I remember Bill and Pat walking home on different schedules.

Although that incident was definitely a low point, their relationship wasn't all downhill. One winter evening following the head-bashing episode, the two went skating on the creek that ran through our property.

"It was a beautiful night," my brother recalled. "The ice was perfect and we skated back and forth under the stars holding hands." Probably the reason the event seemed special was because neither Bill nor Vivien received much encouragement from Mom and Dad when it came to the social aspects of life. Most friends they chose simply failed to measure up to their elevated standards.

A taste of social life was the main reason Vivien joined Girl Guides. She'd go to the meetings, then "party" after. Bill hardly got away from home except for school, but one evening persuaded Mom and Dad to allow him to go to school chum Hank Willem's home to watch the Saturday night hockey game. Televisions were scarce in our neighbourhood, making this a much anticipated event.

Wouldn't you know it...that happened to be the night the Willems' TV suffered cardiac arrest. Hank's father even slugged it a few times to see if he could revive it, but to no avail. Bill listened to the game on the radio for a while, then went home.

The spring season of 1957 witnessed our family on the move once again, this time to a farm in Perth County. Throughout the previous autumn with our parents spending an increasing time away from the farm, Bill was forced to spend an equivalent amount of time away from his studies. In secondary school now, Bill's grades soon reflected this chronic absenteeism. So with only two months of grade nine under his belt, it was agreed my brother would call it quits, with the understanding he return the following year to school, wherever that might be.

For a while Bill enjoyed the freedom from classes, but even with a new and larger farm the novelty soon wore off and all too soon it was the familiar challenge of snow-clogged laneways, hard-starting vehicles, frozen hands, frozen feet, and frozen water pipes. It was days such as these Bill wished he was back in the classroom, or perhaps just in a warmer climate.

My brother often imagined what it would be like to farm in Virginia or Kentucky or the Carolinas or maybe Georgia...someplace far away from winter winds and blinding blizzards. He read with interest advertisements in *Hoard's Dairyman* and *Holstein Journal* requesting herdsmen in these more temperate regions. He actually answered an ad from a Georgia operation but lost his nerve when a genuine position was offered. Bill had mentioned not a word to anyone of his farm fantasy...especially Dad and Mom, and being just sixteen he never would have been allowed to go anyway.

Although Bill never did return to school, Vivien continued her studies, favouring typing, shorthand, and book-keeping as opposed to more general subjects. With some effort she floated along for a couple of years managing passing grades, but hit a cement wall in the final semester of grade twelve. A number of subjects shared in the downfall, mathematics being the most noteworthy.

For whatever reason, their math teacher recited the results of the exam out loud for all to hear, beginning with the highest mark first. It was certainly no surprise to Vivien when the magical "50" mark passed without her name being called. She knew she'd fared poorly so wasn't even overly alarmed when "40" disappeared without recognition. However it was total embarrassment by the low "20s" with no mention, and through the "teens" Vivien secretly prayed the floor would open and she could simply disappear.

What's incredible at this point is there were still students waiting to hear results...but finally the torture was complete..."Vivien Turner...3."

As we leaf back through the years and observe Vivien's academic record, it almost seems pre-ordained that mathematics would be her downfall. From that first day of school a dozen years earlier, remember how those goddam "2s" gave her such grief?

If there's any consolation at all for my sister, I guess it centres on the fact that her "3" wasn't the worst...no, that unrewarding title was reserved for her chum Gwen Stevenson...Gwen received a 0.

A Little Imagination
Goes a Long Way

IT'S SURPRISING TO WHAT LENGTHS A LITTLE IMAGINATION AND ingenuity can elevate a handful of kids...especially "car crazy" kids growing up in the flashy automotive world of the 1950s and '60s. It proved the ultimate challenge for my brother Brian and cousin Doug Watt to dream up new and interesting ideas to help pass the summer holidays. When you are still within that magical eight- to ten-year-old range, imagination knows no boundaries.

Doug, because he was an only child, had some neat toys in our eyes. One intriguing item was a hand-held telescope with which the three of us would spend hours spying on cars on the highway that passed a half mile from our farm. During this era of the mid-20th century, it was easy for anyone with a little automotive knowledge to recognize the various models. Dual, and even triple-toned colour combinations; fins that varied in size from tasteful to grotesque and swept in every conceivable direction; distinctive tail-light and side chrome treatments and unique grilles...all aided in identification.

With the help of a good telescope, the job was a piece of cake. First step of this game was to guess the passing vehicle's make and model, utilizing just the naked eye. The telescope's role was to merely confirm or deny your guess. "It's a '59 Ford"..."No, it's a Meteor. See the extra chrome on the side?" "You're right, okay your turn." "Let's see...a '58 Chev" "Sorry, a '58 Pontiac." "What, you're crazy! Let's see that scope...oh I guess you're right, they're practically the same." "They're not the same at all, you idiot!...Pontiacs have that wide stripe on the side." The game inevitably descended into a name-calling shouting match.

Time to bring on the "go car"...an idea that surfaced seasonally but seldom passed the dream stage; but this summer we'd do it!...and thus began our elaborate plans.

"Alright, first we need a box. That's no problem. There's plenty of scrap wood around." "What should we use for seats?" "How about that old buggy seat in the loft above the implement shed. I hope there are no wasps in it this year." "Okay, wheels?" "We'll use those ones from Vivien's old doll buggy. Maybe we could use the springs too." "There's that old steering wheel I found in the dump, that'll work good, as that speedometer I carried on my bike for a while." "Wow, this is going to be the best 'go car' yet!"

"We could install headlights on it, there's a couple of burnt-out tractor lights in the shed...and we could probably construct fenders with some old roofing steel." Someone even suggested lifting the Briggs and Stratton engine from the lawn mower. "Before we get too carried away," cautioned Doug, "what about axles?" Well...uh...what should've appeared a straightforward procedure always seemed to be the stall point each season.

...But not this year! Out to the scrap pile on the north side of the implement shed we trudged. "Any steel rod will do" "It has to fit the hole in the wheel" "Maybe we could use wood." "You can't use wood, stupid!" Suddenly I remembered that great junk pile in the bush at the back of the farm. All sorts of treasures had been tossed there over the years. The problem was the distance, nearly a mile, and the heat. It was one of those sticky August afternoons... much too hot to tramp away back there and perhaps not find anything suitable when we got there.

"What about Donnie?" someone suggested. That seemed an avenue worth discussing. My little brother was about three or four at that time, quite capable we thought of handling this little chore. He could walk back and check out the pile for anything that resembled an axle. No sense all of us going.

Donnie didn't seem overly enthusiastic about the adventure so we promised him first ride when the "go car" was completed. He still wasn't convinced, so we had to add candy to the bribe. The entire project derailed shortly after, however. Dad was mending fence along the creek when Donnie came huffing by. Upon hearing his son's destination and mission, Dad relayed a return message basically stating what we could do with our axle. Oh well...maybe next year...

Many of the truly great inventions of this world are discovered purely by accident. James Watt, idly watching the lid of a boiling kettle bounce up and down, hit upon the idea of harnessing that pressure of steam to power machines.

A more modern invention, Velcro, was hatched while its Swiss inventor was removing burrs from his dog's coat. With the way the burr hooks clung to fur or fabric, he recognized the potential for a practical new fastener.

"Post-it" notes basically came about due to a batch of poor quality adhesive with only "marginal stickiness," and 3M turned it into an office phenomenon.

Although much more isolated, an invention for which we take credit was launched on our very farm in the summer of 1958. Doug, Brian and I were rummaging through the scrap pile for something...probably axles...when Doug picked up an old tire that was in the way and tossed it out onto the laneway. Instead of merely making a couple of bounces then falling down, the tire rolled along past the house and all the way down the grade of the laneway before coming to rest in the ditch. "Tire rolling" was born!

It took a few minutes to establish some ground rules, but once set, the regulations were simple. The three of us would line up single file. These positions depended entirely on a person's showing in the previous match. We employed the "handicap" system. The person whose tire travelled the shortest distance stood first in line in the next heat. We figured it kept the games more even and encouraged competitiveness.

At the "go" signal, the three of us would begin running, slapping our respective tires along in front of us. At a predetermined point, you had to let go and just hope for the best. Doug employed a 14" Goodyear snow tire that was fast but somewhat erratic. I used a 15" Firestone that was a respectable all-around tire...just enough heft to stay true to the course but still compact enough for good speed. Brian's favourite was a 16" Dunlop, a tire that simply lumbered slowly and steadily along without fanfare, its sheer weight often the deciding factor as it scattered any competitor in its path into the burdock and thistle-lined ditch beside the laneway.

Any chance we could get would witness the three of us running those tires up and down our laneway...for hours at a time and days on end. We were still rolling tires when I was 11 or 12 and Doug a couple years older.

By now, Mom and Dad had long since become embarrassed by the whole affair. "You look ridiculous!" Dad informed us one hot steaming day, "running up and down the lane in this heat. If I asked you to get the cows, unload hay or help with some fencing, there'd be an outcry of how hot it was!"

Then Mom had her say. "You look ridiculous alright... and sound like a herd of horses galloping by the window every few minutes. I wonder what the neighbours think when they see boys your age clomping up and down the lane chasing a bunch of stupid tires! They'd think the sun had fried your brain, that's what!"

Okay, so maybe Mom and Dad weren't entirely behind us; any revolutionary idea creates opposing factions. But they were right, the writing was on the wall; tire rolling had simply run its course, soon to become just another memory.

Although it never occurred, it had always been my intention at least that perhaps the three of us should have reunited some summer for a "rolling reunion." Maybe a whole new generation was just waiting for the rebirth of this lost art. I can almost visualize it...country laneways, secluded town streets, school parking lots, all alive with the activity of running shoes and rolling tires. And possibly in some sports hall of fame, there'd hang a photo of the three visionaries who started it all.

Old Dogs and Chickens

DURING MY TRAVELS EACH MORNING, PASSING BY FARM GATES of children waiting for the school bus, it's surprising how often a dog forms part of the group. Dogs with exotic pedigrees accompanied by their poop bag–carrying owners are certainly part of the town and city scene, but it would seem plain old running-free farm-bred collies are still a dominant force of the rural landscape.

For a kid growing up in the 1950s, dogs were certainly a fixture of our daily farm life. Fetching cows for milking, controlling the groundhog population, and warning of the arrival of insurance salesmen were all tasks expected of a farm dog of that period. This class of dog slept outside or in the stable, depending on the season, went everywhere the farmer and kids went, ate scraps discarded from the kitchen table, and for the most part just minded its own business.

Tanner was one dog I recall...a dog that didn't make many friends the year or so he was with us. Tanner chased everything on wheels from kiddie cars to milk trucks, ripped Uncle John's pants, and tore Aunt Alma's dress on two different occasions. And it wasn't only humans who fared badly. My sister Vivien owned a doll, Shirley, with beautiful blue eyes that opened and closed depending if the doll was sitting up or lying down. One day with nothing better to do, Tanner decided to chew off Shirley's left arm.

There was Scamp...a shaggy terrier-spaniel cross we got as a pup. A very affectionate dog that loved people...and chickens; Dad caught her chasing a couple of hens soon after her arrival and gave her a good licking from a branch from a nearby tree. During the episode while Scamp howled, my brother Brian and I bawled, at the same time letting our father know he was the meanest person who had ever lived.

Scamp was a slow learner, for just a few days later a similar harassment occurred...another session courtesy of Dad...another round of dog howling and kid bawling.

In 1957 our family moved from Simcoe County to Perth. It rained most of the 75-mile journey, with Scamp riding in the cab of the truck mesmerized by the windshield wipers. For a while after her arrival, I recall the little spaniel walking around with her head cycling from side to side.

It was around this time my sister Vivien was looking for some cash income and invested in a hundred or so leghorn chickens. Scamp wasn't particular about chicken breeds, as long as they would run when chased; hence a couple of "issues" developed that summer. Another solid "reminder" by our father finally seemed to sink into the spaniel's rather thick head.

Raising poultry in the 1950s didn't require highly intensive management as the birds enjoyed a rather relaxed existence. Each morning the small "chicken door" would be opened, allowing the birds to amble down the ramp in their own good time. The day would be spent scratching for worms and bugs and bathing in water puddles. Feed consisted of oats from the granary and if one could afford it a bit of protein supplement, although with free-range chickens it wasn't all that important.

At dusk, again at their own pace the hens would make their return up the ramp to roost, and once safely inside it would be someone's job to secure the door. As with most agricultural endeavours of the 1950s, little money was earned from raising poultry. However every dollar counted, and economics aside, a small chicken flock was as much a part of the rural environment as cats and dogs.

Ah yes...dogs. With the exception of her poultry vice, Scamp was a well-behaved dog. She didn't chase cars or cows. She'd never bitten a soul...not even an insurance salesman. She ate what was offered, came when she was called, never wandered, and earned her keep with a healthy quota of groundhogs each summer. Most of all, Scamp provided faithfulness, love, and affection. Especially to Brian and me, who had the time to spend with her.

Upon one day's arrival from school, no dog met us as usual. It was planting time and everyone was busy, but after a brief search Brian and I discovered her lying quietly on the cement floor of the stable. "Hi Scamp!" Scamp made no effort to get up. "Come on, Scamp!" holding the door open. Scamp still never moved.

Dad appeared at that point. "What's wrong with Scamp?" we asked. "She got run over by the tractor this morning... Bill was cultivating and she came out of the fencerow right in front of him. The front wheel of the tractor went right over her." I could feel tears welling up in my eyes.

"Scamp probably won't live," Dad added coldly. "She's probably all squashed inside." Well that did it!

For a long time I thought Dad's attitude callous, but I suppose he was certain of the dog's demise and could see no use offering false hope. "We'll get you another dog."

However, Scamp wasn't ready for the big doghouse in the sky. It would take more than a tractor wheel. Two weeks later, she'd returned to her old self...Now, if it just wasn't for those damn chickens!

We'd just returned from the Turner reunion in Collingwood one fine summer Sunday, and upon arrival were greeted by Scamp lounging on the front lawn with a chicken close by...a dead one, I might add. Out on the laneway between the implement shed and barn was another. I can recall the colour in Dad's cheeks rising as we followed him into the upper storey of the barn. Immediately inside the door lay another dead bird. But scattered around the floor was the grisliest sight of all...where at least a dozen of our flock lay massacred. Amongst the carnage were enough feathers to stuff two pillows. The remainder of the flock were huddled in a tight group in the corner of the henhouse in utter pandemonium.

Strangely, Dad never laid a hand on Scamp. Instead he merely locked her in the woodshed. "There's nothing we can do about it now," he said, "so let's get at the chores."

Well, that was the last we ever saw of Scamp. Her time had finally run out along with Dad's patience. When pressed regarding her whereabouts a day or two later, Dad simply stated that she'd "run away." Yeah...I guess that's the "end of story" Brian and I prefer to believe as well.

There was another dog that comes to mind as I write this: Paddy...an old border collie that really wasn't ours at all. He belonged to Ritchie Canning, from whom my parents bought their first farm in 1953. Perhaps because Ritchie was a bachelor, he and Paddy had a close relationship...a rarity among farm dogs of that period. Paddy was probably fourteen or fifteen at this point and when the transfer of the farm was completed, Ritchie asked Dad if Paddy might stay on. As he was moving to an apartment, taking Paddy was out of the question.

"He's pretty old and can't get around too well," Ritchie pleaded. "He wouldn't be much bother. I just can't bear to have him done away with!" Dad wasn't too enthused about having the old dog around, but understood his anxiety, so agreed.

That final morning while Ritchie loaded his truck with the last of his belongings, his "best friend" stared from the front lawn, trying to understand where all the possessions they'd shared these many years had gone, and who were these strangers settling on *his* farm? Ritchie gave the old dog's ears a scratch. "I'll come and see you as often as I can." That poor old dog must have known Ritchie wasn't making just a routine trip to town, for he lay on the driveway, staring toward the road until darkness settled.

But true to his word, Ritchie Canning did drop in from time to time over the course of that summer. Paddy would recognize the sound of his truck before it came into view, and with as much speed as his arthritic limbs could muster, hurry to greet his master. However as the season progressed, the visits petered out. Ritchie, I suppose, didn't want to appear a nuisance, and probably figured it was better for both him and Paddy if he simply stayed away.

As kids we never paid much attention to Paddy and not being used to children, Paddy responded likewise. By autumn the old dog had failed noticeably, both in hearing and eyesight, and seldom ventured further than the front lawn.

Paddy's last night began as usual in the woodshed. As he drifted off to sleep, his canine dreams recalled vividly his days as a pup. Ritchie plowed with horses then, and Paddy could picture himself running along behind the team and plow as the fields were turned to black, one furrow at a time. Later the tractor arrived, and although frightening at first, Paddy soon discovered he nothing to fear.

Each morning was a set pattern. After the cows were milked and the chores completed at home, he and Ritchie would journey over to the barn on the adjoining farm that Ritchie also owned. Quite often, man and dog would cross the hilly pasture together, or if Ritchie drove, Paddy, still taking the same route, would be sitting there proudly when his master arrived. "You beat me again, Paddy!" giving his ears a good rub...Paddy stirred slightly as he recreated that portion of the dream.

The next scene portrayed the day those strange men began erecting a fence across his pasture field in readiness for the new super highway to be built, in effect cutting off his travel path to the second farm. After that, Paddy was forced to take the road along with Ritchie, and although a bit of the fun had been removed from the morning exercise, Paddy soon adjusted.

His dream recalled other visions: Lying on the kitchen floor in front of the stove while Ritchie listened to evening radio. Sometimes it was the Grand Ole Opry from Nashville or maybe the Barn Dance from Chicago. Saturday night hockey with Foster Hewitt...Paddy had heard it all from his berth on the kitchen floor...Then he heard Ritchie calling, signalling bedtime. Paddy didn't really mind going to the woodshed, but always pretended not to hear the first time. Ritchie called again...

Paddy opened his eyes and stared blankly at his surroundings. Ritchie was nowhere in sight. A harvest moon sent a shaft of near daylight brightness through the open woodshed door. Pulling his old frame to the entranceway, he surveyed the yard outside. Still seeing no sign, Paddy walked out onto the lawn. Away to the west the pasture field lay clearly defined...clearer than he'd seen it in years.

His old heart quickened as he realized from where the voice originated. Forgetting his aching bones, he hurried towards his destination. Reaching the woven wire fence, Paddy stopped...confused by the barrier separating him from the one he loved. Back and forth he paced along the wire wall, searching for an opening. Eventually sighting a low spot between two posts, Paddy crawled under.

But everything seemed strange and unusual...the gravel shoulder...the asphalt; suddenly a bright light appeared in the pasture field. Paddy turned, blinded by the oncoming beam. And then all was blackness...

Paddy was discovered on the shoulder of the highway the following morning and Dad buried him beneath the grass of the pasture he'd roamed for 15 years. For Paddy, the long lonely hours of waiting for his master's return were over.

Milk...Our Bread and Butter

IN 1953, AFTER A TEN-YEAR STINT AS HERDSMAN FOR CHARLIE Cerswell's dairy operation at Bond Head, Ontario, my father purchased a 65-acre farm near Bradford Ontario. Dad had been around dairy cattle long enough at this point to realize if any cow could pay the mortgage it was Holsteins. Bond Haven Farms extended a major boost to our fledgling operation when Charlie contributed ten cows free of charge...well sort of. Charlie got the first heifer calf, we got the bulls and all subsequent heifer calves if the cows lived long enough. They were all in their "senior" years and anyone familiar with heavy producing Holsteins knows as the years pass, their udders "go." Some of the cows we inherited...their udders had "gone," sagging enough to make milking a challenge, but they did provide the foundation for our herd, and as Dad often reminded us, "We couldn't have started farming without them."

Dad purchased a DeLaval milk cooler with a capacity of eight 80-pound volume cans. The cans were placed on steel racks inside the cooler, while two tight fitting, rubber-sealed, front mounted doors provided access. A compressor system formed as much ice as was needed, while water continually circulated over this formation; a multitude of holes from an assortment of pipes running around the interior of the cooler shot jets of icy cold water onto the cans. As time passed, some critics complained that during very warm weather the centre portion of the can received insufficient cooling, but it sure beat the system employed by most small to medium dairies of that period...merely dunking the can in the nearest water trough.

During summer, the cans were taken from the cooler just prior to the arrival of the milk transporter and placed on a rickety old wagon Dad bought for expressly that purpose. The milk truck simply pulled alongside, the driver lifted the cans into the truck and returned the empties from the day before. Each producer had a cardboard numbered tag wired to the handle of the can. No tag...no pay.

In winter, once the laneway became plugged with snow, the cans were transported to the road by our trusty Allis-Chalmers pulling an old horse-drawn sleigh. It was my brother Bill's job to steady the cargo...not an easy task for a ten-year-old, as the sleigh pitched and tossed over the hard-packed drifts. Once, two cans got away, rolling off their shaky platform into the ditch, spilling their contents in the process. Bill began to cry, he felt so bad. Dad probably felt close to tears himself, as two cans were half our daily production in those days.

When we moved to Perth County in 1957, we moved as well to a new system of handling and shipping milk...

the bulk system, a revolutionary idea in our neighbourhood at the time. As word spread that Dad was in the market for a bulk cooler, a platoon of representatives descended upon our farm, everyone wanting to be the first to install a new machine in our area. I recall one particular afternoon a salesman in our yard, one leaving and another arriving.

A kid growing up on a dairy farm soon learns hard work, and long hours are normal practice. When my brothers and I were very young the tasks were simple, usually feeding calves. A calf received whole milk for a couple of weeks then powdered "milk replacer" was gradually introduced into the diet. Purina was especially easy to mix and smelled great too. It was a more expensive product and Dad would sometimes experiment with Shur-Gain or some other brand, but nothing seemed to go over like Purina.

Other jobs we were expected to perform as time went on included feeding cows hay and grain; feeding hay constituted climbing the wooden ladder to the haymow and tossing down maybe two dozen bales. I recall how bitterly cold that hayloft was on a winter's evening, and how the steel roof cracked and snapped in tune with the frosty air. In summer, driving our dairy herd back and forth between field and barn was a regular exercise for small boys. Washing milking machines and cooler were routine, as were cleaning stables and, of course, carrying milk.

I believe I was about eight when first I began that job. At that age, half of a three-gallon pail was my limit. To enable me to reach the cooler, Dad provided a big block of wood on which to stand. The milk was poured into a metal strainer on top of the cooler while a gauze "filter disc," fitting tightly against the bottom of the strainer, prevented foreign objects from floating into the cooler. Although this deterred flies from entering, many remained clustered on the inside surface of the strainer. Dad always gave the strainer a tap to disperse the fly population before pouring in the milk. Not me...I enjoyed seeing how many I could drown. If you were quick, you could sometimes snuff out a dozen or so. I wonder if that practice might have had anything to do with the reason our city relatives often brought their own milk with them!

Flies were always a nuisance to dairy farmers, so Dad invested in a "fly fogger" to combat the problem, a machine that sort of resembled a paint sprayer. Once the cattle were in for milking, Dad would switch it on and begin walking around the stable, the fogger blasting out DDT or Agent Orange or whatever it was he used. He'd practically disappear in the chemical mist but never wore any kind of protective gear. In five minutes the stable would be blanketed with chemical and not a fly left breathing.

Despite the former acknowledgement of "drowning flies," producing a sanitary and marketable commodity was our first priority...well our fathers' at least. Each time the milk was picked up from our farm, a sample was taken, the results tallied over a 30-day period and returned via a pink, envelope-sized card. At one point we were kicked off the fluid market, forcing us to send our entire milk supply to the local cheese factory for a couple of days until the problem was rectified. Did we ever get a "tuning in" from Dad over that one! "There will be no more shortcuts!" as he finished his tirade...Imagine our father thinking we might cut a few corners!

A considerable amount of accounting was involved with shipping milk. In accordance with the rules of Record of Performance testing, every drop of milk from every cow, every milking, had to be weighed and documented. This figure was accumulated over a cow's lactation, usually nine or ten months. The higher their production record, generally the more saleable they and any future offspring were worth. A spring scale with a hook in which to hang a pail calculated each milking's results. Admittedly, we were pretty liberal with our figures: 19 lbs. became 20 or 21, 24½ would inevitably be 26 or 27, depending on the mood of the bookkeeper. You couldn't...well cheat isn't a very nice word...inflate the figures too much, as an official ROP inspector visited once a month and if figures varied too widely, he'd demand a retest.

Thinking back on this practice, seemingly riddled with loopholes...what was the point of the ROP exercise if the figures were continually skewed? I doubt we were alone when it came to occasionally "adjusting" the totals to suit our favour? If so, it makes one wonder just how accurate those "official" production records were?

Our mother never cared for the monthly interruptions by these inspectors...and that's putting it mildly; for two days, meals and sleeping accommodations had to be provided, plus at this period of time, many were war veterans with ailing stomachs and worse nerves. They'd grumble at length about the food being served, the racket we kids were making, and numerous other issues. As time passed, personnel became more agreeable and the inspection period reduced to one day; however it was a ritual with which Mom never fully came to grips.

There were eight or ten different inspectors serving our area of southwestern Ontario. One lived right in our neighbouring town of Palmerston, three miles away, and went home at night, providing one less issue for Mom. There was an overweight man who thought our torsion-bar kitchen chairs the most comfortable he ever sat upon. Mom was always nervous the chair would collapse under his bulk.

We had a German inspector and I recall one of his associates commenting, "You know...judging by Paul's age, I'll bet you anything he served in Hitler's Youth Army!"

It was almost like the United Nations: Scottish, English, Canadian, Swedish, Dutch, Danish...There was one guy...a nice chap who regularly treated us youngsters to ice cream and movies, but I did realize even at that tender age he was a little different in the way he liked to "play" with me and my brothers.

Personally, I looked forward to the inspector's visit, meaning I could skip my milk carrying duties as the inspector weighed the milk, took a sample from each cow, and carried the milk to the cooler; even brought his personal weigh scale. And you can bet that 19 lbs. was 19 lbs.!

Calculation of butterfat percentage, which for Holsteins was in the 3.6–3.8% range, was an important part of the inspector's job, and a rather dangerous one as it involved sulphuric acid. A glass gallon jug of the liquid was always hidden mysteriously away in a darkened corner of our cellar, with strict warnings never to touch, or even go near it. As a kid we were constantly reminded of horror stories of what just one drop of this stuff could do. One recount told how this acid had burned someone's pants completely off.

The milk sample the inspector collected from each individual cow for the morning and evening milking was placed in a glass vial. It was at this stage the sulphuric acid was added to the sample and the vials put into an apparatus containing individual metal cups and operated by a hand crank. Centrifugal force was the scientific factor that separated the butterfat, enabling a reading to be taken.

My brothers and I would sit at the kitchen table where the inspector had set up his little laboratory, our faces just inches from the spinning vials of acid-induced milk. It took about fifteen minutes to spin out each batch sample, and when done the butterfat reading could be clearly seen as a darkened portion in the neck of the vial. A compass was used to measure this darkened amount, and through a conversion the butterfat percentage was calculated.

After a few years, a special metal "suitcase" was furnished for testing. All specimens were safely sealed out of sight while the rotation process was ongoing, now handled electronically...the inspector merely flipping an electric switch. I guess it was at this point the testing procedure lost its appeal as a spectator sport.

Rubber, Glass and Steel

WHEN I THINK OF AUTOMOBILES, OFTEN MY MIND WANDERS back to the 1950s, to my Uncle Percy Magee's Grey County farm at Rock Mills. Out behind his barn I could always look forward to at least a half dozen cars of 1930s and '40s vintage strewn among the thistles, burdocks, and barnyard grass. One had to contend with ill-tempered geese, spider webs, bee hives, and snakes, but it was worth the challenge to sit behind the wheel, dreaming I was driving down some carefree Ontario highway.

A few years later, a trip to Carl Shoemaker, the local auto wrecker, was the highlight of my day. Only here instead of a mere handful, perhaps a couple hundred relics from the past would be my playground. There were challenges as well...the most notable, "Joe" the junkyard German shepherd; provided sudden moves were avoided, Joe was reasonably tolerant.

Another automobile-related memory of that era was the Automotive Building at the Canadian National Exhibition in Toronto. Each August this huge complex was jammed with new cars, mostly from Detroit but including several European models as well. At that point no one even considered a Japanese model. What a great place for "car nuts" and what a great period of time. A time when styling ran rampant and every year was a major restyle. Nothing was too much. Many of these cars of which I was so awe-struck have long passed into obscurity. Meteor, Monarch, Hudson, Packard, Nash, Desoto, Imperial, Studebaker, Kaiser, Frazer...even Pontiac and Plymouth...all gone.

It was a time of automotive boasting and bragging. I remember some Dodge propaganda: "THE NEW DODGE IS ACTUALLY ONE FOOT LONGER THAN ITS LARGEST SELLING COMPETITOR." Chrysler Corporation donated free rulers to prove the fact.

Back a few years ago when the automobile was celebrating the end of its first century, every auto magazine was offering their view on which cars they thought had truly made a difference in the world. The Ford Model T and Volkswagen Beetle were on everyone's list but after that, opinions varied widely. I was thinking about this subject myself recently and came to my own conclusions. The Volkswagen certainly qualifies and I have already dedicated an account of the little German wonder in another story, as a 1958 model was my first car.

I'm not at all surprised that the Model T belongs in that exclusive group. Although it was long before my time... forty years actually...I recalled so many stories my father related about Henry Ford's Model T, it almost seems as if it was part of my life as well. Someone wrote that "automobiles gave men dreams but the Model T gave men mobility."

This new Ford changed the landscape of North America, its main attraction being simplicity...in workmanship and colour. Henry Ford's quip "you can have any colour you want as long as it's black" was legendary. There was hardly a thing that a hammer, a pair of pliers, or a bit of wire couldn't fix. The four-cylinder engine rated at 20 horsepower was low-powered even for its day, but was still more than adequate for the chassis' high centre of gravity, anemic two-wheeled brakes, skinny tires, two-speed transmission, and shaky steering.

Henry Ford claimed four cylinders was all a car needed. "I have no interest in a car that has more spark plugs than a cow has teats." The Model T had no oil pump, water pump, or fuel pump, all considered non-essential by Henry. Cups on the crankshaft "threw" oil up to the pistons, gasoline flowed by gravity, and water simply circulated in its own good time. The "heater" was no more than a hole in the dashboard radiating only the slightest hint of mild air from the manifold. Defrosting? Forget it. Generator capacity was borderline; operating at night in high gear, headlights were little more than a candle glow. Shifting to low, consequently speeding up the engine, things brightened considerably.

Starting a Model T was always an adventure, especially if the battery was weak and the self-starter wouldn't turn the engine. In this case you walked to the front of the car, yanked the choke wire beneath the radiator, then returned to the dashboard, turning on the ignition coil. To lower the compression, thus making the engine easier to turn over, retard the ignition with the spark control lever situated on the left side of the steering wheel and set the throttle until it's "about right." Then return to the front and give the crank a lusty swing. Careful though! More than a few became innocent victims of a broken wrist due to crank mishandling.

If you were lucky and the engine started right away, a quick run to the driver's compartment was a necessity to advance the spark control. Too slow, and the engine would stop, forcing a repeat performance. Only after switching off the coil, returning the choke lever to the off position, and adjusting the throttle until the car was running smoothly were you ready to embark.

The final step...depress the left pedal engaging low gear, while simultaneously pulling down on the throttle lever. Once under way, releasing the left pedal automatically engaged high gear; re-adjust the throttle to suit road conditions and "happy motoring"!

Henry Ford's Model T had never been designed for grace, style, or charm. It was aimed at the farmer and blue-collar worker...a "working man's car" Henry described it. That was how it was built and marketed...from the first one in 1908 until the 15 millionth in 1927.

Another interesting automobile enterprise in my mind was the Tucker...though it hardly made a ripple on the automotive scene. My mother recalled being at the Canadian National Exhibition in Toronto in the late summer of 1947 when the Tucker was introduced.

For months, newspapers and magazines had been discussing Preston Tucker's innovative new car. Compared to what was being offered at the time in the automotive world, this car was almost space-age: doors that slid into the roof; headlights mounted on swivelling fenders that turned in the direction of the front wheels; a periscope for 360-degree vision; as well as a centrally located steering wheel. This new car needed no clutch, transmission, driveshaft, or differential as hydraulic motors at each wheel received power from an air-cooled helicopter engine to provide motion.

The car supposedly was capable of a top speed of 130 mph (over 200 kph) and delivering 30 miles to the gallon. It was big and wide and roomy; "seven inches wider than a Cadillac," Tucker boasted. Also furnished were seatbelts, a windshield that popped out in a rollover, padded dash, air-cooled disc brakes, fuel injection, and a 24-volt electrical system.

In the preceding weeks of the initial launch, sales personnel had managed to raise $26 million...a substantial amount for 1947! However the entire affair began to unravel when it became apparent that the showroom prototype was much less than promised.

First to go had been the swivelling front fenders as they simply could not be designed to operate properly. Instead a centrally mounted third headlight was installed, but it did revolve with the direction of the front wheels. Next to go were the sliding doors. They couldn't be made to work satisfactorily either so were replaced by conventional units.

The seat belts didn't make the cut either. Apparently a survey at the time discovered the public somehow considered a car inherently unsafe if it had to have seat belts. The hydraulic torque converters failed the test and were replaced by a regular transmission...which also didn't work. For several days the prototype had no reverse. The massive air-cooled helicopter engine was a massive headache and was exchanged for a water-cooled version.

Despite being much less than advertised, the prototype surprisingly was still garnering huge attention on the car show circuit, although potential customers were growing impatient waiting for this wonder on wheels to actually be available. Shortage of steel, shortage of key components, but mostly shortage of cash was the underlying theme for lack of production.

And the last thing the new enterprise needed...the American Securities and Exchange Commission began hearing complaints that ranged anywhere from false advertising to outright swindle. The SEC had been established in the 1930s by President Roosevelt in response to the unregulated stock trading that led to the Great Depression.

A lot of ink has been utilized through the years, discussing and debating how the SEC was acting on behalf of the Detroit automakers, conspiring to shut Tucker down, but most hold little substance. All Detroit automakers were struggling to get raw materials following the war and no doubt they received first choice. General Motors, Ford, and Chrysler had fulfilled large military contracts on limited time schedules for the government so naturally they received whatever was available. That's just business.

Preston Tucker also made a few enemies in political circles with his "against the establishment" practices, and more than likely it was from this camp the SEC was alerted. Tucker certainly wasn't the first to raise capital through networking and a promise-based stock offering... entrepreneurs had been using this strategy for decades, but it certainly would have been enough to get the SEC's attention. Their biggest concern seemed to hinge on Tucker's rather unorthodox methods of raising capital such as selling accessories and dealer franchises before the car was even close to production.

The commission warned Tucker of the impending investigation and asked for his cooperation...and his books. Tucker refused on all accounts; perhaps his books weren't all in order. Whatever the reasoning, customers began cancelling orders, dealers panicked, and stock value plummeted. At this point Tucker had no choice but to shut down his assembly line and declare bankruptcy. On evidence supplied by the SEC, Tucker and seven of his associates were indicted on over 30 counts of mail fraud, conspiracy, and other violations, but over a period of time all charges were rescinded. The damage was done however and the party was over.

As stated, $26 million was a handful of cash in 1947, but as events proved, not near enough to launch an automobile with such high expectations. That issue along with the aforementioned material shortages and assembly problems no doubt had as much to do with Tucker's failure as all the other challenges associated with the venture. With just 51 cars produced, Preston Tucker's dream car was destined to become just another colourful page in the often turbulent history book of the automobile industry.

William Carruthers, 1909.

Rebecca Ellen (Reba) Turner Carruthers, Wedding day, 1910.

Grandpa Will, front seat passenger.

Viv and Bill, 1945.

Doug Watt, David, and Brian, 1958.

Final load of hay, 1958.

Down the Dusty Road

A LTHOUGH JUST 19, MY SISTER VIVIEN WAS MAKING PLANS for her wedding in the summer of 1961. For Mom and Dad it must have seemed a period of short duration since they had first held her in their arms. The school years had raced by and suddenly she was a grown woman.

Four years earlier when our family moved from Simcoe County to Perth, Vivien was finishing her second year of high school. But finding the change in schools too great, she opted to take a break. My parents agreed...but only on the condition she return to classes come autumn. This decision attracted a visit by the truant officer...the second that season.

My brother Bill, who was a year younger made the same resolution, but never did resume classes. "Being 15, he's legally entitled to remain home," the officer informed Dad, "but I'd give it plenty of consideration as a good education is not to be taken lightly."

With Bill's decision fresh in his mind, the officer was even more vocal in his comments. After he'd wound down, Dad restated his case. "Vivien is staying home for the summer and will return to school in the fall." End of discussion.

Vivien put in her three years although not without difficulties (There was that score of "3" in grade 12 math you'll remember.) However she excelled at typing and shorthand and secured two part-time positions; secretary of the Palmerston Public School and simultaneously receptionist at the Palmerston Hospital.

As far as a social life, there were a couple of boys in elementary school she kind of liked. Jimmy Boudreaux stood out in particular. He apparently had "nice warm hands."

Filling the gap later on was Dalton Hilflinger, a tall skinny fellow who drove a nice candy apple red, 1960 Ford Falcon, a brand new model only introduced to the public that year. Dalton was a nice chap who drove the "Royal Mail" truck for several years until he saved enough to realize his dream as a pig farmer.

Then there was Grenville Uppenlicher. Grenville didn't have a fine car to impress my sister. He didn't have a car at all or even a driver's license. Grenville had never adapted to things mechanical. His father bought a new Avery tractor in 1950 and most boys his age you wouldn't have been able to keep them off the seat. Grenville, however, couldn't stay far enough away. He hadn't even mastered a bicycle when he graduated from public school. With no bus service, his father clearly stated he learn to ride or else walk the four-mile trek to school. Grenville practiced throughout the summer and although shaky, managed to pedal his way to Palmerston when the autumn semester arrived.

Grenville's sister was a close friend of Vivien. During their frequent visits, Grenville tried his best to make his feelings known, but never knew exactly how to approach Vivien. And Vivien simply wasn't interested. One cold late fall day, Grenville walked the two-mile distance to our place, stood at the end of the laneway for the longest time, then turned and walked home, obviously losing whatever nerve he had for whatever he was planning to say.

He then took to writing long flowery letters to better convey his thoughts. I remember one correspondence where the things about which he felt particularly passionate were transcribed in red ink. Vivien was at a loss as how to handle the situation, so Mom and Dad helped her compose a letter of her own that finally put the matter to rest, but at the same time cushion the blow to Grenville's fragile ego.

Then down the dusty road came Glen Walter Cober... Vivien had heard about this "cute guy" who was working for our friend/neighbour/trucker/dealer Doug Hamilton, so Bill introduced my sister and the rest is history. Glen was just another in a long line of characters who over the seasons would find temporary work with the Hamilton organization. Glen's brother had laboured there the previous two summers while readying himself for his teaching career. This vacancy opened the door for his younger brother in the summer of 1960.

Glen had spent the previous summer cutting grass along the roadsides for the Department of Highways. Hour upon hour under a summer sun with only the monotonous drone of a tractor engine for company prompted Glen to pursue something more challenging. As all employees learned through time...if it was a desire for challenge, there was no better place to be than the Hamilton farm! However this job only had to fill the void until Glen began a full-time position at the Imperial Bank of Commerce in the nearby village of Wroxeter that autumn.

Although far from new, Glen had a cool car...a grey 1949 Plymouth "business coupe," meaning it had no back seat... just a huge trunk. As the name implied, it had originally been designed for salesmen and others who spent their life on the road and needed the extra room for whatever products they might be selling.

Glen liked that car but yearned for something with a little more potential, which in Glen's book meant power and speed. A 1955 green and white Ford Fairlane was more to his liking, its V-8 engine providing plenty of opportunity to burn rubber.

Glen was a personable guy...definitely outspoken, but at least in that regard you knew where you stood. He was particularly nice to us kids...even when we were a pain in the ass nuisance!

He was sort of a shade tree mechanic and I always enjoyed watching him tear apart some mysterious component of automobile, tractor, lawnmower, or whatever, and most of the time put it back together. Glen's family resided in the town of Fordwich, about 10 miles from us. Since the death of his mother several years earlier, Glen's father had raised their seven children on his own while working as an auto mechanic in the little town.

Glen got to utilize his own mechanical skills during the winter of 1960–61, replacing a faulty connecting rod bearing in Bill's Chevrolet pickup. It seemed a good arrangement for my brother as Glen donated his labour, although I suspect the real reason for his generosity was to visit Vivien. She was only too happy to hold his flashlight, tools, or whatever. Mechanically, the results of working on the engine in a frigid barn proved disappointing as he never did get it operating properly. Romantically, however, the outcome between Glen and Vivien proved much more successful with no shortage of heat.

A couple of weeks before their wedding, the church congregation where Glen's family attended, the "Brethren in Christ," staged a shower for the duo. The affair was an eclectic mix of old-time hymns, prayers, games for kids, speeches, presentations, and lots of neighbourhood chat about crops, weather, gardens, grain and livestock prices, and so-and-so's new Plymouth.

My sister's wedding day dawned grey and unseasonably cool for the last Saturday in June. Even by mid-afternoon, warm jackets were still the prescribed apparel. The attendants, my brother Bill and Glen's sister Ruth, drove the lovers to the Presbyterian Church in Palmerston...an obvious concession on Glen's behalf. Our family were Church of Scotland advocates, centuries old, so I guess from the outset Glen figured there was no better way to smooth the waters with his new mother-in-law than a conversion to Presbyterianism.

Following the simple ceremony, Bill, in an effort to liven things up, chauffeured the wedding party uptown for the customary horn honking. However in that a funeral was in progress, and not to offend anyone, the foursome simply rolled out of town without fanfare.

Following the photo shooting, the wedding party returned to our place, where Mom provided a supper for the two families. The bride and groom utilized Dad's car that day as Glen was afraid someone might sabotage his. Neither seemed overly concerned about our car. This plan misfired anyway when Glen's brother-in-law asked my brother Don, who was just three at the time, where Glen's car was hidden. "In there," pointing towards the implement shed.

No doubt there was more than a little sadness on their part when later that evening my parents watched their first born and only daughter disappear into the darkness of that June night. We younger kids were less sentimental. Asked my next oldest brother Richard, "Do I get Vivien's room now?"

By the time of their wedding in June 1961, Glen had been transferred to the bank in the town of New Hamburg, about a three-quarter-hour drive away. Bank personnel were shifted often in those days and February 1963 witnessed another transfer to the town of Lakefield, situated in the Kawartha District of southeastern Ontario.

Our friend, neighbour, and all-round trucker Doug Hamilton volunteered to move their belongings the three-hour-plus trip. He and Dad left for New Hamburg early in the morning and the well below freezing temperatures meant Doug had been unable to remove the layer of manure that had accumulated on the truck floor from the previous day's cattle haul, now the consistency of hardened cement. "Well, I guess if it's that hard," reasoned Doug, "it should present no problem."

It turned out to be a beautiful day, with the mid-February sunshine providing surprising warmth...enough that by the time they reached their destination the manure was no longer in a solid state. Why Vivien was upset I don't know...it was just a matter of wiping the excess manure off the bottom of all furnishings before they were carried into their new apartment.

Doug Hamilton, as you might have guessed, wasn't a professional mover, but as he didn't have to concern himself with such trivial issues as licenses and insurance, customers were generally willing to put up with a few "disadvantages." As Doug stated, "our rates are reasonable."

I guess my brother-in-law grew disenchanted with the nomadic style that banking demanded in that era, for just four months later he accepted a position with Canadian Tire and moved his family, which now included an 18-month-old and a four-month-old to the city of Kitchener.

In July of that same year, while recovering from an appendectomy, I was invited to Glen and Vivien's apartment, situated in the downtown core of the city. I enjoyed my week there. Their next-door neighbours had a nephew my age visiting at the same time. George was a fan of anything on four wheels so we had plenty of common ground and it was he who introduced me to the hobby of model building.

In the evenings, Glen would often take us for tours of the city and countryside in his '55 Ford. One evening on a barren stretch of county road somewhere outside the city, we met up with Glen's brother Lloyd, who lived and worked in Kitchener and except for colour, drove an identical car to Glen's machine. The match-up was too good to let pass and immediately a drag was arranged between the two Fords. I was as excited as a 14-year-old could be, never having been involved in a drag race before. I wouldn't that night either; Vivien and Glen had two kids by this time and Vivien mentioned something to Glen about "being an idiot" and "growing up," pointing out his responsibilities for a carload of kids...well damn!

An experience that comes to mind when recalling memories of Glen and Vivien is snowmobiling, as Glen had purchased a "Sno-Jet" snowmobile in an effort to provide a bit of fun and help offset the horrible winters we were experiencing at the time.

During the early 1970s especially, we suffered some severe winters in succession. Storm after storm, bitter winds, sub-zero temperatures, frozen pipes, hydro interruptions; at one point our lane was blocked for an entire month with drifted snow reaching halfway up the hydro poles.

Glen left his machine at our place one Saturday while he was on some errand and I decided he wouldn't mind if I took it for a little run. Soon after he'd gone I pulled on the warmest clothes I owned and trooped out to the yard. Snowmobiles were still relatively rare in our neighbourhood so Mom and my youngest brother Don were watching from the kitchen window as I settled onto the seat.

When it had refused to start after several attempts and afraid I'd run the battery down, I resorted to the "Armstrong" method. Following about two dozen pulls on the recoil and sweating like a horse, I gave up, frustrated and angry. "It's nice and quiet!" said Don as I trudged back into the house." I learned later I'd neglected to activate the choke, which I didn't even know it had.

The next time he left the machine I was ready to redeem myself. No problem starting it this time...I circled the yard a couple of times to get the feel then headed the machine out into the field just west of the house. What an exhilarating feeling as I opened the throttle! I'd heard snowmobilers rail about the thrill of gliding over a snow-covered field and quickly understood their enthusiasm. I'd only planned to circle the field a couple of times but was having too much fun and raced almost to the back of the farm, making a few sweeping power turns in the process. Boy...was I going to have one of these!

I was beginning to feel the January chill as I didn't have proper snowmobile outerwear so headed back to the house.

Don was looking out the window and I decided to get even with him for laughing, showing off with a nearly top speed blast around the circumference of the field...and then about halfway around it stopped...dead. Trying the starter several times proved fruitless. I checked the fuel; I checked the spark plug. I didn't know what else to do.

So here's Glen's snowmobile sitting in the middle of the field, 500 feet from the house. I did my best to ignore Don's attempt at humour concerning my predicament as I walked into the kitchen and asked as nicely as possible if he could help me push it up to the house. "Not really," he answered. I finally persuaded him to give me a hand and we both trudged back through the three feet of snow to the disabled machine. I figured if we could get it up to the house where Glen left it, he'd never have to know I "borrowed" it.

I had no idea how heavy a stranded snowmobile was, and after several unsuccessful attempts, Don voiced his opinion we were wasting our time and headed back to the house. I knew he was right, but hated to leave it there. I stewed the rest of the afternoon, but there was no other choice, so there it sat.

After supper, Glen and his friend Vernon Heise appeared on Vernon's machine in anticipation of an evening of snow-mobiling. "Where's the machine...in the shed?" asked Glen.

"Uh...well I just took one little circle around the field and it stopped."

"What's the problem, Glen?" asked Vernon, who was standing outside. "The snowmobile stopped on him...it's out in the field."

"I'll get my rubber boots," I volunteered quickly.

This time with Glen at my side I slogged the familiar route to the scene of the crime. Glen incidentally never said a word about "borrowing" his machine. Although knowing his nature, he'd have said "sure" in a second if I had asked.

Vernon shone his headlight on the stricken machine while Glen tried to start it without success. "Let's get it up by the yard light," he suggested. Vernon retrieved a rope from beneath the seat and tied it to the rear of his machine. His snowmobile spun and dug itself into the deep, crusted snow. We tried again, and with Glen and me pushing with all our might, we finally managed to get it up the slope to the house. My rubber boots were completely filled with snow by this time and I could feel the chill penetrating through the soles of my feet.

By yard light's glow, Glen and Vernon set about inspecting the machine while I merely stood there gradually freezing in the bone-chilling January air. I certainly wasn't contributing anything to the diagnosis...I just thought it only right I be there. They never did get the damn thing to go and had no recourse but to leave it where it sat, Vernon taking Glen home. I realize it was a disappointing conclusion to Glen's evening, but my day hadn't been so great either. One thing for sure...that "exhilarating feeling" I'd known several hours earlier had certainly dissipated.

One Minute to Midnight

FOR AS LONG AS I CAN REMEMBER, MY COUSIN DOUG WATT had spent the second week of August, the final week of his Dad's yearly holiday, at our farm. Starting in 1960 when I was 11 years old, I began the first of three summer vacations at his home in Toronto. Doug relinquished his bedroom, where I found myself surrounded by a fascinating mixture of automotive posters, magazines, comic books, model cars, and airplanes.

Doug, an only child, was blessed with an array of toys and games. A real stopwatch; a remote operated helicopter; a "Minerva" transistor radio forever tuned to CHUM. He owned a wonderful set of "Dinky" toys too. When he became more interested in model building, Doug donated the entire collection to us, which we gradually managed to lose over the years.

A week in Toronto went by quickly. Each day began with us watching morning television while Doug's mom cooked breakfast. His dad, a draftsman at Westeel Industries, was always gone by the time we arose. Doug and I would place our order, pull a TV table up to the living room couch, and sip tea while waiting to be served. Once breakfast was finished, we'd clear out, allowing his mom to clean up our mess.

We'd spend at least part of one day with my grandparents and another with Doug's grandmother, a charming Scottish lady. She would always ask about Mom…"Such a lovely lass…and on such a fine estate she lives!" She always referred to our farm as an "estate."

Doug's grandmother had been widowed several years earlier when her husband, returning on his bicycle from work, was hit by a car just around the corner from where he lived and died of his injuries. Mrs. Watt then had to go to work to support her family, finding employment repairing carpets at a factory on Toronto's waterfront, a job she held until retirement.

A favourite pastime of ours were the stock car races that ran on a 1/3-mile asphalt oval in front of the grandstand at the Canadian National Exhibition grounds. There were two classes of cars, "Hobbies" and "Super Modifieds." Most of the former were of '30s and '40s vintage, with "flat head" Fords being the favourite. The Modifieds were apt to be anything. The most common practice was to take a small car…an Austin or Willys perhaps…and stuff a then modern V-8 engine beneath the hood.

I'll never forget that wonderful odour of gasoline and burning rubber, hot asphalt and overheated engines, mixed with the sound of unmuffled engines ricocheting off the grandstand. Fans yelling, tires squealing, crumpled metal… green, red, black, white, yellow, and of course checkered flags.

Fire extinguishers, fire trucks, tow trucks, ambulances, and a crackling public address system are all etched in memory.

The Canadian National Exhibition itself was a high point...a decades-long tradition to which our family had looked forward. When I had been with Mom, the CNE midway had merely been a noisy section one rushed through to get to the other side. With Doug, I found it fascinating. Especially at night; that's when the biggest crowds became evident, swelling the midway to one solid mass of humanity. Blaring music; shouting barkers; screaming roller coaster riders; and the ever present clicking of the prize wheels, cranking out an endless array of stuffed animals and other useless trinkets to those choosing to part with their dimes and quarters...all added to the orchestra of sight and sound.

Entertaining the nostrils was the odour of almost any fried food one could imagine, while underfoot, thousands of empty paper cups, food wrappers, and popcorn boxes littered the asphalt. The seemingly millions of lights that bathed the midway; the fireworks at day's close; multicoloured flares discharging into the inky blackness, before falling in a cascading shower of stars into Lake Ontario.

An avenue that had always been persistently off limits to us was "real" CNE food. While eating the so-called wholesome products dictated by our parents from the Pure Food Building, I had been noticing with increased interest the hot dogs, hamburgers, and French fries. Mom, however, informed us this food, in addition to being non-nutritious, couldn't be trusted and would no doubt invite indigestion or even food poisoning.

Doug, I soon learned, agreed with this viewpoint...with one exception. Any food consumed within the walls of the agricultural coliseum was somehow exempt. A perennial favourite of mine...corn beef on rye slathered with mustard with an ice-cold Pepsi...I can taste it now...I can also easily resurrect the smell of the swine exhibit directly upstairs! Lots of great memories...but my Toronto vacation trilogy ended in 1962. The following summer, Doug went north to work at a Muskoka resort. That 1962 vacation proved to be my least enjoyable. Doug and I still frequented our favourite haunts...the car races, the downtown stores, the waterfront...but that summer was different. I was scared. It sounds a bit silly now perhaps, but you have to appreciate the political climate of the time and the years preceding.

The "cold war," as it was called, began immediately after World War Two, with the U.S.A., Britain, Canada, and a few others known as the Western Powers refusing to allow the Soviet Union to extend any more influence into Eastern Europe. Canada's distrust and opposing views of Soviet politics stemmed from the fact we were simply linked, both economically and culturally, with the United States. If it came to a showdown, our country would be no match against an enemy that size without help. Political analysts of that era claimed the only logical way for the Soviets to attack the U.S.A. would be through Canada.

For years seemingly, the world stumbled along, crisis after crisis: the Suez Canal project for instance, where Egypt's President Nasser seized the canal from international control, then solicited financial aid as well as armaments from Russia to finance it, and at the same time protect his "investment" from outside aggression. This ticked off neighbour Israel, which attacked Egypt. Britain and France prepared to back Israel, while Russia prepared to join the fight with Egypt.

It must have been about this time that my father proclaimed the best thing to happen to Nasser would be for "someone to drop a bomb on him!" Fortunately, the United Nations under the leadership of Lester Pearson managed to gain a truce before total war broke out.

Then came the summer of 1960, when an American U-2 reconnaissance plane was shot down over Russia. President Eisenhower assured a startled world the pilot had merely taken off from an American base in Turkey on a weather research project and "wandered off course." Russian Premier Khrushchev had failed to reveal that the pilot was alive and in their custody. He also produced a taped confession from the pilot clearly stating he had been on a spy mission.

Into this turmoil came a new U.S. president, J.F. Kennedy, but things didn't improve. Germany had always been the "hot spot" in this period, as East Berliners, alarmed at the increasing Soviet military presence, began fleeing to the west in ever increasing numbers. To stop the exodus, the Russians began the construction of a cement and barbed wire wall between the two halves of the city of Berlin. "The wall" almost instantly restricted Easterners from travelling to the western sector of Berlin, theoretically making them prisoners in their own city.

Bonds between Canada and the U.S. began to unravel as time went on as well. Although Prime Minister Diefenbaker and former U.S. President Eisenhower had a good relationship, Diefenbaker, a strong Monarchist, did lament the increased American influence upon our culture and their friendship gradually soured. With Kennedy it hit bottom. The two simply disliked each other.

It didn't help relations when Canada reneged on its promise of employing squadrons of nuclear-powered U.S.

anti-aircraft missiles as stated in the NORAD agreement. Some U.S. politicians simply told Canada it could kiss goodbye any aid from their country and we could just "blow up" for all they cared.

The nuclear threat heated up another notch that autumn when Russia resumed nuclear bomb testing in the atmosphere. The U.S. retaliated by resuming underground testing, and then the following spring, above-ground testing was reinstated.

And on and on it went...Practically all anyone talked about that summer was the threat of global war. Millions of pounds of powdered milk, tons of grain, as well as countless dehydrated products were being stored in underground silos away from the dangers of nuclear fallout. People were making plans for going underground, with nuclear fallout shelters selling briskly. Prime Minister Diefenbaker had his own underground walled retreat just outside of Ottawa, dubbed the "Diefenbunker." Even President Eisenhower's $76-billion highway system of the 1950s wasn't just for regular traffic. "If a nuclear holocaust should happen," he warned, "military vehicles would need good roads to travel as well as moving tens of millions evacuees quickly."

When I was in Toronto that summer, the radio stations would frequently run tapes of air raid sirens, familiarizing the city's population with the sound of the "real thing" for when it happened and they could supposedly make plans for escape. All evacuation routes had been methodically laid out by city planners with nuclear foresight. I recall one editorialist of the day raving that the only answer was a third world war, "...a war that will clean up the mess we're in and start over with a clean sheet!"

Doug explained how they had regular air drills at his elementary school, training the students to run to the gymnasium at the signal, or if no time allowed, simply hide beneath their desks. He surmised we wouldn't stand a chance in a nuclear war anyway, as it would be over in a flash. It was for all these reasons I wanted to get back home that summer and as far from Toronto as possible, somehow rationalizing that 90 miles northwest might guarantee my safety.

"I'd just as soon be in the epicentre," reasoned my cousin, "that way you'd never know what happened. Living on the fringe would only mean horrible radiation burns or just die a slow agonizing death from cancer"...and you wonder why I was scared?

Nearly everyone, whether admitted or not, was scared or at least nervous that summer. I imagine the feeling was rather like that summer 23 years earlier, with World War Two imminent. Unlike 1939, war was a not a sure thing in 1962, but the emotion was similar. Only this time, with nuclear capabilities, the future could be decided in minutes.

...And as if we needed more tension: Cuba had been a pain in the ass since 1959 when Fidel Castro overthrew the local government and established himself as president. Castro detested Americans and over the next couple of years stated his position by seizing all American-owned sugarcane plantations, cattle ranches, and oil refineries. Figuring perhaps he'd gone a little too far too fast, Castro became convinced the U.S. was planning an attack against his country, so turned to some of the western nations for help in securing armaments for protection. Under severe U.S. pressure to do so, they refused, forcing Castro to turn to a willing country just waiting in the wings...the U.S.S.R.

They responded by not only sending materials to build launch sites, but missiles as well. In October, American spy photos captured pictures of these missiles and things really hit the fan! President Kennedy immediately ordered a naval blockade to prevent any further shipments and demanded Khrushchev dismantle all existing launch sites...or else:

We have no wish to war with the Soviet Union for we are a peaceful people who desire to live in peace. The cost of freedom is high, but Americans have always paid it. And one path we will never choose, and that's the path of surrender or submission...

Two days went by...and in the interim that's practically all people talked about, although seemingly reserved, almost as if one erroneous comment might in some way tip the scales. Finally after another tension-filled day, Khrushchev relented to Kennedy's demands, provided the U.S. agree not to attack Cuba. A few months later, the U.S. and Russia signed maybe their most important treaty to date. Following the signing, Kennedy announced:

Yesterday a shaft of lightness cut into the darkness. Negotiations were concluded in Moscow on a treaty to ban all nuclear tests in the atmosphere, outer space and under water...According to the ancient Chinese proverb, a journey of a thousand miles begins with one step...and if that journey is a thousand miles, or even more, let history record that we, in this land, at this time, took the first step.

Predictability Postponed

Back in the 1950s attending a one-room public school in Perth County, a typical day would commence at 8:40, when our teacher Mrs. Ashmore arrived in her 1956 two-toned blue Buick. At 8:57 the belfry bell sounded its appeal, ordering us to quickly move to our assigned desks, standing at attention, arms at our side.

"Good morning boys and girls"..."Good morning Mrs. Ashmore." While standing, we recited The Lord's Prayer and sang "God Save the Queen" with Mrs. Ashmore keeping us on key and in proper time via the corner piano. Taking our seats meant that Bible scripture was next on the agenda, where the senior students participated in reading the text. Lastly, "current events," when a previously assigned student was required to bring a newspaper clipping or story on some world or local happening.

At 9:20 it was down to business, and that meant arithmetic until first recess. Although I found arithmetic relatively easy, it always seemed like a long period. Following recess was reading and spelling and after lunch grammar, science, history, geography, and literature were the assigned subjects, depending on the day. Penmanship and artistry received their turn one day a week. This agenda was as predictable as dawn and dusk.

Because the schedule of subjects was so strictly enforced, it was a bonus when the occasional diversion interrupted routine. The first departure from normality for the school season was the local "Field Day" held in the village of Kurtzville some six miles away. I only entered running-oriented events and seldom won a top prize, but I was always a "contender."

Although not associated with the actual field day meets, baseball tournaments between competing schools were regular features. I never played baseball if I could help it. I couldn't throw. I couldn't catch. I couldn't hit. In fact in my limited little league experience, only two hits stand out as memorable...one square in the chin...the other in the back of the head! I was pretty fast on the bases, but since I stank at the plate, it was an extremely rare event that my running talent was put to use.

Most of the time, no one cared whether I played, but in the days leading up to the tournament, the school team would sometimes recruit me for "a wider range of defence practice." With my athletic skills, little practice was gained.

Rather than participate in sports I didn't enjoy or was no good at, I preferred to spend my recess period "walking the fence." Completely surrounding our schoolyard was a woven wire fence with wooden posts every ten or twelve feet. Nailed to the top of these posts were 2 by 6 inch hardwood planks. I walked miles on that narrow wooden walkway over the years, my mind contemplating the more important aspects of child-hood...memorizing license plate numbers or dreaming of that new accessory-laden bicycle featured in the spring Canadian Tire catalogue. Excepting a couple of short broken sections of plank necessitating a "portage," one could walk the complete perimeter of the schoolyard.

"So, what's wrong with your little brother anyway?" someone would inevitably ask Richard. Sometimes he'd counter with an entertaining remark of how I'd fallen out of my carriage as a baby and landed squarely on my head. Most times, however, he merely looked at me and shrugged his shoulders.

Another escape from educational routine was Arbour Day. Originally Arbour Day was established as a holiday when Canadians were expected to plant trees as part of a global reforestation project. I don't know if it exists at all nowadays, but when I attended school in the 1950s it was yearly event held sometime in April when winter's remains had finally disappeared and the ground dried out. Raking dead leaves and grass, picking up broken branches, and just generally sprucing up the schoolyard was our annual objective.

Part of each year's program consisted of a walk to Gordon Nelson's woodlot a quarter mile from the school. Here we would re-establish our knowledge of trees, wild flowers, and other species of vegetation. Plus, there would be the annual cautionary reminder of the painful and irri-tating effects of poison ivy and poison oak or even more lethal plants like water hemlock.

The day's finale was setting fire to the pile of grass, leaves, branches, and other debris we'd collected, and after the fire died down we'd roast marshmallows on sharpened sticks over the glowing embers.

Some extracurricular events were of short duration, maybe just a half hour or so. Remembrance Day observances and Red Cross meetings would fall into this category. World War One veterans would drop off poppies at each school in the section every November for which students could donate a few coins of whatever currency they could spare. Mrs. Ashmore would read some background material to familiarize us with some of the events of both world wars, then close by reciting John McCrae's poem "In Flanders Fields."

Red Cross meetings on the other hand were held three or four times a year, basically summarizing for those who didn't know, or had forgotten, the organization's achievements and goals. At the end of the proceedings a collection was taken up among the students. At a nickel per student it doesn't sound like much, but added up from schools all across Canada, the campaign gained more significance.

The "Skating Party" was another occasion on which to free ourselves from the doldrums of the "3 R's." On a designated Friday in the middle of February, we'd all be car-pooled to the Palmerston arena, where the experienced skaters would spend an enjoyable hour or so circling the arena. Meanwhile, the inept, unfit, and uncoordinated, to which I belonged, merely skidded around in our galoshes in the centre of the ice surface.

When recalling childhood skating experiences, I'm reminded of a mile-long trudge to the frozen pond in our bush. My feet were cold by arrival and exchanging galoshes for skates while sitting in the deep snow only added to the discomfort. After lurching around on the rough ice surface in ill-fitting skates for twenty minutes, my feet would have absolutely no feeling...and there was still that bone-chilling walk back to the house!

But I digress...this skating event was sponsored by the Women's Christian Temperance Union, of which Mrs. Ashmore was a member. Believing that alcohol consumption was the foundation for unemployment, disease, poverty, prostitution, and every other world problem, the WCTU organization decreed the only resolution for all this social decay was total abstinence.

Someone from the WCTU would show up at our school each week throughout the month of January and as compensation for enduring their monotonous monologues on the evils of alcohol and even writing an exam...we were rewarded with the skating event. After the actual skating was through, the good ladies would serve a hot lunch. The menu seemed to alternate from year to year between "soup and sandwiches" and "beans and wieners."

Upon completion of the course, WCTU personnel donated a book from which Mrs. Ashmore would read in regulated installments throughout the rest of the winter. One could always count on a good wholesome story, high on family values and morals.

Other events that helped relieve the day-to-day drudgery of regular classes were Halloween and Valentine's Day. On Halloween every student was expected to come to school in costume. My best remembered costume was a "native person." Nowadays I suppose that choice would be classified both politically incorrect and socially unacceptable. Hand made by Mom from burlap feed bags enhanced with scarlet trim, this costume also sported a headband sprouting a single red feather. It was well crafted, as Richard wore that costume first I and I know it was passed on to my younger brother Brian when I outgrew it.

The previous afternoon's effort of cutting dozens of pumpkins, witches, goblins, and black cats from bristle board lent a spooky atmosphere to the proceedings. Prizes for best costume and "apple dunking," where the big kids would see how long they could hold the little kids' heads under water before they drowned, were characteristic of each year's festivities.

Valentine's Day was pretty low key, where it was simply anticipated that every kid would give every other kid a valentine. Take 30 to 35 students, square that figure, and you can figure a large box was needed to hold the cards as well as some time to distribute them. There was a girl in my class, Mary Patterson, who I kind of liked, so instead of the standard 50 valentines for a dollar variety, I shelled out a whole dime and bought her a somewhat gooey card that conveyed she was special. Mary moved away later that year, but we corresponded by mail for a while and she told me she still had that card.

Probably the best remembered diversions from routine were the annual bus excursions, for which a student qualified upon reaching grade five. Over the years our school had travelled to such diverse destinations as Fort George at Niagara-On-The-Lake, Casa Loma in Toronto, the Provincial Reforestation Centre near Lake Erie, and the Kellogg's factory in London.

Because it was my first, the bus trip I recall best was to "Ste. Marie among the Hurons" at Midland. Constructed in 1639, it was the first European settlement in Ontario. It probably wasn't coincidental that our class had studied the various native bands that semester, including the Hurons of

Central Ontario. We were told how the Jesuit fathers had tried to bring Christianity to the Huron Indians, but with the various warring tribes had their hands full. After several Jesuit priests were killed, the settlement was abandoned, but not before being burnt to the ground lest it suffer desecration from enemy bands.

Beginning in 1941 over a 10-year period, a partial reconstruction was undertaken. Through meticulous documentation, the entire central section of the settlement was rebuilt until it appeared as it had 300 years earlier. That was the stage of the settlement when we visited in 1960. (My brothers and I re-visited the site in the summer of 2012 to discover an extensive and continuing reconstruction has been carried out through the years and the settlement now boasts a museum, research library, and an archaeological laboratory.)

Just across the road from the Huron village is Martyr's Shrine, a church built in 1926 to commemorate the aforementioned Jesuit missionaries who lost their lives. With its two great steeples dominating the skyline that overlooks the beautiful countryside around Georgian Bay, the huge church made a bold and impressive statement to a ten-year-old. The interior was even more inspiring with its ultra-high ceilings, scores of golden candlesticks, statues everywhere and acres of stained glass.

To that point I thought our Presbyterian church in Palmerston with its soaring spire and stained-glass windows was pretty special, but it was no match for this structure. But that day more than 50 years ago, we were all strangers to the grandeur of Catholicism. My brothers and I were the lone representatives of the Presbyterian faith. The United Missionary entertained several followers plus a sprinkling of United and Lutheran. The remainder garnered no particular faith. The only person familiar with the surroundings was Mrs. Ashmore...an Anglican.

The first indication we were out of our realm became evident as we filed into the pews for a short history of the Shrine by one of the priests. Such a commotion as we crashed and clattered our way over those "planks" on the floor..."Watch the kneeling boards!" Mrs. Ashmore whispered in disgust, "Huh?...oh is that what those are!"

Of all the excursions from school, our most notable field trip took place in 1958 and travelled less than half a mile. Destination...Harlyn Farms.

Mrs. Ashmore had somehow become aware of the bulk milk system in operation on our farm and wondered if our father might be kind enough to demonstrate its capabilities to an eager class. The following Friday was the suggested date. Dad accepted the challenge, but did mention that on that particular Friday the cooler would be empty. As the milk was picked up on alternate days, Dad suggested perhaps another date would be more suitable. Once Annie Ashmore was committed to a certain avenue, however, she seldom veered. The Friday in question would remain as planned.

The only other field trip closely resembling this outing was the previous year when we visited the local cheese factory, which had gone over quite well. Once protocol was established for this venture, Mrs. Ashmore made the official announcement. To be honest, the class didn't go wild over the proposal. "Who the hell wants to look at a stupid milk cooler?" I recall a voice barely audible from the back row.

Maybe it was the beautiful weather that June Friday, for by the time of our scheduled appointment a fair bit of excitement had been generated. There were a few last-minute instructions on how to conduct ourselves and Carol

Bender, one of the grade eight pupils, was asked if she'd rehearsed her "thank you" speech. A few girls rode with Mrs. Ashmore in her Buick, while everyone else walked.

Once assembled, the milk house presentation began. Whether it was a dry performance or just too many other distractions, but when Dad finished, his audience had dwindled to just basically a few of the smallest kids and Mrs. Ashmore herself. Dad was probably correct in his assumption that an empty cooler was a poor drawing card. Most of the girls had gravitated to our front yard and were being entertained by our baby brother. Donnie was just three months old and proving to be a big hit. As for the boys...my brothers included...we were everywhere but the milk house.

My parents thought it would be a nice gesture to treat their guests, so purchased three dozen "Dixie cups" of vanilla ice cream. Contained in a small round cardboard cup and eaten with a wooden spoon, the refreshing dessert was a definite crowd pleaser. Once the festivities were over and following a gentle prompting from Mrs. Ashmore, Carol Bender on behalf of the entire school thanked Mom and Dad for their generosity and being such gracious hosts.

The following Monday however, we received a blast from Mrs. Ashmore. "I never was so embarrassed in my life!" she began. "Mr. Turner was giving an interesting and educational lecture...and when he was finished I looked around to ask the class if they had any questions and all that remained were a few of the little ones!" Her voice was rising now.

"And where was everyone?...up in the haymow or up the silo or goodness knows where! It was the rudest excuse for behaviour I've ever experienced and I'm sure Mr. Turner agreed!" She looked at me and my brothers perhaps for comment or at least acknowledgement, but received nothing as we were as guilty as the rest.

Following a few more wry comments on our "offensive," "ill-mannered," and "disrespectful" conduct, Annie Ashmore brought her tirade to a close..."I hope you enjoyed this little excursion because rest assured...it's the last you're going to get!"...and it was.

Another Season's Promise

IN 1953, MY FATHER HAD BEEN A HERDSMAN FOR A SUCCESSFUL southern Ontario Holstein breeder for many years. Agriculture was all my father really knew, and like so many born to the land, it was only natural for his dream to be a farm of his own. What Dad missed most was the "part of the earth" feeling so important to one raised in the country. He also thought my sister and four brothers needed some steady work and responsibility by this time or we'd end up "useless."

That year, Mom and Dad put a $1500 down payment on a 65-acre property north of Toronto in Simcoe County. Being that we'd never farmed, financial obligations dictated a little money had to go a long way. An Allis-Chalmers model CA tractor with two-furrow plow and cultivator, an old Massey-Harris disc, and a John Deere manure spreader was as good as it got in those early years. Practically everything else was hired from neighbouring farmers.

Herb Hounsome handled our hay and straw crops with a John Deere wire-tie baler, and harvested our oat crop with his Massey-Harris Clipper combine. Herb also provided a home-made wagon to haul the grain to the barn, where either Mom or my sister Vivien would operate the wooden sliding gate while my brother Bill shovelled from inside the flat-floored wagon. No resemblance to an auger existed, simply a bushel basket placed beneath the chute.

When full, Dad would hoist the basket to his hip, lug it all the way up the steep incline of the gangway, then across the floor to the granary situated in the farthest corner of the barn. This procedure would be repeated until the wagon was empty. After a day like that, no wonder he fell asleep the minute he settled in to his favourite living room chair!

Dad offered another neighbour, Wilfred Faris, who owned a John Deere 45 SP, the job of harvesting our wheat. Sometimes looking from afar at Wilfred combining, one had to set one's eyes on some distant object in the background to prove the machine was moving at all. Most importantly in Wilfred's mind was the number of bushels in the bin rather than acres harvested. However, when Wilfred pulled into your field, he was there for a full day. No "wasted time" at the dinner table for Wilfred, as he consumed his sandwiches and refreshment sitting on the machine's open platform surrounded by a maelstrom of dust, chaff, and weed seeds.

Winter brought its own challenges and stress to farming: frozen water, frozen milk, frozen hands and feet, cold houses, and even colder barns. Small farm snow-blowers were non-existent in that era. Some used a manure loader for snow removal, but the first couple of years we didn't have one of those either. Our manure spreader was filled by a good old-fashioned five-tined dung fork.

Getting milk to the dairy was the most pressing job each day, and in winter that meant transporting the cans out our long laneway to the road. This involved starting the tractor, and as we never used anti-freeze, a couple of jugs of hot water first had to be poured through the system. Then the drain cock was closed and the radiator filled with another round of hot water. This always worked but was time-consuming as every gallon had to be heated in the reservoir on the kitchen stove. Once started, the Allis-Chalmers was hooked to an old horse sleigh and the cans loaded for the trip to the road.

In 1957 we relocated 75 miles further west to a larger farm in Perth County, and along with the move came some machinery additions. It was a notable day when our brand-new used machinery arrived from Crawford P. Cowan, the Massey-Harris–Ferguson dealer in nearby Harriston.

A Massey-Harris 101 Junior stretched our tractor fleet to two. This particular 101 probably had fifteen years under its drawbar at this point. However, with its new coat of shiny red paint and contrasting yellow wheels, in my eyes it might have just rolled off the assembly line.

Despite its age, the Massey 101 was a tractor with an excellent reputation. The 101 series, in fact, had been the mainstay of Massey-Harris's tractor business throughout the war years, when the rest of the tractor range had made only a small contribution.

Along with the Massey tractor came a Cockshutt seed drill painted in Massey colours. (Their colours were close anyway) and a New Holland 77 baler. It too was an old machine with tens of thousands of bales to its credit, but Crawford Cowan enjoyed working with a paint sprayer, and the baler along with everything else had not been spared.

I'll admit we were a long distance from state-of-the-art agriculture...but we'd reached a plateau of independence only dreamed of five years before. Grain and corn harvesting were now the only occasions where we depended fully upon outside help, as a New Idea mower and side rake were added to our machinery list. George Cleland, our local New Idea dealer, also owned a farm, so Dad traded a Holstein bull for the new rake.

As hay consumed our largest acreage, that New Holland baler proved to be our most important machine...although as a kid it scared me to death. The decibel level of that four-cylinder unmuffled "Wisconsin" engine at full throttle could easily be heard the length of the farm. And that huge apparatus perched atop the baler that forced the crop down into the bale chamber always reminded me of a "dinosaur's" head.

With all the various components that required synchronization and timing, there was plenty of opportunity for breakdown, and ours suffered more than its share throughout the seasons, many of freak nature. Like the day the "dinosaur" plunger disconnected and smashed into the engine. Or the day a shear pin (one of about a dozen it gobbled each working day) flew from the flywheel and landed on one of the huge drive gears, breaking a tooth. Then there was the day the needles didn't clear the bale chamber in time, the plunger snapping the two-inch-thick steel rods like matchsticks. Or when our neighbour Doug Hamilton accidentally rammed a prong of his manure loader into the 36-inch diameter baler tire...

By this time in the late '50s–early '60s, Doug was harvesting our grain in return for our hay baling services. As well as his John Deere combine, Doug owned a grain swather that mounted on the front of his 420 John Deere tractor. Swathers of any kind were in short supply in our neighbourhood; hence a long list of farmers depended on him.

Doug's problems began with the rain, as the 1959 harvest proved to be one of the wettest on record, in conjunction with a design flaw of the machine that dropped the cut swath exactly in the wheel mark of the tractor. Even if two or three sunny days did materialize, the grain swath lying in the furrow of the wheel mark failed to dry enough to resume combining.

Well into September the weather remained inclement, and in some fields the grain had completely disappeared into the stubble. As mentioned, Dad had bought a new rake that spring and a couple of our neighbours had borrowed it to turn swaths. Dad wasn't convinced this was the way to go, however. "I think it shells too much grain."

Instead, he elected to turn the swaths by hand. What a job that was! Anyone who could handle a pitchfork was called into action. We spent hours turning those swaths, many of which were already sprouting from the excess moisture. "This has got to be the stupidest idea I've ever heard!" blurted my brother Bill during one session. We've got a brand new rake that everybody else is using, and here we are forking swaths by hand!"

Not helping matters was the fact that Doug's John Deere combine was showing its age with constant breakdowns, particularly bearing failures. Dad, aware by now of Doug's maintenance program...practically non-existent...wondered if perhaps it was the operator rather than the machine that was at fault. Doug had a livestock trucking enterprise to augment his farming income and as business increased, less time became available for such mundane tasks as lubrication and preventative maintenance. Dad's suspicions were realized upon discovering Doug's grease gun on one occasion crusted with sprouted grain and rusting in a remote section of the combine.

Meanwhile our old baler soldiered on…until 1961 when it gave up the ghost for good, forcing Dad to hire a neighbour to complete the hay harvest. But things really began to look up the following year when Dad purchased a brand new New Holland 270 baler and traded the 101 Massey-Harris Junior tractor on a Massey Ferguson 35 diesel.

I remember how exciting it was settling into the foam-filled padded seat of our new tractor for the first time! The steering wheel, throttle, starter switch, and gear shift all fell naturally into place. The clutch and brake pedals were right where one's feet were, unlike the stretch needed in the Allis Chalmers and old Massey. It was 1963 modern, from its three-cylinder diesel engine to its mind-boggling twelve speed "Multi-Power" transmission. It had oversize tires, the wondrous Ferguson hydraulic lift system, plus another Harry Ferguson invention, a differential lock that locked both wheels together for superb traction in slippery field conditions.

My next oldest brother Richard had always been our baler operator on the old 77, but when he began a series of off-farm summer jobs, I moved up the scale just in time for the new Massey tractor. I'd be about fourteen then.

One particular day, we had just finished baling the final load of hay from the back field of the farm. Dad took one load with the Allis Chalmers and instructed me to bring the baler and second load with the Massey. As the tractor was brand new and my experience limited, his offer certainly wasn't given without plenty of direction.

"Make sure the PTO shaft is locked securely into position after you put the baler in transport position. That's very important! The ground is kind of rough so stay in third gear, low range, and remember to shift the Multi-Power to high range when descending that hill to the river. Are you paying attention?" I assured Dad I wasn't a child and didn't need to be reminded.

(On the surface Massey-Ferguson's "Multi-Power" seemed like a good idea, the unit's high and low range providing a "gear within a gear" similar to a truck with a two-speed axle. A serious drawback, however, MP had to be in high range while descending hills or the tractor would "free wheel," making for one hell of a fast descent, the last thing needed when towing a load of hay or similar heavy load.)

As Dad left for the barn, I placed a rock behind the right hand wheel of the baler and reversed the tractor, forcing the drawbar to slide the machine into transport position. I then hooked the front universal joint of the four-foot-long PTO shaft onto the yoke that protruded from the baler drawbar. The shaft didn't seem to snap into place quite the same as when Dad did it, but appeared snug.

When I reached the brow of the hill, I raised the Multi-Power lever into high position, feeling the compression control my speed down the grade. It was then that I heard something...and glancing back in horror saw the PTO shaft dragging behind the tractor! Just then, the head of the shaft hit a rock imbedded in the ground, bending it back under the front of the baler. I hit the brakes just as the shaft's rear universal joint sheared from the baler flywheel and plummeted to the ground.

Time can dull the memory, but in my 60-plus years, I don't remember feeling much worse than I did at that moment. After staring at the mangled shaft, now bent at a 45-degree angle for...I don't know how long, I placed it on top of the baler and resumed my homeward trek, now more resembling a funeral procession. Approaching the river, I almost hoped God might grant me a favour and simply allow me to drown.

My mind raced with excuses and explanations as I drove slowly into the barnyard. Bill was looking from the stable door and somehow sensed something wasn't right. He walked over to where I sat on the tractor. As he surveyed the twisted and distorted chunk of metal still riding atop the baler, all I could think of to say was, "Well...we've got troubles now!" Bill merely answered... "Well, *you* do anyway!"

At that point Dad and my younger brother Brian appeared on the scene. Brian was brimming with excitement as he anticipated the imminent showdown. But that was never our father's style. While many fathers would have reached for the belt, or at least delivered a verbal barrage...Dad simply looked at me with an expression that varied somewhere between mild frustration and total disappointment.

This "silent treatment" could be as emotionally devastating as either of the former. "Well, there's nothing we can do about it now...we've got chores to finish." With that he turned and headed back to the stable. Totally dejected, Brian followed.

The New Holland dealer wanted over a hundred dollars for a new shaft, so Dad took it to the local machine shop and with a committed combination of heat and hammering, straightened it best they could for $20. I offered to pay the bill, although I probably didn't have 20 cents to my name. "I think you learned your lesson" was Dad's last comment on the subject.

He certainly was right on that point...as I (and anyone else who used it) was reminded every single time the baler was transferred from field to transport position. From that day onward and for as long as we held ownership, that damn shaft would bind and jam, often needing some not so tender persuasion with a sledge hammer to slide it into proper position. Indeed...some lessons can last a lifetime!

Mystical Medium

As I write this in 2014, Canadian television is celebrating its 62nd anniversary. It was 1952 when the Canadian Broadcasting Corporation (CBC) introduced its first programming to Canada on CBFT Montreal. On CBLT Toronto, program transmission consisted of just two nights a week. These were the days when a crowd gathered anywhere a television set happened to be operating. There were no bona fide television dealers or licensing contracts to apply for in those days. It was simply whoever wished to sell the new invention. Record stores, hardware stores, furniture stores, automobile dealerships...one might find a unit for sale just about anywhere.

In February 1952, King George VI died and his daughter Elizabeth ascended the throne. The following June her official coronation was broadcast world-wide from Westminster Abbey. It was this grand event that introduced television to our family, when the arena in our hometown of

Bradford, Ontario, provided an exhibition displaying all the splendour of the occasion.

Featured among the exhibits of Royal nostalgia and commercialism that momentous day was an attraction far outweighing all others: Through the brilliance of black and white, a bank of television sets strategically located around the perimeter of the arena provided hundreds of onlookers, including my parents and brother and sister, a firsthand look at Royal pageantry until then only seen in books.

How time goes...Just two years ago our family watched the festivities commemorating Queen Elizabeth's 60th anniversary on the throne. (My brother and sister noted there was a marked difference in the quality of the television broadcast 60 years later.)

Being a few years younger than my brother and sister, my initial recollection of television was no less spectacular: watching *The Red Skelton Show* at Ben and Ethel Steers', neighbours who lived just down the road. Back in the 1950s it was a common rural practice for "TV neighbours" to invite "non-TV neighbours" over for an evening of entertainment with this new medium.

With our limited exposure to this relatively new invention, little wonder we were excited when on the first Saturday of October in 1957, a panel truck with "Jack's TV and Highway Furniture" stencilled on the side pulled into our yard. The rear doors were opened to reveal an Admiral "floor model" television set...could it be? Dad quickly explained we were "just trying it out." He and Jack Seiler hauled the set up the front steps to our house and placed it in a quickly emptied corner of our living room.

My grandparents were visiting that weekend and Grandpa Carruthers had been listening to the World Series on the radio. Jack hooked up the set to the roof aerial the previous owners had left, for which Dad rather reluctantly had paid them 50 dollars. As Jack tuned in the picture, he turned to Grandpa. "That's better, eh!" Everyone gathered around the 21-inch black-and-white screen as the New York Yankees and Milwaukee Braves battled it out in the third game of what would prove to be a seven game series. Milwaukee, who in another decade would relocate to Atlanta, got thoroughly pasted by the Yankees 12–3 in that particular game, but led by slugger Hank Aaron would eventually win the series.

It was difficult to concentrate on anything else the balance of that day. Following the evening chores we gathered in the newly named "TV room" and watched *Holiday Ranch,* a variety show hosted by a slightly overweight clarinet player, Cliff McKay. We had to wait until the following Saturday before we got to see our first hockey game on our brand-new used TV. By this time, Jack Seiler's "try it out" philosophy had proved successful and the Admiral was officially ours.

How exciting it was to finally see Foster Hewitt talking to the commentator between periods after all those years listening to his voice on radio! The Leafs would lose that game 5–3 to Detroit, their third loss of their three-game season...a glimpse of what lay ahead.

Toronto had been on a slide the last two or three years, losing out in the semi-finals in five games in 1955, and missing the playoffs altogether in 1956 with a second last showing. This particular season would be the most dismal yet, finishing in the basement with only 21 wins, less than half of Montreal, who would eventually cruise to their third consecutive Stanley Cup.

In that era, the weekly televised game from Toronto came on the air at 9 p.m., about the beginning of the second period. ESSO was the only sponsor, and Canadian actor Murray Westgate was their spokesman. Each Saturday game opened with the ESSO jingle...I don't know if I remember it all...it's been a long time...

When the tires are humming and the motor purrs
and your car is eager and the thought occurs,
That it's great to be alive in this land of ours, great
to drive in this land of ours,
What a great new feeling what a wonderful sense
of sheer enjoyment and of confidence...

I can't recall the last line or two at the moment and it sounds unbelievable this day and age...one sponsor for the entire game. It's almost comedic now, but I recall the controversy when the games started coming on at 8 p.m. and Molson Breweries became co-sponsor. An outcry directed towards CBC ensued from a pious segment of the public, bemoaning how the "purity" of hockey was being defiled by allowing a sponsor that promoted the "evils of alcohol."

In this age of satellite signal TV, 200 channels, unbelievably clear images, screens that rival small movie theatres for size, high-tech electronics, and computers...televisions now run for years without service or even an adjustment. In the days of our first TV, one had to continuously "fiddle" with the controls.

"Rolling" was a constant nuisance, necessitating an adjustment with the "vertical" control. Or the picture would "narrow in," meaning the "horizontal" needed attention. If either of the above failed, a good solid whack on the side of the set with the palm of your hand would sometimes bring it around. If the picture tube was getting weak, well there was the "brightness" control to help alleviate that problem. One control we didn't have to worry about was the channel selector. We only got one channel...CBC's CKNX Channel 8 from the town of Wingham, Ontario, just a half hour away.

CKNX was born in 1955 when radio salesman and serviceman Doc Cruickshank's application for a license was granted, making CKNX the first rurally based television station in North America. Cruickshank's Wingham radio station had been operating since 1927.

That the CBC affiliate of Wingham was our only choice was certainly no hardship. Whatever happened to air was just fine. Even the commercials were fun to watch that first winter. Favourite programmes of ours were *Don Messer* and *Country Hoedown,* hosted by Gordie Tapp with Tommy Hunter as one of the featured vocalists.

Front Page Challenge...what a highlight to actually *see* Gordon Sinclair, another radio personality our family had been listening to for years. That show started the same year we got our TV. Sinclair was there from day one and Pierre Berton joined soon after. It was on the air 37 years.

Lassie and *Leave it to Beaver* were favourites of mine, as were a couple of shows filmed in Toronto. Shot at Toronto's waterfront, *Tugboat Annie* was a story about a loud-mouthed widowed tugboat captain, whose trademark was trading insults with her competitors.

Cannonball was filmed at the Food Terminal, the city's main distribution centre for produce. *Cannonball* featured two truckers who endured a variety of mishaps and adventures each week as their GMC 18-wheeler travelled to such exotic places as Buffalo, Sarnia, and Sudbury. They were forever putting up with knife-wielding stowaways, bomb threats, or mechanical malfunctions, such as losing their brakes on the infamous southern Simcoe County downgrade near the village of Mono Mills.

The *Ed Sullivan Show* was good entertainment where "variety" was an understatement. Frank Sinatra would sing a song or two and perhaps Jack Carter or Bob Newhart would perform a comedy routine. The Beatles made their debut on the Sullivan show as did nearly every other musical group of the 1960s. Sandwiched between these acts might be a juggler or somebody's "dancing bears." As far as continuity...there was none, but the Sunday night program from New York survived 20 years.

One of our family favourites, *Circle 8 Ranch,* originated right in Wingham and starred Don and Cora Robertson, Ernie King, Ross Mann, and Reg Bitton among others. This group, known as "The Ranch Boys," was just a small part of what was or had been the CKNX Barn Dance, another inspiration of Doc Cruickshank. This musical extravaganza begun in 1935 was staged at the Wingham studio every Saturday night, where people would block the street to catch a glimpse of the performing artists. Seeing the potential, Cruickshank took the show on the road, where it became extremely popular over the years.

Their most successful engagement by far was in 1948 at the International Plowing Match near Lindsay, Ontario, when 40,000 people jammed the homemade bleachers during the four-day event. At the other end of the scale was a wintry night in the village of Lucan, when just three showed up! That evening, anyone who wasn't performing would sit in the front row, clapping, whistling, and hollering...whatever it took to generate some "crowd noise" over the airwaves.

Besides hockey, the only other sports program Dad watched with any regularity was the Friday night boxing matches sponsored by Gillette with spokesbird "Sharpie" the parrot. Personally, punching somebody in the head enough times that he eventually falls to the floor unconscious never seemed like "sport"...but maybe that's just me. However, hockey remained Dad's true love for as long as he lived.

Although I was once an avid fan, hockey doesn't do it for me anymore...hasn't for probably twenty years. Too many teams, too many games, too long a season, too many playoffs, too much money...Unions, strikes, lock-outs, and breathtaking monetary contracts rule the NHL these days. (A three-month strike delayed the 2012–13 season until mid-January.)

It seems team loyalty has long since passed into history. Whichever franchise can guarantee a player the most cash or the most lucrative advertising contract or the best chance of winning the Stanley Cup...holds the cards. I heard someone talking about a player who just signed a fourteen-year, $110,000,000 contract!

The Stanley Cup was won by the Chicago Blackhawks in 2013 on June 25...that's not a misprint; that previously mentioned strike was the excuse for the late date but in 2012...a "regular" season, the final game, which was finally won by Los Angeles, didn't drag to a conclusion until June 12.

Los Angeles won the title for the second time in 2014 with another mid-June finish. When one thinks of Los Angeles, hockey isn't the first thing that comes to mind, is it?...especially in the middle of June. I don't know how even "real" hockey fans can get excited about hockey at this late stage of the season. I'd imagine those hockey sweaters must have been warm in the 100-degree Hollywood sun during Lord Stanley's parade.

As my mind drifts back through the misty annals of time to the 1950s and '60s when hockey excited me, the regular season began at Thanksgiving and finished about the time baseball was getting under way, and everything including the Stanley Cup was completed by the end of April.

Now we have the NHL draft in July, a two- or three-day event...summer hockey camp (this past August, Canada was playing some hockey tournament in Slovakia)...exhibition games in September...followed by nearly seven months of regular season hockey...before being capped by two months of playoffs. In the "good old days," overtime was an exclusive to playoffs, now to seemingly extend the games even longer it's an all-season event...what was wrong with a tie?...and the less said about "shoot-outs" the better!

Canadian Saturday night hockey now consists of two televised games in succession...one from Toronto and another from western Canada...plus a "pre-game" show highlighting the previous week's fights, concussions, head shots, suspensions, and top four-letter words uttered by team coaches and players. Not to mention listening to "analysts" continually support the ongoing violence in hockey with tired "heat of the game" and "defending the zone" arguments.

But these days it's much more than just NHL saturating television, radio, and arenas throughout Canada. There's OHL, GOJHL, Junior "C," Junior "D," College and University hockey, Peewees, Novice, Tykes, Atoms, Squirt...in both men's and women's leagues...even Tim Horton "Timbits

Hockey." There's the Stanley Cup, Memorial Cup, Calder Cup, Cherrey Cup, Canada Cup...

There's International hockey, World hockey, Junior Hockey, Women's Hockey, and every four years, Olympic hockey. There's the "All-Star" game now lengthened into a two-day venue, as well as awards presentations that slog along for a couple of evenings. If there happens to be a day with no news items pertaining to hockey, sports-writers can always exhume NHL and WHA left-winger Paul Henderson's goal against a Russian team from four decades past.

Even in 1972 I missed whatever significance that goal signified. At the International Plowing Match that year in my home county, while everyone seemed glued to a couple of television sets in the tented city, I recall enjoying the freedom of climbing onto tractors and combines unencumbered by long lines and crowds of people.

A few years ago, Paul Henderson's sweater and gloves... or was it his stick and skates?...I forget now...were exhibited in a tour of hundreds of little towns across the country. In 2012 to commemorate the 40th anniversary of that event, I heard from one source, the socks and underwear Paul was wearing on that memorable day were featured exhibits... but you know how stories go...

Perhaps I'm being unfair cataloguing hockey; it just seems "Canada's game" obsession has no end. All facets of sports are manipulated by mass media these days...and it's not only sports. What now passes for "entertainment" was unthinkable even ten years ago. "Reality TV" is today's buzzword, where terrible scripts, inferior acting, multiple tears, and liberal use of the "f" word seem the only criteria.

But personal cynicism aside of what televised programming has become over the decades...on that long ago October weekend in 1957, Jack Seiler had been correct in his assumption. Once our family got a taste of the world of television, there was no turning back. The $150 price tag for that used Admiral was nearly half our monthly farming income at that time. Dad even took a part-time job that winter to help pay the note. That magical 21-inch black-and-white screen would brighten many a long winter night in the years to come.

Just Another Friday

THE CLOCK-RADIO BESIDE MY BED SIGNALED ITS REGULAR 7:20 alarm but I was already awake. I never did sleep well with an exam to write the following day. I'd written English Literature and French earlier in the week and today's schedule would comprise the "2 G's"...Geometry and Geography.

I walked down the hall to the bathroom in the semi-darkness, noting how dawn took its time in arriving these mornings, particularly a cloudy one like this. But it seemed it had been that way for most of the month. According to the weather stats, this month had been one of the wettest Novembers on record. Today's forecast would do little to change this trend as a "low" arriving from Illinois later in the day could provide an additional inch of moisture.

While Mom made sandwiches I ate my favourite cereal... hot oatmeal...and collected my thoughts for the day. The Geometry exam would probably be the most challenging. As it was on this morning's agenda and with time to spare before catching the bus, I committed myself to one last evaluation of Geometry theorems. An almost legendary conviction passed down through students with years of educational experience declared that even if one fared poorly on the actual geometric calculations, correctly memorizing the theorems was worth 50% of the final mark. I hoped so as a good memory was about all I had going for me.

Twenty minutes later with sandwiches packed in my binder and mental images of transverse angles and congruent triangles racing through my brain, the yellow "Bluebird" rolled to a stop in front of me. Although the November dawn was still fighting a sluggish battle against the overcast of grey, the temperature was pleasant enough that only a light jacket was needed as I stood waiting at the end of our driveway.

Being the second last stop on the bus route each day meant good seats were always a premium. There was a certain group of students whose morning entertainment was the delight of denying me a seat with them and seeing how long I could wander the aisles before the bus driver would holler "give him a seat!" At least that would be one less issue to deal with today as the staggered exam schedule would mean a noticeable reduction of riders.

Upon arrival at school and following registration, all students were assigned their designated room for their particular examination. The Geometry trial proved challenging, but no more than expected, so finished with a reasonably positive attitude...one down...one to go.

After finishing my lunch in the school cafeteria, I took the fifteen remaining minutes to scan my Geography notes. For some reason Geography had always been a roll of the dice for me. Over the years I'd known results both great and disastrous. More times than not, my fate rested with the regional topography maps where one had to identify the various lakes, rivers, mountain ranges, islands...or whatever. This particular semester we were studying Eastern Europe and the Soviet Union, so I spent my last few moments scanning the maps of those areas.

Figuring I was as ready as I'd ever be, I headed towards Room 14. Throughout my high school years, I'd entertained two approaches upon first receiving my exam paper...and never did conclude which was best. The first...the recommended version...was to read the exam through its entirety. Door number two...simply wade right in and take the questions as they appear. The first approach is an asset if you know...or think you know...the majority of the answers. This route then offers a comforting state of mind in which to conclude the test. However if you see dozens of questions for which you realize too late you didn't study hard enough...it can be devastating to your self-esteem.

I don't recall which avenue I chose that particular day, but was just nicely under way when from the corner of my eye I noticed Mr. Burns, the assigned teacher for the room across the hall, appearing uncharacteristically solemn as he chatted with Mr. Graff, our assigned teacher. Mr. Graff then commented something to Mr. Burns, who only replied with a shake of his head.

At this point Mr. Graff returned to our room. "Mr. Burns," he began, "has just informed me that President Kennedy was assassinated this afternoon...he died about five minutes ago."

Those nineteen words were delivered in the same monotone and with as little emotion as Mr. Graff conveyed his daily homework assignments at the end of each period.

Silence dominated the scene for a few seconds as each brain reacted to the announcement. A couple of classmates burst into tears. Following a few more seconds the questions began...where?...how?...when?...who?...All were met with just a shrug of the shoulders.

It may have been only a few minutes but seemed much longer as I sat lost in thought. One in particular was something our History teacher had mentioned just a week or so before. Mr. Edmunds had been commenting on the fact how every U.S. president to hold office in twenty-year increments since 1860 had died in office...Lincoln, Garfield, McKinley, Harding, and Roosevelt..."I wonder," he said, "if President Kennedy is a superstitious man?"

To this day, I'm at a loss as to why Mr. Graff didn't wait until the completion of the exam to inform us of Kennedy's death. I'm sure I speak for almost everyone in that room that day how difficult it was to get our attention back to the exam and resume writing. Mr. McCoag, our Geography teacher, declared when marking the exams he could tell in some instances exactly at what point certain pupils were when the bulletin was issued. Some, who'd been doing favourably, went completely to pieces, forgetting information they never would have under normal circumstances. McCoag claimed even the handwriting changed in some cases.

The hour or so following "the message" is somewhat blurry, and I retain no recollection of how I fared in that Friday afternoon exam those many years ago, but I recall shortly before the 3 p.m. deadline handing in my paper and leaving the room. As the cut-off approached, Mr. Graff, with at least a stab at compassion, announced he would be "lenient" on the three o'clock rule.

It was strangely quiet as I made my way towards the exit doors. What a difference from the usual chorus of student chatter, slamming locker doors, and general hallway chaos. Outside stood random knots of young men and women, and with each group passed the subject was the same. The slate-grey skies that had been that day's dominant focus had now turned to drizzling rain...the weather a perfect mirror of how a majority of us were probably feeling.

Up on Main Street, people gathered wherever there was a radio or television set, straining for scraps of information of this shocking event. The rain was beginning to fall with more authority and although I didn't have a raincoat, rather than wait a half hour for the bus, I decided to hitch-hike home. A little water wouldn't hurt and for some reason I just wanted to get home.

Two or three cars passed by before a two-toned green '56 Pontiac slowed to a stop. A man, probably in his early 50s, was behind the wheel. From his dashboard radio speaker crackled the one subject that was probably on every radio in the country at that moment.

"Well, I guess they got him, eh!" he said after a few seconds. I didn't really know how to respond so said nothing.

It was less than a five-minute drive from town to our side road, but during that interval I learned President Kennedy had been in Dallas, Texas, and that a high-powered rifle from a distance of more than 250 feet had felled him as he rode in the presidential limousine. "Boy...that's a pretty good shot from that distance...especially a moving target...250 feet...yeah, that's good...must've been a pro!"

Again I didn't respond but couldn't believe the man's coldness. While he was still marvelling at the assassin's marksmanship, our concession came into view and he slowed and pulled to the shoulder. I was relieved to get out.

At home, Mom of course had the TV on, where I learned that a suspect, Lee Harvey Oswald, had been captured hiding in a movie theatre a short distance from the murder site.

Over and over as the afternoon and evening wore on, we were subjected to the same scenes. The presidential motorcade making its way along the streets of Dallas; as it passed the Texas School Book Depository, shots from a sixth-floor window were heard, then mayhem as people ran for cover and security officers and media personnel poured over the scene, while the Lincoln limousine accelerated away. The official announcement from Parkland Hospital confirming Kennedy's death, and Vice-President Lyndon Johnson taking the oath of office to become the 36th president of the United States.

The presidential plane as it landed in Washington and the removal of the casket to a waiting hearse. The new president appearing haggard and tired, issuing a brief statement promising, "I will do my best. That's all I can do. I ask for your help...and God's."

And of course Jackie Kennedy, still attired in the pink outfit she'd been wearing during the motorcade, now splattered with her husband's blood...It was like a recurring nightmare.

If there wasn't enough happening that weekend, on Sunday while President Kennedy lay in state, Lee Oswald, accused assassin, was shot to death on live TV while being transferred to the basement of the Dallas police station. A Dallas nightclub owner, Jack Ruby, wandered onto the scene and in a glaring and questionable breach of security, somehow went undetected...until he pulled out a gun and shot Oswald at point blank range.

On Monday while I was writing Chemistry and Latin, President Kennedy was buried at Arlington cemetery, amidst prayers, taps, rifle salutes, a fly-over of 50 jet fighters, followed by "Air Force One," Kennedy's personal jet for the roughly 1000 days of his presidential term. An eternal flame was lit by Jacqueline Kennedy, as it had been her suggestion to have "something living" at the gravesite... Only then was the long dark weekend over.

Looking back with the perspective of 50 years, I'm fully aware of how many people in the generation following smile or roll their eyes, or show some other sign of boredom when we "baby boomers" start reminiscing about the Kennedy assassination. But in the context of the times, both the Eisenhower era as well as our own political periods in Canada seemed dull and stuffy in comparison to the Kennedy years. Because of their exuberance and youth, John and Jacqueline Kennedy had brought previously unseen colour and vitality to the White House...and hope to a troubled world. That this picture could be shattered in mere seconds was something with which our generation couldn't easily come to grips at the time.

Just to illustrate the significance of that day, a friend of mine related how she remembered her mother ironing in the living room..."which she never did"...watching "something" on TV and crying. "I don't recall anything about what was on the television or anything else about that day...just this crystal clear image of my mother in tears."

And I should note...my friend was just a few days short of her *third* birthday!

Different generations recall different happenings and events within the framework of their own life span. For many, the deaths of Elvis Presley or John Lennon no doubt stir emotions every bit as significant as we experienced.

Certain calendar dates are forever etched in the minds of individuals who recall where they were and what they were doing in a particular moment of time...November 11, 1918...October 29, 1929...September 3, 1939...December 7, 1941...June 6, 1944...May 8, 1945...

Not on a scale anywhere near those momentous events, but for me, October 15, 1954, when Hurricane Hazel roared into Ontario, still evokes strong memories. The 600 million people who were watching their TV sets from around the world on July 29, 1969, will not forget that extraordinary day, and September 11, 2001, will certainly remain a memorial milestone.

But for the majority of my generation, time will not diminish the impact of November 22, 1963...so tolerant smiles and subtle facial gestures aside...recalling that Friday afternoon will never cease to remind us "where we were" and..."what we were doing."

Peggy and Hugh

IN THE SPRING OF 1931, MY MOTHER WAS COMPLETING HER fourth year at Toronto's Parkdale Collegiate. Like most of her peers, she was beginning to doubt whether career plans made years before would ever materialize. The economic climate was still spiralling downward from the stock market crash eighteen months earlier and future predictions held nothing but gloom.

It had always been Mom's dream to teach school, but it was obvious now it was just that…a dream. With her father facing wage reductions and shorter working hours at his job at Massey-Harris, finances for teacher's college, or "normal school" as it was then known, were out of the question. It was indeed a disappointment, as Parkdale Collegiate was one of the top academic institutions in Canada at the time and she'd already earned her "junior matriculation," the first of two major steps for Normal School acceptance.

So, conditions being what they were, my mother chose to spend her fifth year of post-elementary education at Western Commerce, a more diversified education centre whose emphasis was business rather than academics. The school, situated in the Runnymede and Annette Street area of Toronto, was a long walk from home, but to save the nickel streetcar fare, that's exactly what my mother did... morning and night for a year regardless of weather.

Helping pass the time on the homeward trek of this daily marathon was a fellow Western Commerce student, Peggy Phillips. Together each day along Bloor Street to Landsdowne Avenue, the two would walk, where Peggy headed north to her home and Evelyn, south. The two met early in the school year, and throughout the next few months began cementing the foundation of friendship that would last a lifetime.

Moving the calendar ahead eight years, we find Mother married and living on a farm with her in-laws in the desolate isolation known as Grey County near the village of Eugenia. No hydro, no running water, no indoor plumbing, friends, few and far between...comprised a long winter for a city girl. No wonder she looked forward to a visit from her old friend Peggy Phillips.

Accompanying Peggy was her fiancé, Hugh Hayes. Peggy was driving a brand new Studebaker, which they were able to drive only as far as the crossroads community of Rock Mills, some three miles from the Turner farm. That final three-mile trek was courtesy of horse and sleigh, provided by Mom's father-in-law. Roads were plowed as long as they could, but as no "wing" existed on the snow plows of that era, the machine simply burrowed through the snow, leaving in its wake a trail just wide enough for two horses to meet.

"It was a beautiful sunny day," Peggy recalled, "and such an exhilarating feeling to be gliding along under that brilliant blue sky, snowbanks towering above us on both sides and the harness bells jingling as we went. It was as if we were right in the middle of a scenic Christmas card."

Hugh was especially taken with this winter wonderland and had the foresight to bring a camera. One particularly huge snowbank impressed him, stretching some twenty feet above the road's surface. He showed the snapshot around work and everyone was equally impressed with its magnitude. However, when he and Peggy returned the following summer, most of the "snowbank" was still there. It turned out to be a pile of gravel with just two or three feet of snow on top, but Hugh enjoyed the amusement his mistake had caused as much as anyone.

Hugh quickly fell in love with country life and couldn't wait to "help" with anything that needed to be done. Chopping wood was a favourite, but my grandfather would usually make a point of hiding the axe when the city lad was around. "I guess he was afraid I'd hack my foot off or something," Hugh surmised.

Except for a twist of fate, the story of Peggy and Hugh might have ended in the late summer of 1939. Peggy and her father had planned to sail to England to visit relatives. Passage was booked on the British ocean liner *Athenia,* but as developments in Europe deteriorated and the threat of war loomed ever nearer, they decided to cancel their cruise plans. Instead, the money for the passage went towards the new Studebaker.

The night of September 3, a German submarine was patrolling the North Atlantic, 200 miles west of the Hebrides. It had left its base a week before with a score of others to be ready when war broke out. Germany had officially been at war with Britain only since the noon hour of that September day, when the submarine's periscope zeroed in on the huge passenger liner...

I guess there's no way to imagine what might have crossed the minds of Peggy and her father when they read this head-line in the *Toronto Star* the following morning...a headline Peggy confessed she would never forget as long as she lived!

OCEAN LINER ATHENIA WITH 1400 ABOARD TORPEDOED OFF COAST OF ENGLAND

It's to the credit of the crew and the close proximity of another ship that a majority of the travellers of the *Athenia* were rescued, but well over a hundred passengers still perished in the waters of the North Atlantic that night.

The sinking of an unarmed passenger ship stunned the world, but as it turned out, the *Athenia* was only the first blow in a battle that would witness the destruction of twenty-five million tons of shipping and the loss of count-less lives before World War Two was over.

My parents made a series of moves over the course of the next twenty years: Brampton, Bond Head, Bradford... and our most regular company, summer or winter, contin-ued to be the Hayeses.

Peggy, after graduating from Western Commerce, worked for Manufacturers Life Insurance, a company notorious for their low pay scale, but a popular starting point for recently graduated commercial students. She and Hugh married in 1942 and Peggy worked there throughout the war until their son Warren was born in 1946. In Peggy's words, "We were short on staff so the company insisted I work as long as possible. When I could no longer fit between my desk and the wall, my boss admitted maybe it was time to leave."

Hugh worked at a munitions plant in Toronto during the war, a job considered essential service, thus excusing him from overseas duty. After the war Hugh secured employment with Admiral Electronics, eventually becoming head of Purchasing, a position he held until retirement. Despite their frequent visits, the Hayes certainly weren't freeloaders, always bringing a cache of goodies, things like smoked hams, oranges, bananas, fancy baked goods, or "store bought" jams...items we rarely saw but at Christmas perhaps. Hugh continued to take an active interest in the functioning of our farm. Whatever the task...Hugh was up for it. Pumping water, forking silage, forking manure, carrying milk, chopping wood (unlike his father, my father allowed Hugh to take his chances with an axe).

Both lovers of nature, it wasn't surprising that Peggy and Hugh purchased an acre of land on the outskirts of the town of Port Credit, on the north shore of Lake Ontario. It was a delightful setting, complete with woodlot, plenty of grass, and even a small stream trickling through a section of the property.

Over a series of four or five decades, the quiet towns of Port Credit, Cooksville, Streetsville, Clarkson, Erindale, Malton, and others quickly ballooned into a jumble of townhouses, office complexes, apartments and mini-malls, collectively known as Mississauga. The Hayes were forced to continually fight the expansion and expropriation plans of city planners, hell bent on developing the area in order to make some "real" money from their little patch of green.

With our move to Palmerston in 1957, we doubled the distance our Toronto friends and relatives had to travel. This was a non-issue for the Hayeses, who still held the attendance record. As we had a dairy operation, carrying milk to our bulk cooler was an unfailing and consistent job, every pound transported by three-gallon pail. In accordance with milk marketing rules, all milk had to be weighed morning and night. As recounted in an earlier story, Dad would sometimes suggest an "adjustment" in the weight, especially if a particular cow needed a slight push to reach a certain level of production.

At this point I was just entering my teen years and had carried milk long enough to know which cows needed a little "adjustment," so when I placed the milk pail on the scale and it read 27 pounds, I jotted down 29. It was at that moment I noticed Hugh peering over my shoulder. He looked at the scale...then back to the weigh sheet. "How come you wrote 29 when it's 27 on the scale?"..."Well... uh...sometimes...we add just a little...just once in a while." To be honest, he'd kind of startled me.

"Hey Harold," Hugh called over to Dad, "this lad's juggling the books!"

Dad sort of explained to an amused Hugh why the odd cow's record was "adjusted." The next pail I weighed, Hugh was standing there. As I picked up the pen, he whispered over my shoulder. "What do you think...should we cheat a little on this one too?"

Hugh was one of the greatest storytellers I ever knew. He could choose any subject, and where it would simply be regular conversation for many...in Hugh's hands the story would have the most sombre individual grinning. If he noticed his audience was paying particular attention to a certain aspect of his story, he'd repeat that part, emphasizing in the retelling what his listeners were finding so stimulating. No one could recount his stories with justice, because Hugh Hayes didn't simply tell funny stories... rather he simply told stories *funny*.

A pastime that Hugh relished was target practice. He owned a then state-of-the-art semi-automatic rifle complete with telescope, and he and my father enjoyed a healthy rivalry. Dad's firearm was his old .22 calibre Cooey he'd owned since the age of 11.

Somewhere a safe distance from buildings, a wooden target would be set up and the duo would test their competitive skills. Although a near relic at this point, Dad's rifle seldom missed its mark. Plenty of practice of eradicating groundhogs over the years had paid off.

During one weekend's competition, Hugh was experiencing remarkable hard luck. Dad's brother-in-law Aubrey MacDonald happened to be visiting as well and gladly joined the competition using Dad's rifle. When it was Hugh's turn, Aubrey watched patiently as shot after frustrating shot went astray. "There's definitely something wrong with the scope!" exclaimed Hugh as another bullet missed its intended destination.

"Do you mind if I try?" asked my uncle. Hugh relinquished the firearm; Aubrey took careful aim and fired off several shots, each one hitting the target, dead centre. It wasn't difficult to see the exhibition had rankled Hugh. Aubrey savoured the moment by staring at the distant target. "Well boys...I guess there's nothing wrong with the gun!"

Another passion of Hugh Hayes was cars. The first car he owned that I recall was a 1953 Vauxhall...a car they had for years. It was a cute little medium grey machine that Hugh liked to drive for all it was worth, a throwback to his days when he would spend his weekends dirt track racing. A half mile away, one could easily recognize the distinctive sound of the tiny Vauxhall engine revving to the limit with each gear change. When Chevrolet introduced its "pony car" the Camaro in 1967, Hugh figured this was the car for him and ordered a brand new unit. Hugh was nearing 60 at this point and I recall Peggy commenting; "I don't know if it's second childhood or last fling!"

Peggy and Hugh remained loyal visitors to the farm throughout the 1970s and into the '80s when my parents retired to town. When Mom and Dad celebrated both their 40th and 50th wedding anniversaries, although it was officially "just family," the Hayes were the exception. By the time the '90s rolled around, time was catching up with the foursome, making driving less appealing, so phone and mail became the prescribed means of communication.

Hugh passed away in June 1997, in his late 80s, while Dad followed just four months later. Mom and Peggy continued their regular telephone conversations and letter writing. Reading remained a common bond as it had since they met, and proved invaluable now as they adjusted to life alone. Through their letters and phone calls, discussions on the particular books they were reading at the time would invariably dominate their conversations. "Thank goodness for the comfort of a good book," commented Peggy, on one occasion.

Then came that day in the summer of 1999 when Mom received a call from her sister Alma, who'd seen Peggy's obituary in the *Toronto Star*. Alma had been away for a few days and was catching up on the papers when she saw the notice. By this time, the funeral was over. Mom never learned of the circumstances of Peggy's death...whether her life-long friend passed away at home, in hospital, had been ill, died suddenly...no idea. Peggy and Hugh had one son, but he never thought or bothered to inform anyone in our family... not much of a way to end a seventy-year friendship, was it?

Artemesia's Wonder

THE HAMLET OF EUGENIA, ONTARIO, IS SITUATED ON THE EAST-ern edge of the Beaver River in the Township of Arteme-sia, Grey County. In 1869, my great-great-grandfather Samuel Turner emigrated from Lincolnshire, England, and purchased crown land in the valley just below this settlement.

In the latter part of the 19th and early 20th century, Eugenia, despite its diminutive size, was a thriving commu-nity, boasting a couple of saw mills, grist mill, barrel and stave factory, casket factory, and two general stores, one serving as the local post office. Also there was a blacksmith, cobbler, veneer mill, shingle mill, two churches, and a two-room schoolhouse with two teachers administering educa-tion to 60 children.

Working with the surveyors when the new commu-nity was in its planning stages were several young soldiers who'd recently served in the Crimean War, a religious war fought in the mid-1850s between Russia and an alliance of

France, Britain, and the Ottoman Empire...better known as the Turkish Empire. One of the soldiers suggested the new community be named for Princess Eugenie, wife of Napoleon III, who'd commanded the French army in the aforementioned war. Thus, many of the seemingly strange street names evolved from battles fought in the Crimean Peninsula, such as Inkerman, Balaclava, Zouave, and Conrobert.

Town fathers had great expectations for Eugenia, but when the Toronto, Grey and Bruce Railway bypassed the new municipality, further development stagnated and population never did reach the size necessary for incorporation as a village.

But Eugenia didn't just fade away. It had something far beyond what most communities could even imagine: Mother Nature, eons ago, had chosen Eugenia as a very special place with a spectacular landmark as its focus. The first settlers of Artemesia Township and all who followed were drawn especially in spring to a distant roar, which upon closer inspection revealed one of nature's wonders: on the Beaver River, a thundering wall of white water cascading into a narrow limestone gorge nearly 80 feet below.

An early resident of the township, William Hogg, foresaw the potential of this phenomenon and in 1895 purchased a turbine and constructed a small generating plant capable of supplying power to Eugenia and neighbouring village of Flesherton. This was the same time the city of Toronto was looking for an electrical source and Hogg made a valiant effort to persuade Toronto that his plant could handle the feat. Hogg was no match however for Adam Beck's newly formed hydro-electric development, which had a pretty good power source itself...Niagara Falls.

Working independently of both of these proposals was a group of Toronto businessman who spent an enormous amount of money and time excavating a tunnel through the large hill beside Eugenia Falls. Their ultimate goal was to divert the Beaver River through this tunnel, theorizing the extra fall would increase the effectiveness of the turbines. After they had built a tunnel nearly 900 feet long but before a gallon of water passed through, the venture went bankrupt.

This cleared the way for Beck's consortium to move in, his Hydro Power Commission immediately beginning an extensive land acquisition program with area farmers. Those most affected were between the 8th and 12th concessions of Artemesia running east from Eugenia, an area encompassing approximately 1700 acres. A northern section of my great-grandfather Solomon Turner's farm was in the proposed flood area but was mostly woodlot.

Although they'd receive much higher compensation, some township residents would see their entire farms threatened. Owners were given time to dismantle and move buildings and remove any logs cut, but not standing timber. Everything didn't happen as planned; a solid brick house owned by the Plantt family was jacked up and awaiting removal when the water in the new lake rose faster than expected and the Plantt house simply dissolved in the tide.

Before all this took place of course a dam had to be built, and one of the biggest tasks was getting a huge steam shovel to the site to dig the foundation. The only way to bring a machine of this magnitude was by rail...except the railway had bypassed Eugenia, you'll recall, the closest spur being Ceylon Station, seven miles away. The dilemma was solved by placing temporary rails in increments of 100 feet and pushing the giant shovel onto the rails. The machine was then stopped, the 100 feet of track taken from behind and placed in front of the shovel, which was then rolled onto that particular stretch of rail...and so it went all the way to Eugenia.

This mega-construction project provided many hours of pay for the estimated 1,000 workers who flocked to the site for the 25 cent per hour wage. But it was hard labour and unrelenting...seven days a week, three gangs each working an eight-hour shift with no actual meal break... "a shovel in one hand, a sandwich in the other."

If you couldn't cope it was goodbye. It was said only half in jest of the three groups involved in the project, there was one gang walking in from the train in Ceylon...one working...and one walking back to catch the train home after being fired.

My grandfather Oliver Turner made his contribution to the dam's construction, hauling and levelling gravel courtesy of a team of horses and a "gravel scoop." For this service, he received a coveted $5 a day.

When the Eugenia dam was completed, it was an impressive structure with a girth of 1700 feet, towering 50 feet high at its centre point. Backed by the man-made lake... referred for generations locally as the "Hydro Lake"...this reserve of water was sent gushing nearly 3300 feet through two 48-inch wooden pipes constructed of Douglas fir to a surge tank, then a further 1500-foot drop to the newly constructed power station on the valley floor.

Perhaps there wasn't a lot of choice where one purchased generators and turbines in 1915, as the first shipment originated from Switzerland. The First World War was well under way at this point, and the ship carrying the three turbines bound for the Eugenia Hydro project was sunk by a German U-boat as it entered the St. Lawrence River. This caused a several-month delay while a second order was submitted, this one much less complicated and much closer to home...Wisconsin, U.S.A.

Finally on November 18, 1915, the flooding of area farmland began when the Eugenia Dam was officially opened, its three generators producing 4500 kW of power. This output was sufficient capacity to provide electricity to every village in a 30-mile radius, including the busy seaports and shipbuilding centres of Collingwood and Owen Sound.

By the time the snow melted the following spring, township residents could barely recognize their surroundings. Of course those in the direct flood plain had moved, but others on the fringe of this new lake suddenly found themselves isolated from previously close neighbours.

My great-grandfather's farm was completely severed from the village, as the 10th concession west to Eugenia was now entirely under water. During winter it wasn't as restrictive, as one could cross on the frozen ice, but routine travel on the concession was a difficult habit to break. Once automobiles began showing up in rural communities, the detour wasn't so tedious, but until such time, those affected had no other recourse but adjustment.

By the 1950s Lake Eugenia (its official title) had become an attractive tourist destination with private cottages ringing its shores, but before the end of that decade, serious cracks were discovered in the concrete dam. The Hydro Commission believed the repair bill of half a million dollars to be economically unsound so decided instead to lower the level of the water in the lake by four feet, thereby easing pressure on the dam. Cottage owners, who'd enjoyed water literally at their doorstep, suddenly faced a shoreline 50 feet away. With the value of their property seriously compromised, the resulting protest travelled all the way to the provincial legislature in Toronto. After considerable pressure, the government granted funds for a new earthen dam, enabling the reservoir to be raised to its former level.

While the new dam was being constructed, the lake was completely drained and all the trees left when the area was flooded nearly 50 years earlier were removed. I recall on our frequent trips to visit relatives in the Eugenia area that summer how strange the drained lake appeared. And it seemed the Hydro Commission couldn't win when it came to appeasing lake residents, the "lake clearing" angering those who'd enjoyed fishing, as the trees stumps, etc., had provided a mecca for their sport.

Recreational interests of cottage owners had shifted over the years, however; small fishing boats had been traded for powered watercraft, and this revitalized waterway, like it or not, was the future. A compromise was reached when an area of the lake south of the eighth concession was left as nature intended and the fishermen could enjoy their recreation in relative peace.

By the 1980s, modern technology, including nuclear energy from a mega-generating plant on the shores of Lake Huron, had relegated small water-powered generators such as Eugenia Falls to the back burner when it came to hydro-electrical output...but in its day!

For interest's sake, two of the three Wisconsin-purchased turbines installed in the Eugenia generating plant back in 1915 were still in operation at this point seven decades later.

Today, Lake Eugenia is most noted for some 400 cottages scattered around its circumference, the ground on which several of these cottages reside being farmland once owned by my ancestors. My uncle, Eldon Turner, fourth generation of Turners of Eugenia, spent considerable time and money throughout the 1960s severing lots from his farm that bordered the lake.

This past April, I was walking through Artemesia Township's Salem Cemetery, final resting place of generations of Turners and their neighbours; it was a peaceful Sunday morning, and while strolling the grassy walkways between the gravestones I became aware of a distant sound. It was difficult to decipher at first...sort of a hissing. With the passing of the occasional vehicle on the side road, the sound would subside then re-establish itself as it had before the interruption.

Finally the source of this mysterious whispering occurred to me. A two-mile drive brought me into the hamlet of Eugenia, where on the Beaver River a thundering wall of white water, fresh from winter's run-off, cascaded into a narrow limestone gorge some 80 feet below...the same sight and sound the first settlers to Artemesia Township discovered more than a century and a half before.

I have visited the falls many, many times in my life, but never did that rushing torrent affect me as it did that April morning. Perhaps the reaction was triggered by that leisurely ramble among the marble memorials earlier, each inscription helping me to connect the dots of my lineage and compelling a closer examination of my ancestral roots.

As I stood mesmerized by the surging tide of water, I tried to imagine the overwhelming emotion my ancestors experienced when initially setting eyes upon this phenomenon of nature. On this Sunday nearly 150 years and six generations later...the falls on the Beaver River stirred the same emotion within me.

Yes Sir...Mr. Gray!

ANYONE FOLLOWING THESE RAMBLINGS OF MINE KNOWS HIGH school was not a particularly enjoyable part of my life. An occasional distraction, however, temporarily at least freed me from the daily apprehension and anxiety I endured those teenage years.

Immediately following Christmas break, Norwell Secondary School launched its extracurricular activities. A broad range of subjects were offered, from language, home economics, and music classes to firearms and emergency response training. Being a non-joiner, I of course did nothing...except on Tuesdays. Beginning on the first Tuesday after the holiday, every first-year male student got "drafted."

"Tonight we begin cadet practice" boomed Principal Gray's voice on the intercom. "All boys in grade nine will assemble in the east hall where you will be joined by Mr. Edmunds; and let me make myself clear...cadet inspection is compulsory!"

Ephram Gray, a true core army man had initiated cadet training at Norwell in 1943, believing it to be an integral part of the school curriculum. Another reason, the provincial government offered a grant depending on how many students participated. Mr. Gray functioned as Commanding Officer, while Mr. Edmunds, Modern History teacher and Guidance Counsellor, dusted off his Second World War captain's role.

Fifty or 60 raw recruits stood waiting in the hall for the first practice. "Captain" Edmunds explained briefly how we'd be meeting regularly each Tuesday until April, then more often as needed, up until cadet inspection in late May. We were stationed in three long lines and began some basic drill formations. "Left turn!...right turn!...a...ten...shun!" We repeated these moves repeatedly while the kids in the upper grades entertained themselves by staring, pointing, and laughing at us through the double glass doors. After a half hour of drill, plus a reminder that absenteeism would not be tolerated, we were excused.

As fellow classmate Laverne Mahood and I embarked the bus, I recall overhearing an upper level student comment to someone, "I'd hate to depend on that sorry looking group to defend our country!"

Well, we got better...slowly. Weekly practice had now moved to the gymnasium, where our marching abilities could be more finely honed. "Left...left...left right left...left...left... left right left. Left turn...right turn..." and on it went week after week. Mr. Gray would drop in on an irregular basis to monitor our progress and check the attendance roll.

After a couple of months we were fitted with rifles from World War Two surplus, an advancement compelling an entirely new set of manoeuvres; practice...practice...practice. We were now stationed in permanent platoons each with its own sergeant, someone who was good at bossing people around, usually a fourth-year student.

For the first two months attendance was nearly 100 percent, but as time wore on and pleasant spring days became more frequent, a noticeable amount of absenteeism crept into the ranks. Laverne wanted to skip the exercise one night and asked Chris Van de Water and me to join him.

"What if Mr. Gray happened to show up?" I asked nervously. Chris shared my apprehension, but Laverne stated we could do what we wanted; he simply wasn't going. Chris and I sort of hedged our bets, deciding to leave it to fate. "Heads we go to drill."

The spinning coin indicated what was called and we headed towards the gymnasium. It seemed the warm spring air had claimed a few more soldiers than Laverne, for the ranks were noticeably reduced. With a thin smile, Mr. Edmunds asked. "Is there a plague of some sort circulating the school of which I'm unaware?"

Next morning during Physics class, Mr. Gray marched unannounced into the room. "Excuse me Mr. Burns...but I would like to see Matthews, Mahood, Dixon, Murray, and Armstrong in the hallway...now! Laverne hadn't shown up for classes that day, so just four timidly made their way towards the door. Mr. Gray closed the door behind him while Mr. Burns resumed teaching, but his voice was no match for Eph Gray's as the hollering began right away.

"Mr. Edmunds has informed me we had a few "no shows" at cadet practice last night. You boys are in 9A5A, so I presumed you knew what "compulsory" meant. Obviously you don't!...Do you know what compulsory means?... well then what's your excuse?" We couldn't hear all what was said, the explanations varying between "uptown"..."I forgot"...and "a sore leg."

"I don't give a damn if you have two broken legs, Dixon! When I inform you to take drill I expect you to take drill and I will be the one that decides the reasons! Now get back to class and if this ever happens again, you'll receive a military exercise from me you'll never forget!"

The four filed back into the room and once inside acted like heroes, joking...a couple even laughing as they took their seats. I guess they laughed too soon; Mr. Gray was watching through the glass-panelled door, which immediately opened.

"So you think it's funny, do you? Well come with me, laddies, and you can decide for yourselves if it's funny!" I guess not...as there wasn't the hint of a smile from anyone when they returned a few minutes later. Yes...that was a lucky coin Chris tossed the previous evening!

In April, we received uniforms to aid our transformation to something more resembling military personnel. These uniforms were regulation World War Two product, and since that war was fought by grown men, you can imagine how a bunch of scrawny cadets appeared, stomping along in our oversized jackets and baggy trousers.

At last the big night when all the platoons gathered at the Harriston arena for inspection. Plenty of pageantry and spectacle was in force with the Norwell Brass Band providing the rhythm to keep us reasonably in step. Following some awards of merit and a few speeches, the platoons circled the arena one last time, then led by the band, marched downtown to the cenotaph. As each platoon passed the marble monument, their sergeant hollered, "Left...face!" Someone in the platoon...I don't recall who...issued the same order as we passed the pool hall.

Unlike today's students who have a wide range of options when it comes to subject matter, "compulsory" was still the key word for our generation...Latin for instance. Our teacher, Maurice Audet, was an interesting character who'd travelled the breadth of the globe, spoke French fluently and three or four other languages as well. He'd also spent three years interned in a Japanese prisoner of war camp during World War Two.

I suppose I learned something about vocabulary and the root words from which our language was derived, but was unsure what good the subject was actually doing. Inside the front cover of my textbook, I penned the verse handed down from generations before.

> *Latin is a subject as dead as dead can be. It killed*
> *the ancient Romans and now is killing me.*

An interesting phenomenon began in our Latin class during late March. A fellow student decided he simply didn't like the subject anymore and asked Mr. Audet if he could quit. "Okay" was his answer. Another tried. Same result. Apparently it was Mr. Audet's belief if a student didn't want to learn, he didn't want to teach. Pure and simple; after a third classmate dropped out, I made my decision.

"Mr. Audet...I don't think I'll be taking Latin anymore." He simply nodded and made a gesture with his hand as though he were dismissing some annoying insect. A week later, Chris followed suit. There were six of us now. The weather was warm at this point and since Latin was first period following lunch, we'd go "up town" or to the park and simply blend in with the senior kids who were on their rightful noon hour.

This utopia lasted well into May, until one morning Mr. Gray announced over the intercom that he wanted to see six students in his office...now. I was one of them. Even a person with just half his mental capacity could figure why we were being summoned. As we filed quietly along the corridor leading to the principal's office, the atmosphere resembled what I would expect just prior to an execution.

"We really didn't do anything wrong," someone finally ventured, breaking the gloomy silence.

"That's right," I agreed. "We did have Mr. Audet's permission." With our spirits buoyed, we walked purpose-fully into Mr. Gray's office. That buoyancy evaporated fast. Eph Gray as usual wasted no time on preliminaries.

"Well boys," he began loudly. "I understand you haven't been going to Latin class!" He studied our reaction, then with a yardstick for emphasis, added in a much more subdued tone..."and on whose authority?"

No one else spoke, so I bravely piped up, "Mr. Audet, sir." Quickly wheeling in my direction, Mr. Gray pressed his yardstick into my belly. "Mr. Audet has no damn authority! I'm the only one around here that makes that decision! Has anybody got a problem with that?" We all sort of mumbled "no sir." Any other answer would have been suicidal.

"So Mr. Turner, you seem to have all the answers...I'd be interested in hearing why you decided to drop Latin?" I knew he was expecting some sort of answer and quickly, so just said the first thing that came in to my mind. "I don't like it, sir"...could I've said anything more stupid?

"Oh, so you don't like it...well I don't like gravy on my potatoes. So you see we all have our crosses to bear." To what

subject do you think your talents would be more suited?...
whittling?... basket weaving?...how about pillow embroidery?"

He wrapped up his short tirade by waving the now
familiar yardstick in our faces to make his final point. "Now
boys, you will go to Latin class today and tomorrow and
every day until the end of the semester, at which time you
will write the exam and you'll pass if you know what's good
for you!...now run along."

As we shuffled out, Chris played one last card. "Sir...if
we get a note from our parents can we quit?"

Gray exploded. "I don't care if you get a note from your
goddam Sunday school teacher! You're in "A" class laddie...
and that means Latin and the sooner you get that through
your thick head the better. Now all of you...get the hell
out!" We got out.

Skulking back to Latin class that day we wondered what
reception awaited. I don't know if he was still stinging from
his own "talk" with Principal Gray or what, but Mr. Audet
never so much as acknowledged our presence. For the rest
of the semester it was as if we were invisible. I studied a
reasonable amount and managed a "50" grade, whereas
Chris and Laverne both fell short of the mark. It was all
redundant anyway, as none of us picked Latin, which would
finally become an optional subject the following year.

One positive aspect of my third year at Norwell was the
fact I finally succeeded in dumping Physical Education, a
pain in the ass from day one. My release was even legal...
sort of. On one of the first days of winter I took a header
on a patch of ice outside our house, and as I reached to
gather myself my index finger bent backwards causing a
slight sprain. That was on Saturday and my finger did swell

up a bit...really! It was still sore Monday, so I managed to persuade Mom to write a note to the principal.

My reputation obviously preceded me, for instead of simply signing his name and granting me indefinite leave, Mr. Gray wrote across the bottom of the paper in big red letters, ONE DAY ONLY! Well, that kind of miffed me, but I presented it to the gym teacher...and never went back. And the teacher never said another word. All too familiar with both my athletic abilities and attitude, he probably thought "good riddance."

Laverne hadn't darkened a gymnasium door all year because of some arm affliction that he never did fully explain. But he had discovered that some senior students had a spare class every day during sixth period that coincided perfectly with our Phys. Ed. class. So, each afternoon we simply melted into a couple of back row seats and minded our business.

One day the door opened and in walked Mr. Gray. Those eyes that missed nothing settled on Laverne and me. "Well now...what have we here?" strolling back to where we were seated and placing his imposing frame between us. I happened to have a text book open, at least giving the impression I was studying.

"So, how long have you boys been in senior grade?" It seemed disrespectful not to answer but anything would have sounded stupid, so we said nothing.

"So you just skipped a couple years and went straight to the top! ... that's funny... I never thought either of you were particularly bright enough for such advancement!"

"So where are you lads supposed to be?" staring straight at me.

"Phys. Ed.," I answered rather weakly.

"And you're not there...why?"

"I have a sore hand." I thought that sounded more severe than a sore finger.

"What's your story, Mahood?"

"I have a sore arm."

"I see...a sore hand and a sore arm. What do you do, hit each other with a hammer every night?" A couple of stifled laughs could be heard around the room, then Mr. Gray simply turned on his heels and left the room and no more was ever said.

That remark about not being "particularly bright" certainly contained an honest dose of truth as I'd barely scraped by on my Christmas exams and the upcoming semester's results would prove to be a total disaster. Academically I was...to borrow an expression of the day... "bummed out."

However, less than two months following that encounter I would be gone, and Norwell Secondary would be but an ill-fated footnote of my youth.

Different Is Not Always Better

I DOUBT IF MY PARENTS FULLY REALIZED OR APPRECIATED THE long hours my brother Bill expended over the years in the operation of our dairy farm. When Dad and Mom purchased their Simcoe County farm in 1953, Bill was 11 years old but performing adult tasks. Milking, feeding, watering, and cleaning all had to be attended night and morning. Nothing changed but the location when we moved to Perth County four years later...milking, feeding, watering, and cleaning.

If my parents needed a reminder, the situation presented itself on an August morning in 1961, with my brother waking up with a sick stomach and sore abdomen that failed to improve as the day progressed. Next youngest brother Richard was working at a resort in Muskoka that summer, while that particular week I was visiting my cousin in Toronto.

"Do you think you're good enough to do the evening chores?" my Dad asked. Realizing how critical help was, Bill agreed with reluctance.

"I'll do the morning chores if you don't feel any better," Dad promised. For that Bill was relieved, for he felt worse the next day. By that evening he could barely stand. At this point Dad and Mom finally came to the conclusion perhaps this was more than a usual belly ache!

The doctor was called (they still made house calls then) and immediately diagnosed acute appendicitis. By the time Bill was wheeled into the operating room the appendix had burst and events simply went south. Following the operation, peritonitis developed and Bill spent the next few days in varying degrees of delirium and seemingly endless vomiting. When at last my brother arrived home, he walked like an old man and it was October before he fully recovered.

Our milking stable at this point in time was archaic even by 1960 standards...especially where the younger cattle were housed. Homemade wooden partitions secured by the farmer's "best friend"...baler twine...were no match for imaginative and resourceful animals who had all the time in the world to plan and practice escape procedures. Consequently, any time of the day or night one could discover cattle wandering the stable, eating from the feed barrel, tearing up bales of hay, or untying feed bags...the opportunities were limitless.

Bill would grumble how things would be different on *his* farm. Only steel partitions would suffice. And heated water bowls. No more carrying water in pails because the bowls were frozen. And an automatic stable cleaner would relieve the drudgery and monotony of manure removal. "You'll find out when you're on your own there isn't enough money for all the extras," Dad would remind him.

Bill and Dad would argue at length on feeding practices, ventilation issues, breeding choices, pedigrees…"If we fed our cows as the Department of Agriculture recommends, we'd have more milk without feeding as many cows."

"All those protein supplements do is make the feed companies rich," Dad would counter. Bill insisted we should have ventilation fans. "No sense blowing all the warm air outside!"

"But it would be *dry* air," Bill replied. "Okay, next time you complain about frozen water bowls I'll remind you it's a *dry* cold that's freezing the water."

For the most part, Dad took the criticism good-naturedly. When he was Bill's age he had similar exchanges regarding farming practices with his father. The exception, however, was if Bond Haven Farms, where Dad had worked for 10 years, was mentioned in unfavourable fashion. This organization had provided Dad with ten cows practically as a gift, serving the foundation of our own herd.

Truthfully, some of these Bond Haven cattle had been around for a while and Bill figured they were no longer earning their keep. "What are you going to do…wait until they die of old age?"

"They've got good pedigrees and can still raise good daughters" was Dad's argument. "It doesn't cost any more to feed a good cow than a "hay burner," replied Bill. It would be about this juncture of the seemingly never-ending discussion that Dad would remind his son we wouldn't be farming at all if it weren't for these "hay burners."

It was Bill and his mother who had the greatest scraps. Unlike Dad, who could let a remark pass, Mom's temperament dictated the direct opposite, and a heated argument would erupt. They'd argue about anything and everything and simply wore on each other's nerves.

When Mom and Bill became involved in a "discussion," I'd automatically take my brother's side, as he was my hero. It was Bill who'd taught me to differentiate between makes of cars and sparked my interest in license plates. It was he who explained the variety of crops we grew and how to identify weeds. How certain animals hibernated, how different birds built their nests, and which species migrated in winter and where they went. How snakes in our area were harmless and so were bees if left alone.

It was Bill who taught me the *full* names of all the cows in our stable and would regularly test me. He taught me lyrics to country songs and how to count in French. I also thought he was the funniest guy in the world. "Knock, knock"..."Who's there?"..."Madame"..."Madame who?"... "Madame foot's caught in the door!"

He also performed great animal impersonations. My personal favourite was a snake, where he'd stare straight ahead motionless with this stupid blank look on his face... Okay...perhaps you had to be there.

Of course the routine where he wiggled his ears causing his hat to cycle up and down was legendary.

The result of this hero worship meant I owed him my allegiance in a quarrel. There was never any trend to these arguments between him and Mom. The most trivial issue would ignite the powder; their conflicts became so programmed that my three-year-old brother Donnie would head to the kitchen closet to hide until the storm passed.

Events came to a boil one morning during breakfast. What or who started this particular squabble and what it was about who would know, but Mom bopped Bill over the head with a Melmac (hard plastic) saucer and Bill retaliated by hitting her over the head with a piece of toast and honey. Dad then literally booted Bill out the door.

I figured a piece of toast paled in comparison with a saucer for a weapon and was quite vocal in my opinion that Bill had come out on the stinky end of this deal. A whack on the side of the head courtesy Mom's hand, quieted me down.

This continuous combination of tension at home and the fact that Bill was now 21 dictated an alternative arrangement. His own farm seemed the obvious solution... a farm discovered by accident one afternoon on a remote side road about three miles from home while he and Dad were avoiding a Department of Transport safety inspection.

Any honest evaluation would've placed this farm on the lower rungs of the progressive ladder. A rickety wooden-partitioned cattle stable, a couple of horse stalls, a pig pen, and chicken enclosure within the barn was complemented by a small drafty frame house heated only by a kitchen wood stove. Small rail-fenced paddocks completed the snapshot of the 100-acre property.

Dad purchased the farm then transferred ownership to Bill the following year after the Junior Farmer Credit Corporation financed a more modern stable as well as a milk house. Over the years, Dad had given Bill the occasional cow and calf to provide a foundation for his own herd. Charlie Cerswell, owner and manager of Bond Haven Farms, had provided a similar arrangement with our father, and now offered Bill the use of some of his older stock in exchange for the first heifer calf. Bill didn't have to be coaxed at this point to take the "hayburners" off Charlie's hands.

These proved to be dismal times for my brother. His new farm proved in desperate need of tile drainage, hence crops were lean. The meagre milk cheque was no match for mortgage, milk cooler, and machinery payments as well as repairs, seed, and fertilizer. All those lofty claims to Dad about how *his* farm would operate surely must have haunted him.

An oil furnace installed in the house made conditions more livable by the second winter; however Bill was mainly existing on peanut butter sandwiches, canned stew, and pork and beans. After a while the kitchen table became so stacked with farm magazines, newspapers, mail, and dirty dishes, Bill could hardly find a corner from which to eat. He solved that dilemma by bringing in another table.

Sometime during that year, my sister and her husband, tired of city living, struck a deal whereby they lived in Bill's house and boarded him, a deal that seemed to benefit everyone...and only one kitchen table was needed.

Both 1964 and 1965 proved to be wet seasons and Bill's poorly drained acreage felt the full effects. Our self-propelled combine had to be pulled out of the mud on two or three occasions...once by a bulldozer. I believe my brother would've been farther ahead growing rice.

While the aforementioned seasons were notorious for an over-abundance of rainfall, 1966 proved the opposite, with drought conditions. A heavy thunderstorm on June 6 was the last precipitation we saw until mid-July. Coupled with extreme temperatures, what should have been lush pasture was no more than brown, dried up grass dotted with ragweed and thistles. Hay, normally stored until late autumn, had to be fed throughout the summer until sufficient rainfall could provide pasture re-growth.

The Ontario provincial government offered a $5,000 "drought relief" package presented at a 5% interest rate designed to replenish hay and grain stocks. The money didn't go far as inflationary prices spawned by short supply...and in many cases simple greed...quickly consumed the principal. And since it was a loan not a gift, it simply meant one more payment in an already stretched budget.

Due to the nature of Bill's farm, crops had been less than inspiring even in the so called "good years." A drought merely exacerbated the situation. With the prospect of more hay and grain to buy plus other debts accumulated over the course of the last three seasons, a decision was made to "work out" for a while. It was the familiar road our father had often travelled. Dad kept three or four of Bill's favourite cows at our barn and the balance were sold.

Fifty miles away in Brant County, Bob Brown, owner of Browndale Holsteins, was in the market for an experienced herdsman, and Bill, who had been milking cows and monitoring the Holstein-Friesian Association practically since he could walk, certainly qualified. August 1, 1966, with a promised monthly salary of $400, Bill headed out to meet the challenge.

With the exception of the cows mentioned, all that remained of Bill's herd were the heifers. When winter came, they were transferred from pasture to his stable along with a few of our own, as our barn was chronically overcrowded. Morning and evening I drove down to Bill's to feed the cattle and clean the stable. I don't recall any remuneration but I don't think I really expected any.

Bill remained in his capacity as herdsman for Browndale Holsteins exactly 14 months, although I don't believe he accumulated much in the way of savings. He attended every country music concert that came to the nearby city of Brantford, went on a bus tour to Nashville, purchased records by the score plus a $400 stereo on which to play them. Dad questioned his son's wisdom on spending so much on a "record player," adding how that $400 would have gone a long way towards paying off some of his debts. Bill countered with this analysis: "With the money I owe...$400 is just a drop in the bucket!"

Bob Brown seemed to become quite a hero to my brother. Any weekend he was home we'd be treated to "Bob Brown" stories; Bob Brown's stable cleaner; Bob Brown's silo unloader; Bob Brown's milking system; how Bob Brown fed his cows and what bulls he used in his breeding program. Bill even pointed out to Dad on one occasion how he wasn't fixing fence properly. "This is how Bob Brown does it."

Being in the shadow of a so-called successful farmer for more than a year whetted Bill's appetite for change in his own operation waiting back home. The first item was to dispose of what remained of that eyesore of a cobbled-up horse stable. Sixteen new stalls complemented the 13 installed two years earlier. A stable cleaner was a must and Bill had forever grumbled how damp stables were prime candidates for pneumonia, so he installed a series of exhaust fans.

Bill purchased three or four "new cows" but both Browndale and Bond Haven Farms continued to loan and finance cows, and some of the heifers were on the milking line now as well.

When the stabling was completed in February 1968, it stood second to none. By the time the herd was moved in and the milk began to flow, only one item remained unfinished...the installation of the stable cleaner. Bill didn't seem to be in a hurry...after all he had me to clean the stable the old fashioned way, by wheelbarrow, fork, and shovel.

For two months I continued that drudgery. Bill was living back home as his house was rented until April, so every morning he and I would arise at 4:30, trudge out to the truck often parked at the road and negotiate the snow drifts to his place, as we were always at least an hour ahead of the township plow. I can't recall any time in my life being as cold as on some of those mornings.

Bill's Ford pickup, to its credit, never failed to start, although I remember one particularly frigid morning when the accelerator pedal was frozen to the floor. Consequently we made the three-mile trip in record time, with the engine screaming wide open. A pail of hot water thrown over the engine before our return seemed to thaw the components in question.

Was I sick to death of cleaning stables by the time April rolled around! Two hours each morning and an hour at night. Plus, I was cleaning our own stables twice a day while Dad milked and tended other chores. At the close of that winter, I felt and probably looked like a wheelbarrow load of you know what.

I recalled three years earlier just after I'd quit school and was cleaning stables at our place when a couple of my former classmates, Chris and Laverne, dropped by. I knew they'd be in some day, but I always pictured myself out on the tractor some glorious late spring day, rather than slopping around in rubber boots in manure-filled gutters in a stinky stable. Following a short conversation, Chris said they had to be going..."We're keeping you from your chosen career...shovelling shit!"

Recalling that episode and after the winter I had endured, I couldn't help but think perhaps Chris had been correct...maybe I was destined only to "shovel shit."

With the arrival of the planting season, I quit working for Bill. He could clean his own stables and see how he liked it! I guess he didn't like it much. Before a week passed, the stable cleaner was installed and operating.

Same Dream...Different Time

IT WAS FEBRUARY 2011 AND I'D JUST RETURNED FROM THE Auto Show in Toronto, and among the dizzying assortment of metal and plastic being offered, the automobile gaining the most attention seemed to be the new Volkswagen Beetle. It was déjà vu, as I recalled a similar scene a dozen years earlier when the then "New Beetle" was released to the public. Maybe they'll name this third generation reawakening the "new, new Beetle."

Appearing as if some giant "baby boomers" convention had been unleashed, middle- to upper-aged men and women with varying degrees of grey hair, hair loss, and wrinkles, stared in misty-eyed adoration at the latest German resurrection. Everybody seemingly had an "original Beetle" story to share with whoever happened to be standing near. It took me back as well...back to April 1965 and an advertisement in our hometown newspaper:

FOR SALE: 1958 VOLKSWAGEN...
AS IS...WHERE IS...$99.00.

I was just one month out of high school, basically broke until my summer job began, but in need of my first set of wheels. I drove the family station wagon into town, not sure what to expect for $99. Parked behind a large, sprawling house was a rather tired looking, gold-coloured Volkswagen. The running boards were missing and extensive rust had intruded on both rear fenders, a condition uncommon to Volkswagens. The interior, however, was perfect, and so was the engine according to its owner. While he went to retrieve the key, I continued to examine the car. I could already visualize myself behind the wheel. So who cared about a little rust!

Returning shortly, the Volkswagen owner inserted the key in the ignition. "Just see how quickly it starts!" The engine turned over...and over...and over, but never fired. Not even a splutter. He tried a second and third time.

"I can't understand it!" said the embarrassed, owner. "It's never failed to start...I'll tell you what. You take the car, find out what's wrong, and I'll pay the bill." Well, it sounded fine to me; now to convince Dad.

Dad wasn't quite as excited and after a thorough inspection turned to me. "It's pretty rusty and I think if it was me I'd look for something better...but if you insist this is what you want, we'll pull it home."

For the rest of that weekend, I fussed and fiddled, opened and closed doors, tightened and re-tightened anything that was loose, read and re-read the owner's manual, all the time making mental observations and visualizing the possibilities that could be achieved with a few dollars and a little effort.

The following Monday, we pulled my new prize to our mechanic in Listowel, where the problem was diagnosed as a faulty ignition coil. The charge, including labour, $14; as I had no money at the time, Dad sent an $85 cheque to finalize the deal, which if memory serves, I never paid back. This was long before safety certificates, so after bolting a set of license plates (which Dad also paid for) to the bumper, I was ready for the road. Dad also provided the insurance premium, and whenever I needed fuel I simply nosed up to the farm gas barrel. I couldn't understand why everybody complained about the high price of owning a car!

I drove that little gold machine right through to snowfall, had no problems whatsoever. Okay, it had its shortcomings...what European car of that era didn't?

There was no ventilation. You simply opened a window or suffocated. In cold weather, the heater provided only a mild breath of air and the defroster didn't function at all. As for the tiny wipers...one could do a better job wiping your mitt across the windshield. There was no gas gauge. A wooden fuel measuring stick was calibrated in both Canadian and American gallons, as well as litres. (Little did I know our country would actually use that strange system one day.) As far as power...there really wasn't any. For a fully loaded car, even medium hills proved a challenge. Factor in a strong headwind and you felt as you were driving into a wall of Jell-O. The horn didn't work and when you were reversing, the gearshift had to be manually held in place or it would disengage.

...But I loved that car! There was something about a Volkswagen that provided something greater than mere transportation. Volkswagens were more like old friends. More like the Model T Ford, 50 years earlier. They were designed with the same thought in mind...a car for the masses. That had been Henry Ford's objective in 1908, as was Adolf Hitler's 25 years later.

Hitler, however, had difficulty convincing the German automakers of that era the need for such a car, as most were interested only in expensive automobiles for the wealthy. The only one who showed interest was Ferdinand Porsche, who went to work on the project and came up with a rear mounted, air-cooled engine prototype. The Volkswagen or "People's car" was born.

Seldom does the future take a direct path to its place in history and this was certainly true with the Volkswagen. Before production got under way, a World War interfered, and by the time the devastating conflict ended, the Volkswagen factory, like most German factories, was not a pretty sight.

Automakers from across the globe were invited to take over the ruined plant...free of charge...just to get production under way. Henry Ford II went to Germany with the intention of reopening the plant, but was persuaded otherwise by his advisors. England's Lord Nuffield considered building his Morris car there until he surveyed the bombed-out plant. Rootes Group, another British automaker building Humber, Sunbeam, and Hillman vehicles, discussed the venture but declined, surmising the Volkswagen simply wasn't suited for the modern world.

However, the German people, as well as the occupational forces, were in desperate need of cheap transportation. Therefore, a major re-salvaging effort was begun and before 1945 ended, nearly 2,000 vehicles had been assembled from left-over parts. By the end of the following year, enough of the factory had been reclaimed to produce nearly 10,000 Volkswagens. In 1949, nearly 70,000 were built and Germany figured it was time to test the United States market. Let's just say Americans weren't ready for the Volkswagen at this point. Two cars were sold.

Two or three years later, the funny-looking German car began to dribble into Canada. I remember sitting with my brothers beside the "400" highway that passed through our farm when the first Volkswagen I'd seen – a black one – trundled by. So out of place it seemed among the large, chrome-laden American cars dominating the roads of that period. However, by the time my 1958 model was manufactured, nearly half a million Volkswagens had been built. Before the assembly line at Wolfsburg, Germany, shut down in 1978, more than 16 million cars had been produced. I'm certain Volkswagen management would've sold their very souls for even a small percentage of such a loyal following for subsequent Beetles!

The original Volkswagen that rose from the ashes of World War Two was truly a phenomenal success story, considering it was not a perfect car by any stretch of the imagination. Spartan interior, noisy engine, uncomfortable seats, anaemic heating, compromised foot room; but at the same time, the Volkswagen was economical, extremely reliable, and built to a quality unknown at North American auto plants at the time.

But most importantly, Volkswagens were fun to drive. Even a person unaccustomed to manual transmissions could manipulate that four-speed unit with minimum practice. With its engine behind the rear wheels, and storage space behind the back seat and under the front hood, cargo capacity was surprisingly generous.

Although at a different time and under different circumstances, Adolf Hitler, like Henry Ford, had envisioned the need for an inexpensive but reliable vehicle for the average person. Due to the facts of world history, however, Adolf Hitler...unlike Henry Ford...will never be remembered as an automotive pioneer.

Christmas 1960. David, Vivien, Richard, Bill ... Don, Brian

Will and Reba's 50th anniversary, December 1960.

Viv and Glen's wedding, 1961.

Mom and Dad's 25th anniversary, 1964.

Don, 1964.

Friend John Smith's '58 Beetle, just like mine.

Have Truck...Will Travel

THOSE WHO FOLLOW MY WRITINGS REALIZE MY PASSION FOR character studies of seemingly average people. However, "average" doesn't always mean mundane, mindless, colourless, and boring, as proven by my life-long friend and neighbour Doug Hamilton.

Since dropping out of school in the spring of 1965, I never had any problem finding work. Our family was operating three farms now that my brother-in-law had also purchased a farm. This scenario meant lots of work...but no money.

My father understood not only the monetary value outside income generated, but the psychological importance as well; therefore when Doug Hamilton inquired about hiring my services on a semi-regular basis for the 1966 cropping season, he agreed.

Working for Doug certainly wasn't new. In the spring of 1958 when I was just nine years old, Doug hired Dad, a couple of my brothers, and me to pick stones at his place. Being the youngster of the gang, I was placed on the seat of Doug's John Deere and proceeded to pull the wagon up and down the field while the rest carried or tossed the rocks, depending on their mass, onto the wagon. For a half day's work, Doug gave Dad ten dollars, which he divided equally, giving me the silver dollar that was left. That was the first off-farm income I earned.

Doug's family had moved to Perth County in 1947 when Doug was 13. Their farm was probably the only one in the area at that time without hydro and still farming with horses, and no one was more aware of this than the young teenager. While walking those monotonous miles behind a team and single-furrow plow, Doug dreamed of the tractor he'd be driving someday. In that visual, the tractor was always a John Deere. He had one more dream as well...an Oldsmobile car.

Although a slow process, over the next several years his father purchased a well-used Fordson tractor along with some matching implements; and the 20-year-old Ford, compliments of a neighbour and interest-free loan, was replaced by a nearly new Plymouth.

By 1952, although still in his teens, Doug was gradually taking responsibility for the running of the family farm. But Doug was a realist and realized John Deeres and Oldsmobiles cost money; therefore off-farm income was crucial. Buying, selling, and hauling livestock always held appeal, but he was without either funds or credit for a truck. Doug solved the dilemma by furnishing a homemade trailer to tow behind the family Plymouth until he could afford his first truck...a 15-year-old GMC for $65.

Doug nearly lost his hard-earned investment before reaching first base. When he had owned the truck just one week, Doug decided to take his prized possession to the Hamilton reunion to show it off. As the battery was weak, the old GMC was parked on the gangway of his cousin's farm, assuring a guaranteed start upon departure. However, while the adults were having their annual meeting in the house, a few of the kids experimenting with matches set fire to the barn. Doug just managed to remove his truck in time but the barn burnt to the ground. As Doug commented later, "The fire kind of put a damper on the reunion."

In addition to dealing in livestock, Doug began experimenting in other fields, the first being cheaply sold horse-related equipment at farm auctions. With the shift to mechanized power, Doug reasoned items such as harness, single-furrow plows and other walk-behind implements could be bought for just a few dollars and sold at a profit to the Mennonite communities in the area.

However it was buggies that really catapulted Doug into the Mennonite trade. The first one he purchased for $4 but only had half the amount so borrowed the balance from a friend and sold it the next day for $15. After that he started buying buggies regularly, generally paying about $5, then selling them anywhere from $15 to $25. It was the Mennonite sect that gave Doug his start and it was they who continued to be some of his best customers for his entire career. The young entrepreneur had figured that formula right away. "Mennonites are closely knit...treat them fairly and you'll have the entire community on your side."

By the winter of 1953, Doug had graduated to a 1950 GMC. It was with this truck that Doug advanced into the binder market. These old reapers were gathering rust in fence corners and woodlots all over Southwestern Ontario, but he made a successful business resurrecting these relics to areas where they were still wanted and needed. Once he cornered the market on the horse-drawn trade, Doug branched into tractors and related implements. Throughout the following years he became heavily involved in the pull-type combine market, making countless trips to machinery auctions in Michigan and Ohio.

Although livestock was Doug's bread and butter, diversity was his dessert. So whether it was furniture or fertilizer, baled clover, bagged cement or bulk barley, whether it had rubber tires or steel spokes, four wheels or four legs...Doug would haul it.

In 1955 Doug purchased a new Mercury truck and as well officially took over ownership of the family farm. The first link in his dream was realized that year when he bought a brand new John Deere tractor and three-furrow plow.

Three years later another piece of the puzzle fell into place. On the lot of Golden Mile Chevrolet in east Toronto, Doug fell in love with a 1955 green and white Oldsmobile sedan; however, the salesman failed to show much enthusiasm towards the young hayseed with the eight-year-old Plymouth.

"I'd just sold a combine to a guy that morning so I extracted $400 cash from my pocket. That seemed to help move things along!" The same year he married his sweetheart of nearly a decade, and the Oldsmobile became their honeymoon car.

As the 1960s dawned, Doug purchased the farm next door. This farm always seemed like it should've belonged to the Hamilton farm from the outset as the barn was a double-length structure shared by both neighbours and the laneways paralleled each other just 150 feet apart. Once the farm transaction took place, the double lane arrangement made for a dandy circular driveway for the trucks, albeit the new one was a whole lot smoother than Doug's rut-infested laneway...but not for long. An occasional load of gravel and some periodic grading would have made a world of difference, but Doug believed in neither.

Doug liked to relate the story about the man he knew who came from England with just two dollars in his pocket and over the years made a small fortune. This man claimed his success hinged on the fact he never wasted time or money on cutting grass, washing cars, or gravelling laneways. To the end of his life, Doug never personally cut a blade of grass or washed one of the multiple Oldsmobiles he owned, and only when his trucks threatened to disappear in the spring mud did he relent and purchase gravel.

During the 1960s when I first began working for Doug, hauling grain during harvest was a regular task. Doug owned a well-used John Deere self-propelled combine and in addition to handling his own crop, offered his services to our farm as well as several neighbouring farms. The combine was showing its age by this time and with Doug as its chief operator...well, let's just say it aged a whole lot more. With his busy trucking schedule, monotonous duties like general maintenance and lubrication quickly fell by the wayside.

Doug's tools comprised a couple of screwdrivers, a hammer with the claw broken off, and a pair of vise-grips... "the best tool ever invented." His tool kit consisted of a six-quart basket which he had a habit of losing somewhere in the field. Eventually it would be located...usually after someone had driven over it.

One particular year featured an especially wet harvest, and between the weather and machine breakdowns, one would expect Doug to be feeling the pressure from irate farmers, yet he always seemed unencumbered by the weight of everyday problems..."We thrive on headaches"...Well Doug may have thrived, but I doubt his wife did, as it was Marilyn who had to answer the irate calls because he was seldom home. He would be either trucking, combining, or fixing...There was a popular song on the country charts at that time by Don Gibson, and Doug would tell Marilyn, "When those farmers call with their hard luck tales, just sing a couple lines of that song...'Don't tell me your troubles, I got troubles of my own.'"

I always enjoyed Doug's witticisms and never-ending conversation throughout the day. "Do you think the rain will hurt the rhubarb?"...or "What do you think of the east European situation?" If I did a particularly good job at something..."You'll make a man before your mother yet!" One of his favourite remarks he reserved for mealtime: "If you don't eat you can't work and if you can't work you're no good around here."

As well as helping on his farm, I also accompanied Doug on his trucking rounds. At that point in the 1960s, Doug was driving Mercury mid-duty trucks with either a 14- or 16-foot livestock rack. We'd start around 6:30 and the entire morning would be spent travelling the gravelled side roads of the neighbouring townships. Depending upon customer choice and the market itself, the load would be taken either to Schneider's Meats in Kitchener or the Ontario Stockyards in Toronto...sometimes both. A couple of cows here...a bull there...two or three steers at another... possibly some sheep...even the occasional horse.

One morning we picked up an old mare, and as nicely as possible Doug explained to the owner how the recent market hadn't been kind to this class of horse; the man insisted, however, and away it went to Toronto...total selling price...$11. Doug received $3, insurance and selling fees grabbed $5, and the owner was left with $3. The enraged owner phoned Doug the day he received his cheque. "You tell me," he roared, "how you and those goddam thieves in Toronto can charge $8.00 for a $3.00 horse!"

In those days, few customers were blessed with a livestock loading chute, so at every stop this hardwood/reinforced steel chute, which weighed about 200 lbs., had to be dragged from its location beneath the truck rack. Then the side racks that were built of equally solid material would be lifted into position. This exercise would be repeated six or eight or as many as ten times before the load was complete; then we'd head off to our destination.

A major remodelling of Doug's previously mentioned double-length barn was undertaken in the late 1960s. An automatic feeder that dispersed corn silage into a long central manger at the flick of a switch was a major time saver. Two silos, a 45-foot and a 60-foot structure, were constructed even if Doug was afraid to climb them. "I don't care how high I climb as long as I have one foot on the ground." He didn't have to climb near as often when automatic silo unloaders were installed.

By the mid-1960s Doug hired a full-time employee to his roster, as his trucking business had expanded to justify a second truck. As well as truck driving, Vernon Heise shared in the farming aspect as well. Trying to classify my particular position with the organization at that time proved difficult...I think Doug's description was "three quarters-part time-half regular."

If Doug thrived on headaches, he was in the right place on a hot humid August afternoon in 1969 when a sudden thunderstorm hit. Doug and Vernon were standing in the implement shed waiting out the storm when a deafening crack signalled a bolt of lightning had struck the barn. Almost instantly the entire hayloft was a mass of orange flame mixed with thick white smoke. The two ran around the outside of the barn to the feedlot where over a hundred cattle were contained and swung open the gate. The crackling timbers in conjunction with the hiss of dry burning hay were driving the cattle into frenzy and they weren't long vacating.

A similar rescue was launched for the pigs, but the heat was more intense than a dozen blast furnaces by now and they had to retreat. With the entire structure completely enveloped in flame, they could do nothing to save them.

Following the fire a great transformation took place. A barn that would feed nearly 400 cattle was erected and Doug built what was and probably still is the largest silo in Perth County. Twenty-six feet in diameter and reaching 90 feet into the air, this giant was constructed entirely of poured cement in a continuous operation. Construction began early one morning, continued throughout the day, all night as well, and finished mid-morning the following day.

For 30-some hours, that expanding tower of concrete was the prime subject of conversation, as well as the prime attraction throughout the neighbourhood. The jealous ones commented what a ridiculous venture it was to build a silo of such magnitude, which nobody of sound mind needed.

To satisfy the cavernous capacity of this new silo, Doug began a major land acquisition programme, buying two nearby farms and renting a couple more. He introduced a new system of corn forage to our area, a method that involved the use of a forage harvester that picked just the corn cobs, grinding them husk and all into instant cob meal. Doug figured this feed to be the most natural forage for beef cattle ever devised. The digestion rate far outclassed anything else, the cattle made excellent gains, and most importantly...they absolutely loved it.

With the trucking aspect of his operation spiralling upwards, a Mack tractor-trailer was added and Doug took on a role as buyer for a meat packing company in the Niagara area of southern Ontario, to where he hauled regularly.

By 1973, a tractor-trailer, two straight trucks, five John Deere tractors, and a long line of green equipment to complement them were part of what had become known as "Hamilton Farms"...had it really been 20 years, while walking behind that horse and plow, since the dream was first envisioned?

In 1974, a second silo was erected...even larger than the previous. It was the same height but a full four feet greater in diameter...another day and a half of continuous pouring while the township watched and commented.

On October 8, just a few weeks following its completion, the last few loads were being added to the huge structure when the forage pipes plugged. The first thought of the three men unloading the corn was perhaps the silo was full. Part-time farm employee and full-time tractor-trailer driver Bob Scott made the 90-foot climb to investigate but found no reason for the work stoppage. Still mystified as to its cause, Bob retraced his steps down the long ladder.

While the pipes were being cleared, a sharp crackling sound echoed from somewhere above. A fissure opened in the south wall and instantly the entire weight of the silo was shifted to this point. A muffled explosion erupted as a thousand tons of silage fought its way through the opening. The silo shuddered momentarily then toppled, cutting a swath through the barn roof as cleanly as a knife through butter. The silo unloader, perched at the very top, catapulted nearly 300 feet out into an adjacent field.

It was over in seconds. Only a light cloud of dust remained in the air as corn silage and concrete chunks came to rest. No one said a word as the reality hit home...especially Bob Scott, who'd been at the top of the silo as the hourglass was draining its final grains.

Two strokes of luck were in force that day. One, the silo had buckled in a southerly direction, giving the men working at the silo the precious few seconds to get clear. Secondly, all cattle that morning had been transferred to the opposite side of the feedlot for cleaning. Therefore the loss was entirely material...but what a mess! More than 200 acres of corn along with scores of tons of concrete, laced with hundreds of yards of twisted reinforcement rod, all mixed with barn timbers and roofing material, were now lying in the barnyard.

Once satisfied no loss of life had occurred, the neighbourhood deliberated as to the cause. Poor cement perhaps? Incorrect placement of reinforcement rods? How about unstable ground conditions below the foundation? Maybe the contractors hadn't followed the pounds per square inch guidelines concerning correct diameter to height ratios? A few simply reiterated their earlier stand on how a silo of such dimensions was bound to fall over sooner or later.

The cause did turn out to be construction negligence. Insurance adjusters discovered that the steel interior reinforcement rods designed to circle the silo's circumference... didn't; hence the rods simply pulled apart like a zipper. By the time the insurance company sued the silo's manufacturer, the company had gone broke and filed for bankruptcy, setting the stage for a five-year battle in the courts.

While the principal players fought it out in court, Doug salvaged what he could. Bulldozers and power shovels retrieved as much forage as possible, piling it in a field beside the barn. During this operation, any large concrete chunks were discarded but the smaller pieces could only be separated during the feeding process. Corn was retrieved from the pile by manure loader and transferred to a temporary elevator hooked into the regular feeding system. The chunks of cement played havoc with equipment, shredded belts and burned-out motors being the rule rather than the exception. Eventually the entire automatic feeding system had to be replaced.

One day when this seemingly endless ordeal was ongoing, I asked Doug how he was able to cope with a challenge of this magnitude along with everything else needing attention at the time. He paused..."Well, David...my mother said there'd be days like this...she just didn't say there'd be so many!"

Muskoka Memories

JUST AS DUSK WAS SETTLING ON LABOUR DAY MONDAY, 1964, my brother Richard arrived from Woodington House, the Muskoka resort that had been his summer home for four years.

It had seemed a long time ago, that June day in 1961, when Mom and Dad dropped Richard off at the home of our elementary school teacher, Annie Ashmore, and watched him and his school chum Grant Burnett leave for the unfamiliar world of the resort business. Richard was just 14, initiating plenty of discussion between my parents whether he should be allowed to go at all. Mrs. Ashmore's son owned and managed the Muskoka resort, and if it hadn't been for the fact she was doing the recruiting and would be heavily involved in the daily operation, Mom and Dad most certainly wouldn't have agreed.

My brother Bill wasn't in favour of the idea either. Because they were closer in age, Bill was perhaps more familiar with Richard's reckless side, and seemed fearful his brother would drown or meet with some other misfortune. When a letter from Woodington House arrived in the mail in early March of 1962, presumably inquiring if Richard was interested in returning for a second season, Bill gave serious thought to destroying the letter.

In its day, Woodington House was one of the premier hotels of the Muskoka region. Built in 1894 by Michael Woods, the lodge overlooking Lake Rosseau boasted three storeys, large dining room and lounge, spacious verandah with built-in gazebos, and a guest capacity of 125. When Michael died in 1927, his daughter Nancy Anderson inherited the hotel and ran it for 30 years, until she ceded managerial duties to Blair Ashmore, who in time purchased it. Already two thirds of a century old when he acquired ownership, the Muskoka retreat was feeling the passage of time, yet still displayed rustic charm. With plenty of labour, Blair Ashmore could see promise as well.

To this point, Blair had not shown himself to be managerial material, but his hands had been tied somewhat by Mrs. Anderson, who was getting on in years and not interested in the financial commitment of a hotel update. However with his easy-going style and flexible rules, Blair proved to be a great boss, as young employees like Richard and Grant soon discovered. Even if his staff showed only borderline talent on occasion, Blair could always find a way to express his opinions without making the kids feel like complete idiots.

The time for instance when a fuse blew on some electrical circuit: Richard and Grant replaced the faulty fuse only to have it blow again. Another was installed and quickly expired. On the fourth try, Blair appeared on the scene.

"Well, boys...we can't just keep replacing fuses all day can we...there's obviously a problem here!"

My cousin Doug Watt, who worked at the resort for three years, considered it to be a firetrap, and seemed generally surprised the place hadn't burnt to the ground. Although it boasted a repeat clientele, Woodington House lacked plenty in guest convenience, the most notable...an absence of bathrooms. Only one was available on each floor and located at the extreme end of the hallway.

Richard also considered the meals on the low end of the scale as far as competitive lodges, although Doug didn't entirely agree. "I didn't think they were that bad... although the sight of Stan (their cook) hanging over the soup cauldron with his cigarette dangling ashes was a little disconcerting."

Stan was as far from a resort chef as one could imagine, earning his training as an army cook during World War Two. His speciality was sausages cooked in beer. One large skillet called for one half bottle of beer; Stan didn't like to complicate his mind with mathematical concerns, so instead of trying to calculate how a single bottle could achieve two batches...the simple answer was to merely enjoy the refreshment of the extra half bottle of brew.

Mrs. Ashmore spent a lot of time around Woodington, trying her best to have the resort operate on the lowest possible budget. Economizing was Annie's forte and there was even a rumour that she drained the varying amounts of juice left in guests' glasses back into the pitcher for the next meal...but you know how stories become exaggerated!

Each male employee received $200 for an entire summer's work. Their main jobs consisted of mowing grass, washing dishes, and hauling garbage to the dump in the lodge's old Chevrolet pickup. Most guests elected to carry their own luggage to their rooms, but occasionally the employees would receive a tip for bellhop duties.

Interestingly, from the guest driving the Chevrolet or Plymouth, they'd receive a dollar or two...as opposed to seventy-five cents from the Cadillac driver. The girls, most of whom were chambermaids, received about $90 for the season, but earned substantially more in gratuities.

When Richard returned home from Woodington House that weekend in 1964, he was ready to start his fifth and hopefully final year at Norwell High, even if career direc-tion remained unclear. Events would prove his return to school studies that autumn short lived. When introduced to subjects like Chemistry and Trigonometry, Rich quickly lost his way and by the end of first semester had become, in his words, "brain dead." Perhaps sensing impending doom, Rich didn't even bother to show up for classes the week following the exams, so I received a daily report from one of his classmates. "Tell Dick he got 42 in Physics"... "Tell Dick he got 38 in Chemistry"..."Tell Dick I don't know what he got in Trig...Mr. Graff just threw his exam in the trash can!"

For my brother it mattered little; he'd already decided to pack it in and help Dad for the winter, while keeping an eye out for any career opportunity that might surface. So as the winter of 1964–65 settled in, Rich did likewise for a season of milking cows and cleaning stables.

A couple of weeks passed when Dad alerted Richard to an advertisement in the local newspaper by Bell Canada... or Bell Telephone Company as it was known then. Rich garnered an interview at the Stratford office, learned the company was looking for "linemen," and they'd be in touch.

They did call and Richard was told to report for work in Owen Sound on January 18…so much for Dad's helper!

With a job on the horizon, Rich needed a car and Dad had the answer. Our '59 Chevrolet had faithfully served for three seasons but was nearing the end of its career. Dad actually wanted a pickup for the farm but didn't wish to give up the comfort and passenger room a sedan afforded. A compromise was a 1963 Ford Fairlane station wagon that could satisfy either role.

Dad had bought the Fairlane straight deal, the Chevy thus ending up parked beside the implement shed to await its fate. With Rich in need of wheels, Dad dug the car out of a snow bank and offered it to his son for $750. The Chevrolet certainly had a few issues, but Dad figured it to be a good "starter car."

Like most cars of that age and era, the body was pretty well eaten away by rust along the rocker panels and doors as well as the tops of the front fenders. So porous were they that rain, mud, and slush methodically squirted through the openings directly onto the windshield. Plenty of "front end" work was needed also. A dip over a railroad crossing would cause the entire car to shake and shiver like a dog just out of water. The windshield was severely cracked and the tires…well, let's just say they were poor.

Before he was even a third of the way of the 60-mile trek to Owen Sound for his first day of his new job, Rich suffered a flat. The tube that had been peeking through a slit in the right front tire and rubbing on the tie rod could only last so long I guess! Plenty of time was wasted trying to change the offending tire as the jack kept skidding on the road's icy surface and toppling over. Suspecting the state of the remaining tires to be no better and not wanting to risk the rest of the journey without a spare, Rich elected to purchase a new tire in Mount Forest before continuing on.

With his new role of supposedly steady employment, Rich decided an update in transportation was in order and purchased a year-old Chevrolet Biscayne. It was probably the best kept Biscayne in Ontario, as Rich was forever polishing chrome and waxing its sky blue paint. But just as he was with his first bicycle, Rich was fanatical about keeping his car that way, and an unfortunate situation it was for either Brian or me if we ventured too close while the car was receiving its weekend shine.

My brother Brian was always pushing the envelope, so by merely leaving a fingerprint on the newly waxed paint, received a healthy slug courtesy of Rich's fist. He placed his "greasy hand" in Rich's words on the car another time, and recalling the incident, explained that "Brian should be able to move his arm in a couple of days."

I was on the receiving end of Rich's knuckles several times myself...most for good reason, like pulling the chair away just as he was sitting down. Or jumping off the teeter-totter when he was on the high end; he had to wait until his wind returned before cleaning my clock that time.

Other times the reasons for altercation were less defined. Rich had just returned from Muskoka at the end of the Labour Day weekend and was retrieving his suitcase from the car's trunk when one of his "summer girlfriends" gave him a passionate goodbye kiss. I doubt if he was in the door sixty seconds when I inquired who she was; "None of your business!"...Pow!...Yeah...good to see you too, Rich.

When Richard checked into the Bell Telephone Company's Owen Sound facility that January day in 1965, it began a career that would last until retirement. After two or three weeks of extensive job training and education of safety concerns, both in house and "in the field," Rich would in the months and years ahead cover a wide area in his occupation of repairing old phone lines and installing new ones. Considerable time was spent in the vicinity of the generations-old Turner farm in Artemesia Township, installing new services to the many cottages that were springing up along the shores of Lake Eugenia. He also worked an entire winter near Bracebridge, gaining a new perspective on an area of Muskoka where he'd spent several summers.

For the first couple of years, no matter where he worked, Rich came home practically every weekend. Initially it proved a novelty to strap on his spurs and support belt and try to climb the hydro pole in our yard. It was embarrassing, however, when your spurs became lodged in the wood and you had to be lifted off. Rich of course would then show us how it was done, although there were times when even he admitted a less than perfect presentation.

Rich was working near the town of Meaford when he noticed a woman watching, so made a point of impressing her with his speed in descending the pole. In his haste, his spurs missed their mark and he slid all the way to the bottom in one very quick motion.

"I wonder what the woman thought of your exhibition?" someone asked. "I don't know," answered Rich. "I just nonchalantly walked away...as if that's the way we always did it."

Whether it was driving trucks, climbing poles, digging holes, etc., the Bell Telephone creed stressed safety above all else. Around the farm, Richard had always been the reckless one and oft times the one who got into trouble or just luckily avoided disaster. Generally, speed, carelessness, or just plain inattentiveness were the culprits, so Dad figured Bell to be the ideal employer for his son.

Bell's insistence concerning safety issues and in particular seat belt usage and checking vehicles and equipment constantly for potential problems or hazards became second nature to Richard. A decal on the dashboard of every Bell vehicle and signs posted in strategic locations around the workplace reminded employees that *"NO JOB IS SO IMPORTANT AND NO SERVICE SO URGENT THAT WE CANNOT TAKE TIME TO PERFORM OUR WORK SAFELY."*

Richard did his best to transfer some of that "safety and common sense" mindset onto me and my brothers; perhaps it didn't always sink in, but I admit it was his coaching that started me wearing seatbelts, long before seatbelt usage was regulated by Ontario law.

Although 1964 proved to be Richard's final year as an employee of Woodington House, ties to the lodge would remain long after. It was there he met his future wife, and in the succeeding years they, as well as many of the old "Woodington gang," continued to vacation at the Muskoka resort that held such great memories.

Woodington House is now just a memory, registering its last paying guest in 1973. Although closed to the public, for another two decades, the century-old resort stood as tall and imposing as ever, overlooking Lake Rosseau, a landmark of a bygone era.

Often referred to as the "ghost resort" of the Muskoka's, in 1987 it inspired Barbaranne Boyer in her excellent book *Muskoka's Grand Hotels* to write:

> *At Woodington Hotel, time has stopped and been too weary to move on. In the lobby, cobwebs and ghostly shadows lurk in the corners, and for a moment, if you close your eyes, you can feel and hear the sounds of yesterday.*

A Change of Direction

F OR THE MOST PART, 1968 WITNESSED THE END OF OUR father's agricultural career...the only career he'd ever really known. That had never been the intention, but the infamous Depression of the 1930s had the final word on that subject, and Dad, like so many others, did what he had to do to survive, and that happened to be farming.

Dad began milking cows on a part-time basis on his father's farm when he was but ten or twelve years old. In this pre-hydro, pre–milking machine era, this operation was strictly a "hand job." The family herd consisted of a dozen Shorthorn cattle, which in summer were milked outside in the orchard.

As noted, Dad never planned for farming to be his vocation; it was the business world that beckoned upon graduation from high school in 1931. But with unemployment at 25%, it wasn't a good time to find a job let alone a career.

Three more years of milking cows followed before a chance to attend Business College in Orangeville, Ontario, beckoned. One year at Orangeville was followed by just eight months as office clerk at a confectionery factory in downtown Toronto before it succumbed to bankruptcy.

Then it was back home on the family farm for five more years before an opening at a dairy operation of 320 Jerseys...a humongous operation for the times...surfaced near Brampton, Ontario. A two-year stint there was followed by ten years as dairy herdsman at a Holstein dairy in Simcoe County, four years on our own Simcoe County farm, followed by another dozen in Perth County. More than forty years milking and caring for cows.

The continual change in milk industry regulations was a constant source of irritation for our father. And there was seemingly no end to these regulations. Dad had complied with many; hot water and insulation were a necessity, so a water heater was purchased and the milk house walls and ceiling insulated. However, it wasn't that simple as new rules governing milk house dimensions were now in effect. Our building, already minimum interior size, would be too small with the added layer of insulation. That problem was only rectified by installing the framework and insulation on the building's exterior walls.

Next, the drain wasn't up to new codes. Size matters, and ours was simply too small and discharged just a few feet from the milk house...another no-no. The only solution was to rip up the cement floor in the milk house and install a larger drain. That, in conjunction with 50 feet of clay tile, satisfied the proper outlet distance requirement.

Flies were always a nuisance to dairy farmers and a major concern for government inspectors. New regulations stated the stable had to be sprayed twice a day during "fly season" before the milking was allowed to commence; another stipulation, calf pens were to be cleaned "regularly" of manure. No more twice-a-year cleanouts, as had been our practice; larger diameter vacuum lines for the milking machine system were also recommended.

The inspectors didn't stop with just the stable's interior. The manure pile, according to them, shouldn't be there at all. During summer, manure was to be hauled away and spread on a daily basis and in winter stored in a location a "respectable" distance from the barn. A cemented barnyard was another recommendation.

Truthfully, most of these new rules and principles had merit; who wants to drink milk from a dirty fly-infested dairy? The trouble was...there were too many, too close together, and in our father's opinion, too late. He was tired of milking cows and ready for some other avenue of employment. Besides, I was keen to take over the farm at this point so why not let me wrestle with government regulations?

Dad found part-time work that summer as a groundskeeper for the Listowel Golf and Country Club. Cutting grass and keeping the greens maintained consumed most of his allotted time. He also worked a few hours a week at Elmer Bean's Menswear store in Listowel. Elmer had been in the clothing business since 1953 and inside, a large sign proclaimed his store featured a complete line of quality clothing for "Dad and his Lad." Our father certainly took the message to heart, bringing home every bargain Elmer couldn't sell. "I don't care about style," Dad would say. "There's a lot of wear there!"

When fall arrived, Dad got a job at the Campbell's Soup plant on Listowel's southern outskirts, as "wash up" person. This involved hosing down the "fryers" and similar machines, plus the floors, walls, and anything else covered with grease. The hot water from the high pressure hoses, the steam, the grease, the slop and humidity and accompanying high temperatures, was no way to make a living, concluded our father, so after one week he threw in the towel. He didn't know what he was going to do for the winter, but it sure wouldn't be sweating in that hell hole!

"You calling it quits?" the security guard asked as Dad punched out for the last time. "Yes, I guess it's not my kind of job."

"Have you ever considered security work?" Dad answered he knew nothing of the profession. "The company provides all the training," continued the guard. "We're short of help right now if you'd like to give it a try." Few things could have been worse than what he'd been doing all week, so he answered yes.

Next day, Dad went to Security Investigations Services in Kitchener, Ontario, filled out an application, picked out a uniform, and was in business. It didn't take long to learn the ritual, which included keeping track of employees as they came and went and checking all trucks both in and out. The company name, tractor and trailer number, what was being hauled, and the driver's signature all had to be documented and verified.

On weekends with only maintenance staff on duty, hourly patrols had to be undertaken. At a good brisk walk, about 20 minutes was needed. Dad would often commence his patrol to coincide with the intermission of whatever hockey game he happened to be listening to. There was no law stating patrols had to be equal intervals apart. In fact, management preferred they be staggered somewhat, reasoning if anyone were lurking in the factory, irregular timing would be more conducive to nabbing the offending party. Mostly however, patrols were regarded as fire protection above anything else.

Whenever the guard went on patrol, his schedule was monitored, thus eliminating any thought of a missed patrol...no matter how exciting the hockey game. This was well before the computer world took effect, so a simple clock with a paper disc inside was carried during rounds; a series of keys placed strategically along the patrol route insured the guard passed a particular station. Once the key was inserted into the clock, the exact time of day or night was stamped onto the paper disc, which was turned over to management at the end of every shift. I guess the most exciting event during Dad's patrols was the day the cafeteria roof collapsed just a few minutes after he'd passed through. As it was a Sunday morning the cafeteria was closed so only property damage was the result.

After a stint at Campbell's, Dad was transferred to Spinrite Yarns, Listowel's only textile mill since Imperial Cloth had succumbed a few years earlier. Spinrite's roots traced back to 1913 when a company known as Perfect Knitting Mills was established on the banks of the Maitland River, operating with the river's water power. In 1952 it was purchased by D.D. Hay, who also owned a lumber yard, hardware store, and building supply centre in downtown Listowel.

Spinrite was a family-run business where Dad enjoyed working, getting along well with D.D. "David" Hay and his two sons and son-in-law. More responsibility was needed with the Spinrite operation as the guards doubled as boiler engineers as well. But no engineering papers or degrees here…it was purely "show and go." Four boilers had to be heated, pressure maintained, and continually monitored. A "real" engineer was called for special service.

The only problem with the Spinrite textile mill was head guard Ross McArthur. Ross considered himself more law enforcement than security officer and was forever in combat with employees, delivery drivers, taxi operators, and other guards. Ross didn't like many people, and the feeling was mutual. He trusted no employee, always certain they were pilfering wool. But Ross did like the Hay family and more importantly…they liked him. Especially David Hay, and that's all that really mattered. The mill was non-union so Ross always had an ear cocked for the slightest hint of union or strike talk. A word to D.D. and the problem was quickly rectified…usually by firing.

Just a year earlier, a strike had been launched despite Ross's big ears. Almost immediately, Ross overheard of an attempt by a couple of strikers to go to D.D.'s house and toss a rock through his window, so he jumped in his car and headed them off…meeting them on the front lawn with a club. The senior Hay was overwhelmed by Ross's bravery and unshakable dedication, and he could do no wrong in D.D.'s eyes from that point forward. Following that episode, any complaint to management concerning Ross simply fell on deaf ears.

On the subject of that strike, my brother-in-law Glen Cober played a key role. Glen and my sister Vivien had bought a farm just a couple of miles from ours in 1965. They fattened a few animals for beef and raised pigs, and to supplement their income, Glen worked at Spinrite Yarns.

It was during this period…and somehow without Ross's awareness…that strike talk began to circulate ever so quietly and secretly. Glen, like most of our family, had little regard for unions, convinced they merely gathered dues you had no choice but to pay only to finance union management's expensive downtown Toronto suites.

Having said that, however, Spinrite was a minimum wage operation and a literal oven during summer's heat waves, with temperatures rising to alarming levels. The union promised they could address some of these conditions with a show of strength. Glen, along with a few other hold-outs, were finally convinced and agreed to join the fight.

As with most strikes, opening day began with fervour and optimism, although far from a total commitment. Nearly half showed up for work; Glen took his place on the picket line to prevent their crossing, puncturing the occa-sional radiator if need be. The strike dragged on through-out the winter months of 1967–68, but each passing week witnessed a few more picketers crawling back to the factory. When the weeks and months of standing in freezing temper-atures in conjunction with lost wages were calculated, the commitment slowly but steadily lost its appeal. By the end of March nearly everyone was back on the production line.

Glen to his credit was one of the last to surrender...but even pride can carry a person only so far. Although acciden-tally and unintentionally, Glen had become a "ringleader" in Spinrite eyes, so any future at the factory was history. He found temporary employment with a construction crew renovating old stables. However, labouring in dirty old barns among rotten timbers, cobwebs, rats, manure, mould, and dust, busting cement with a jackhammer and sledge, was not the way Glen intended to spend his life.

Things were faring badly at home as well. Glen and Vivi-en's farming operation, a borderline economic venture at best, could in no way sustain the loss of months of income, and they were forced to sell. Glen then found an opening as a maintenance apprentice at Listowel Hospital. The Lord works in mysterious ways, it's been said, and this position was seemingly Glen's niche. My brother-in-law worked at the hospital until retirement, a span of some thirty years, working his way to head of engineering in the interim.

In the period following the strike, Glen often came around after work to visit with Dad in the guardhouse. Although enjoying his son-in-law's company, Dad often felt uneasy as Spinrite management had vowed if they ever saw "that Cober" on their property they'd "kick his ass across the parking lot."

"I'd like to see them try!" was Glen's answer when someone mentioned the fact. Glen was a big muscular guy, a little bit stubborn, and certainly someone you didn't push around. I believe a lot of people would have enjoyed "seeing them try" as well!

Dad continued to work at Spinrite for another year or so, but after countless squabbles and altercations with Ross McArthur, asked for and finally received transfer back to Campbell's. Dad spent the remainder of his time until retirement in 1979 at the soup plant.

When Dad retired and for nearly two decades after, Campbell's Listowel plant produced practically all the frozen food products for the entire Canadian market as well as their famous Pepperidge Farms line of frozen foods. At its peak, Campbell's employed between 500 and 600 people. Then suddenly in 2008 after 48 years, Campbell's closed the Listowel plant, creating not only a devastating economic upheaval to the community, but a psychological impact as well.

A couple of years later, Erie Meats, an Ontario-owned and -operated processor and distributor of meat and poultry products, opened a factory branch in the former Campbell plant. Wieners, ground chicken and turkey, chicken breasts, deli meats, and breaded and battered products are the company's mainstay. To date Erie provides income to about 100 employees, nothing like the Campbell's of old, but at least the plant is operating again and hopefully that workforce will continue to increase as time passes.

Meanwhile, Spinrite Yarns soldiers on. Although still one of the top manufacturers of hand and machine yarn in North America, foreign competition, a high Canadian dollar in relation to other currencies, and perhaps most importantly, changing tastes, have all conspired against not only Spinrite, but the North American textile business in general. The "knitting" generation is passing away while their children and grandchildren have discovered different hobbies.

One aspect, however, that has become extremely popular is the company's factory outlet. Several times each year the Spinrite outlet holds a yarn inventory clearance, an event that attracts thousands from various regions of Ontario and even the northern United States.

So important nowadays, Spinrite has seemingly discovered new ways to adapt to the changes in the industry and continues to provide full-time employment for several hundred Listowel and area residents...but there's still no union.

Going...Going...

B ETWEEN THE COLLAPSE OF THE PORK MARKET IN 1971 AND A disastrous corn crop the following year, by the spring of 1973, I was unofficially bankrupt, owing money I didn't have to feed mills, fertilizer and seed companies, machinery dealerships, petroleum distributors, and various financial institutions.

After becoming tired of endless promises and lies, the Bank of Montreal abandoned me and the Royal Bank, although reluctantly, agreed to consolidate most of my small but numerous monthly payments I couldn't pay into one large bi-yearly payment I couldn't pay.

There was one bright star in the sky, however. A new manager at the Drayton Co-op who was eager to score points with the company couldn't wait to fill my barn with contract pigs. He also wanted to sell me fertilizer, seed barley, herbicides...whatever I might need for the upcoming season. As I was already mired in debt with my regular crop input suppliers, this offer appeared to be exactly what was needed.

Two months later with my stable full of pigs and two farms sown to barley, things appeared to be finally coming together...until Garth McGill, the aforementioned Co-op manager, drove into the yard while I was eating breakfast. He asked me to get in the car, then wasted no time in getting to the point.

"We're really concerned, Dave...we just learned all your assets are registered with the Royal Bank in Harriston." That was no news bulletin to me, but I guess the fact that the 250 pigs housed in my stable actually belonged to the Royal Bank and not the Co-op was disconcerting if not scary. If I went down the drain, so did their investment. And for McGill it was personal, as it was his ass on the line for not checking my financial state beforehand.

"You're in pretty rough shape, aren't you?" McGill asked.

I merely shrugged my shoulders. "Well, I know you are," said McGill, answering his own question..."that's why we've no choice but to take the pigs out. You can understand our side..." I said nothing. "We'll give you the promised price per pig despite not being market weight...and here's some advice...I strongly counsel you to go to Avco Finance or similar establishment and apply for a second mortgage. They'll consolidate your debts and give you enough to plant this spring's crop. If you can get your affairs straightened out, we'll consider supplying you with pigs again."

"What did McGill want?" Dad asked when I returned to the kitchen.

"Oh, he's concerned with the volatile pork market at the present time so is taking the pigs out. He says he'll put some more in when the price stabilizes." Although my brain was still reeling from McGill's conversation, events during the last couple of years had taught me how to lie on a moment's notice.

At that moment, however, the only thing clear about my exchange with McGill was the fact I'd absolutely failed to grasp the gravity of the situation. Big deal! I thought... so the pigs are gone...who needs the stink anyway. A break will be good. I'll just carry on with my cash cropping plans.

One rental farm as well as another I leased from the government through their "lease to purchase" program (ARDA) had already been sown to barley when McGill made his announcement.

Two weeks later I was ready to plant corn at home and headed off to the Drayton Co-op to get a load of fertilizer. The guy in charge of fertilizer distribution hesitated when I placed my order. "I'll be with you in a minute!" I waited...and waited...finally McGill himself appeared. As usual he came right to the point. "You never checked out Avco, did you?" I replied I hadn't. "Well, like I told you two weeks ago, until your finances are in order, we can't extend anymore credit."

Finally it hit me! "I thought you were only worried about the pigs...you didn't mention anything else!"..."As long as the Royal Bank has you tied up," McGill interrupted, "we can't lend you a cent."

I'd been standing on the precipice but was too naïve to realize it. "How am I supposed to pay any bills without a crop?" McGill didn't answer for a few seconds. "I'd advise you to forget about corn and plant the rest of your acreage to barley. It will take a lot less fertilizer. "Will you sell me enough fertilizer for the barley?" I asked in desperation. The answer was a cold "no."

Just then a thought struck me. "But that ground at home has been sprayed with Atrazine...I have no choice but to grow corn!" McGill turned to leave. "If you didn't use any more than two pounds per acre last year the barley might be alright...that's a chance you'll have to take."

I drove home in a daze with my empty wagon, sickened and disheartened, my mind racing in turmoil. I still had some credit left for barley seed, so immediately upon arrival phoned my supplier and ordered extra barley to replace the corn. When I cancelled the corn order, the dealer was a little upset that with this large order loss he might not qualify for his free trip to Jamaica...I really cared!

The only fertilizer I had on hand was a few bags of ammonium nitrate left over from the previous season, but as pure nitrogen was no good for barley, I simply planted my home farm without any added fertility, hoping the pig manure over the last two years would provide enough nutrients to grow a crop. It was the herbicide residue that had me concerned.

Was I relieved when the crop emerged healthy and green... until the first big rain washed the remaining residue into the root system and within days the barley began to wither. Not the entire crop...just certain sections. However, those dead brown streaks advertised a very unattractive landscape, not to mention embarrassment throughout the summer.

The Royal Bank manager made a surprise visit later that summer while I was combining barley at one of my rented farms. He was being transferred from the Harriston branch and I suppose before departure was sent by his superiors to authenticate if the bank's investment was paying off. I was thankful it was this farm on which he chose to check me out, as it had been sown before the financial cut-off and yields were good. Incredibly, I think he even believed me when I told him I'd have no trouble making my autumn payment.

Although grain yield was good on the rented acreages, at home it was a different story. With the lack of fertilizer and carry-over of herbicide, the yield was just as depressing as the crop had appeared all year. Even the areas that had appeared normal were low in both yield and test weight. Regardless of from what farm it originated, I sold the grain directly to whatever feed mill screamed the loudest.

A generous amount of custom plowing kept me afloat that autumn. At $5 an acre I travelled far and wide, although that venture wasn't without drama either. The Ford dealer repossessed my plow in late July, but I just managed to squeeze under the 30-day deadline and make my $400 payment, thanks to a load of barley, or else the plow would've been history. The plow was at my brother's place when the repossession took place and I guess the dealer was expecting trouble, for according to neighbours, the police were there, apparently to confront any resistance they might encounter...but no one was home and the snatch passed without incident.

My most notable custom job that year was plowing and cultivating 140 acres of land for Horace Wells (readers of my first book will remember him as the guy who came to my financial rescue a year earlier in the ARDA fiasco concerning Leon Barker). Horace needed someone to ready his land for planting...and I needed a way to repay my debt to him.

Horace had become disenchanted with growing corn, his previous year's crop being every bit as disastrous as mine. Horace had decided therefore to pursue a different avenue this year...edible beans or "white" beans as they were more familiarly called. Unlike today, beans of any kind were foreign territory to our particular segment of Ontario in 1973, and although Horace was committed to this new crop, he definitely wasn't convinced. At least twice a day he'd ask if I thought he was doing the right thing; I certainly was the wrong person from whom to be seeking agricultural advice!

When planting time arrived, past differences were forgotten and our old adversary Leon Barker was hired to do the job. Like me, Leon needed the money, and Horace being the kind person he was, made the offer...but he asked me first. "If it will make you feel awkward working with Leon, I'll find somebody else to plant." There was no better authority on financial adversity at that time than I, and realized it was only under desperation Leon had taken the steps that he did.

Leon Barker had only two speeds while planting...fast and faster! Rocks, tree branches, ground hogs, or seagulls were of no consequence to Leon once he was at the controls. Horace could only shake his head while watching Leon operate. "That Leon...he drives through a gateway...then looks back to see if he hit anything."

It was a hot dry September and I spent most of it custom plowing. Economically, I was living month to month and this added income saved me from total collapse. Those 15- to 18-hour days provided plenty of time to deliberate my future. Although the bloom had definitely faded, I was still dedicated to agriculture. What is it about farming that makes a person fight against ostensibly impossible odds?

One of the most difficult adjustments that summer was watching our barn stand idle and neglected, probably for the first time in its 80-year history. Except for a few hundred bales of straw and some machinery, the structure sat immersed in desolation, its very soul seemingly being destroyed a day at a time.

Often when the world seems darkest a light appears. That illumination was sparked by a visit from my friend and neighbour Doug Hamilton, expressing interest in filling my barn with pigs on a cost/share agreement. "I know you've had some hard knocks," he said, "but I also know you can take care of pigs."

If Doug was going to place his faith in me, I realized I had to make some personal sacrifices...such as dropping all rented land and concentrating on the home and ARDA farms. Scaling my equipment to a smaller dimension would go a long way towards achieving this goal as well.

So it was with a raised spirit not felt in months I settled into the seat of my big Ford that September Friday morning following Doug's visit. After completing twenty acres of plowing for a customer, I was back home by noon. Upon arrival, Mom informed me the feed mill called, reporting they had a cheque for me for a load of grain I'd sold the previous week, and in the mailbox, which usually yielded nothing but overdue bills, I received a grand surprise: a $1,000 cheque from the government pertaining to the disastrous hog prices of 1971–72. One thousand dollars was a noteworthy amount in 1970s currency, especially for someone in my financial straits.

Because the pork market had fallen below what had been established as a "floor price," the provincial government with plenty of prodding from various farm organizations offered a subsidy to producers who'd shipped hogs below that price line. The pay-out had been talked about in farm magazines and newspapers for months but I never expected it to become reality. Talk about a turnaround of events in just 24 hours; first Doug Hamilton's announcement, then this unexpected cheque!

Immediately following lunch I drove to Listowel, stopping first to pick up an item I'd left at the local machine shop to be welded, then to Canadian Tire for a new battery for the truck. I pulled into the parking lot at the feed mill and was just getting out of the truck when the office manager came rushing out the door. "Your mother just called...your barn's on fire!"

Before I reached the village of Gowanstown, four miles south of our place, I could see the billowing black cloud rising into the clear September sky. I remember this cold shiver passing through my body as the reality hit home.

I could hardly make my way up our concession for "rubberneckers" clogging the road. I parked about 200 feet short of the driveway and ran across the field towards the barn. At that moment the main structural beams gave way and the entire roof assembly came crashing down, sending a shower of fire-laden debris out into the very field I was crossing. Immediately a couple of firemen turned their hoses on the grain stubble that was igniting in scattered patches.

I guess if there was a bright spot on that particular day it concerned the direction of the wind...southeast, the ideal direction for carrying the flames away from the house and implement shed and other outbuildings.

Still it was with uneasiness we retired that evening. The flames had died out, but a crimson glow blanketed the entire stable area and just the slightest breeze from the "wrong" direction could send sparks towards the house. Every hour it seemed someone stole a glance from the bathroom window satisfying themselves all was under control. About 4 a.m. a heavy shower helped quench any remaining threat.

The next morning before breakfast I went out to the site. Except for a few chunks of structural beams still smouldering, silence encased the scene. The seed drill, carefully cleaned, greased, and stored in the upstairs area, now lay on the stable floor, bent into a slight curve from the extreme heat. The feed grinder/mixer, of which I'd been so proud of when new, had settled at a grotesque angle atop the steel partitioning, most of which was either mangled beyond recognition or warped from heat. The thick steel posts that just hours before had supported the entire upstairs floor now sprouted from the blackened ruins like cemetery headstones...not an inappropriate simile I suppose.

That weekend is but a blur in memory as insurance agents, insurance adjusters, scrap dealers, friends, neighbours, and total strangers milled around the sight, speculating on the cause. Lightning?..."no it was a beautiful sunny day." Spontaneous combustion?..."there was no hay in the barn." Wiring?..."possibly." Someone even deliberated on the premise that it might have been a bird carrying a lighted cigarette. Maybe it was simply the emotional factor of that weekend kicking in, but I found it utterly amusing picturing this sparrow perched high on a beam, dragging on a cigarette.

It would take a few days before the true cause of the blaze was determined and the result was indeed spontaneous combustion...but from a completely unfamiliar source. The culprit was the dozen or so bags of ammonium nitrate that had been stored upstairs from the previous year. When the Drayton Co-op pulled the plug on my corn cropping plans, the fertilizer wasn't needed. Every environmental element over the previous sixteen months...rain, snow, drought, extreme heat, numbing cold, variations in humidity...all joined forces that September Friday afternoon to ignite an explosion.

Up until this time, ammonium nitrate was known as exactly what it was...a 34% nitrogen fertilizer additive for growing corn. It was when the Irish Republican Army exploited ammonium nitrate's explosive value for car bombing attacks in the 1970s that it became infamous. In 1993, a 1300-lb. ammonium nitrate–based bomb placed in a truck in front one of the towers of the World Trade Center in New York failed to collapse the building as planned, but killed six people and injured several others. But what really brought the potential of this product to the public's eye was two years later, when a 5,000-lb. bomb hidden in a delivery truck completely destroyed a federal building in Oklahoma City, killing 178.

The week following the fire was filled with untold paperwork concerning insurance claims and damage reports. Within 60 days I received a cheque for the mixer, seed drill, straw, plus recompense for the numerous small articles like forks, shovels, tools, etc...that one never realizes one has until they're gone. As for the barn itself, my insurance policy contained a re-building clause, thus no money would be allocated until a replacement building was erected, and I had a year to attend to that.

Talk about an emotional roller-coaster! A day begun with such promise had quickly taken a 180-degree turn, but it seemed as if my entire farming career had been a series of 180-degree turns, peaks, and valleys. One moment I was riding a wave crest of high sensation only to plunge to the ocean floor the next.

Recalling those turbulent times reminds me of a long-ago high school English Literature class, studying Charles

Dickens. The opening lines of his novel *A Tale of Two Cities* seemed to encompass every emotion I'd endured in farming thus far.

It was the best of times; it was the worst of times.
It was the age of wisdom. It was the age of foolishness....
It was the season of light; it was the season of darkness.
It was the spring of hope, it was the winter of despair.

Pickups and Downs

ON JANUARY 14, 1965, I TURNED SIXTEEN. SO LONG I HAD wished for this day when I could apply for a temporary driver's permit for the Province of Ontario. For years there'd been rumours how the age limit would be elevated to eighteen and I lived in fear that would come to pass in my case. My brother Bill reminded me several times that "any new law takes effect the beginning of the year. I'll bet it happens just two weeks before your birthday."

To Bill's disappointment, the magic day arrived without any legal changes. I passed the temporary, then waited the six long weeks for my "real" test.

The designated car for the test was Dad's '59 Meteor station wagon. It was a nice enough car, being the top-of-the-line trim level, the main drawback its unwieldy dimensions. Parallel parking more resembled the docking of an ocean freighter.

It was a little unruly on the road too, especially if one wasn't used to it. The first day I drove home from Listowel while still on my learner's permit, the roads were kind of icy and it was a handful keeping the big boat on the correct side of the road. Dad and Mom shared the front seat and both seemed unusually quiet, I thought. However, with a little more practice I figured I was ready. My brother Richard, who was working for Bell Canada in the Muskoka region of Ontario that winter, reminded me before he left that weekend how he and Bill had received their license on the first try..."so don't let the family down."

It was a cold overcast afternoon as I was directed through the snow-banked arteries of the town of Listowel. I figured I'd done pretty well but one could never be sure. The examiner scribbled a few notes on his page, then turned to me. "I'm going to give you your license, David...however there are a couple of things..."

I was interested only in the first part of his sentence and what he said after I didn't care. I'd passed and Richard was spared any family embarrassment.

I drove Dad's Meteor that first year but by the following spring was itching for my own set of wheels. I found a '58 Volkswagen for $99, which I drove throughout that summer; but as it had no heater or defroster, a more suitable vehicle was in order for the coming Ontario winter.

My solution was a brand new Volkswagen Deluxe. The trade-in price on my '58 model had been established; the only decision remaining was colour. Let's see...garnet red or ocean blue? Dad suggested another decision was in order. How was I going to pay for it?...Well, I was working part time at a neighbour's...Why do adults always have to spoil dreams with reality?

"I think you would be a lot wiser to buy a pickup, which we could use around the farm too," reasoned my father, "and that way I could help pay for it." Well, that part about helping to pay sounded alright...and pickups were pretty nice nowadays!

As both Ford and General Motors had completely restyled trucks for 1967, it was there I concentrated my efforts. One that especially caught my fancy was a jet black Chevrolet with a nice thick slash of chrome that stretched along the entire lower length of the vehicle and around the wheel wells. Inside, everything was red...the dash, the seats, even the rubber floor mats. $2200 straight deal; I knew this was the truck for me! I couldn't wait to tell Dad.

"You should check out a Fargo," he suggested...Oh God...not a Fargo! At that time, I thought they were the ugliest trucks on the road. I apparently wasn't alone in my assessment, as even International Harvester, which by this point had pretty much faded from the light truck scene, was still selling more trucks than Chrysler's Dodge and Fargo divisions that year.

For those not familiar or who perhaps never cared, Fargos were simply Dodge trucks that differed in name-plate only and were sold exclusively by Plymouth dealers in Canada since the mid-1930s.

Dad's reasoning for considering a Fargo stemmed from the fact my brother Richard's fiancée was a niece of the local Chrysler dealer (I didn't say it made any sense, I'm just relating what he said). Since Dad was going to be aiding in the financing, I had no choice but to check one out.

Backed up against the wall of Stan McRae's dealership in my hometown of Palmerston sat a navy blue Fargo pickup with dark blue interior, a painted white dash, "slant six" and "three on the tree transmission." Exciting as used dishwater and that was as good as it got. No radio, no rear bumper, no passenger sun visor, not even a driver's armrest. Talk about basic! $2100 was the price, which included a heavy-duty suspension, the only option on the entire vehicle.

"You know, Dad," I said, "I can get that Chev truck I was mentioning for $2150 without that piece of chrome." (I was still in love with that red interior.)

"I think it would be nice to buy from Stan McRae," said Dad. "He's almost going to be in the family, you know."

I could have cared less. What I couldn't understand was why I had to carry this burden. Richard, the root cause of this dilemma, had bought a new car the previous autumn... and what did he buy?...a Pontiac! "I looked at a Plymouth," he confessed, "but compared to the Pontiac it was a piece of crap!"

So a Fargo it was; McRae's did throw in an AM radio they had on their shelf...and "throw" was the pivotal word... as the radio had to be pulled three times in two years and returned to its factory of origin for repair.

My oldest brother Bill had purchased a new Ford the previous year, and whereas its Twin-I Beam suspension rode like a car, the Fargo's suspension more resembled a Conestoga wagon. When empty, and especially on rough surfaces, the stiffly sprung vehicle bounced along as if it was performing the Hop Scotch polka. At half load, the "helper" springs clattered and clanged enough to drive one insane. Only at full load did it ride comfortably and quietly.

That Fargo was a thirsty old hog too. The 3:90 ratio gear axle might have been an ideal choice if one was hauling borax across the desert, but had the slant six engine screaming its lungs out at highway speeds in the real world. When

I first bought the truck, I announced I would not be using mere "tractor gas." Only clean, "service station" fuel would do. After sucking down a couple of tanks of 13 mpg "service station" gas, I quietly returned to Dad's barrel.

That truck certainly wasn't without problems. I was heading to Palmerston one afternoon when something caused an interruption in the oil flow, the result being a new set of rod bearings. Thank God for Chrysler's five-year/50,000 mile powertrain warranty!

The warranty was certainly no help the day the battery broke loose from its mounting and toppled into the fan, the entire assembly then crashing through the radiator. I'd exchanged batteries a couple of days before and "neglected" to replace the battery hold-down clamps – my belief they weren't all that necessary.

Two faulty fuel pumps, an alternator, plus endless quality control issues, plagued two years of ownership. Wind noise was unbearable, requiring frequent trips to Canadian Tire for weather stripping material as the dealer was little help. "I can hardly hear the radio!" I complained. Their suggestion was "turn it up."

Another headache was the "Slam it shut with one hand" tailgate touted by Chrysler in their advertisements. It had the most annoying habit of opening at the most inopportune time (heading to the feed mill with a load of bulk grain).

I was fast becoming disenchanted and decided something with more flash was in order, so found myself at Stan McRae's dealership once again. I reasoned it would be easier to sell the idea of a new truck to Dad if I stayed with "uncle" Stan, plus he was the only one who would give anything worthwhile for the old Fargo.

The pickup I chose this time was the top of the line Adventurer model. I ordered a more economical 3:55 axle and a 318 cubic inch V-8 to provide the get-up-and-go. Actually the six-cylinder engine that was standard was more than adequate but one can never have too much power! With little effort I could make black marks on the pavement with the V-8, an important milestone when you are twenty.

To the mix I also added automatic transmission, power steering, whitewall tires, wheel discs, and radio. Copper and beige two-tone paint with pin striping complemented a colour-matched interior with thick door-to-door black carpeting...Look out, girls!

I liked to crank the radio up loud and cruise the gravel roads of our township, while Toronto's top radio station CHUM propelled the hits of the day from the single dash-mounted speaker. I'd often schedule my trips from the local feed mill to correspond with when the high school buses were making their rounds. I'd keep the windows wound down, impressing the girls as they disembarked with my great radio. I figured I was pretty cool!

Recalling that scene objectively...I guess a skinny high school drop-out with buck teeth, brush cut, shod in a pair of rubber boots, piloting a pickup truck laden with a ton of cattle feed, hardly constituted "cool."

That '69 Fargo was a world away from the two-year-old truck it replaced, offering style as well as dependable service for well over four years and probably more except...

In September of 1973 our dairy barn burnt to the ground and the Fargo unfortunately was parked a little too close. The fire department managed to drag the vehicle away from the inferno, but not before it suffered major paint damage, shattered glass, and a couple of flat tires. With the $700 my insurance company gave me, I replaced the windshield and side glass, installed a couple of used tires, and just put up with the scorched paint and seat, as well as a few melted trim items.

By this time, a '70 Pontiac, which I shared with my parents, was our main transportation, relegating the Fargo to "farm vehicle" status. So although the Fargo wasn't all that pleasing visually, the fire damage didn't affect the truck's hauling capabilities. From that day forward though, anyone driving it had to accommodate a rather unpleasant stench.

The Awakening

IN 1976 I'D UNDERTAKEN AN EXTENSIVE JOURNEY OF THE STATE of Kentucky, touring the less-travelled routes and visiting the small towns along the way. That excursion only whetted my appetite to explore farther south of the Mason-Dixon Line: the land of cotton and sugarcane plantations, magnolias and Spanish moss, delta dirt and rice paddies, and to glimpse first-hand the magic and romance of "Old Man River."

In the early hours of April 16, 1977, I crossed into the state of Michigan, following the highway through Flint and Lansing until its connection with Interstate 69, then south through the beautiful farmland of northeast Indiana. I covered a lot of miles and sundown found me just north of the city of Indianapolis.

Sunrise found my faithful Chevy circumventing the city, and Interstate 65 had me in Louisville by mid-morning and

Nashville by noon. It was an absolutely gorgeous day and the traffic, except for big cities, light.

Travelling the super-highways throughout the U.S. and Canada over the years caused me to observe how traffic patterns change when entering a large metropolis. One minute it's serene countryside at a steady 55–60 mph, then almost without warning, you're caught in an accelerating torrent of traffic, being swept along in a seemingly fast flowing river surrounded by hurtling metal...then it fades as quickly as begun and you're back in peaceful countryside. Montgomery, Mobile, Knoxville, Nashville, Toronto, or Toledo...the pattern is the same.

Late in the afternoon a huge billboard containing a portrait of Governor George Wallace welcomed me to Alabama, "The Heart of Dixie." I guess I expected to see cotton fields when I crossed the state border; instead I discovered the northeastern part of the state very rugged, where some places sheer walls of rock towered hundreds of feet above the highway. On one particular crest of this escarpment, 100-foot high Desoto Falls against a backdrop of dark green southern pine, under a cloudless Alabama evening sky, made for a photographer's dream.

The digital thermometer on the roof of the Alabama Savings and Loan's building recorded 85 degrees as I entered the state's largest city the following day. Birmingham was my initial introduction to the magnolia. As I stepped from the truck, the overpowering sweetness almost drove me to nausea until my olfactory glands learned to harmonize with the heavily perfumed blossoms.

My next point of interest centred around Montgomery, 90 miles south. The terrain flattens considerably approaching the city, situated on the eastern edge of Alabama's famous "Black Belt," a 30-mile-wide strip of rich black earth that stretches completely across the state into neighbouring Mississippi.

A century earlier, this region of Alabama harboured some of the greatest cotton plantations in the southern states, a land where cotton was absolute king. In 1915, the boll weevil, a small beetle that feeds inside the boll, or seed pod of the cotton plant, caused major damage to Alabama's premium crop. In the years following the infestation, plantation owners were forced to rotate to alternate crops in an effort to lessen the dependency on cotton in the region. Even as of this writing, the "Black Belt" is still rich, fertile farmland and cotton still grows...it simply no longer rules.

I discovered the city of Montgomery typified the appearance of a pre–Civil War city with historic and attractive homes set on quiet streets lined with mighty oak trees. Azaleas reigned supreme and everywhere the air was saturated with the scent of magnolia.

In early 1861 when many northern states were demanding the government outlaw slavery, Alabama, in response, seceded from the Union, claiming the government had no right to impose such a resolution. It was in Montgomery in February 1861 that Jefferson Davis was sworn in as the first (and as it turned out, last) President of the Confederate States of America.

Texas, Arkansas, Louisiana, Mississippi, Tennessee, Florida, Georgia, North and South Carolina, and Virginia also seceded. Virginia actually split over the slavery debate with the "new" state, West Virginia, staying with the Union.

To say the least, it was an uneasy time for the South. As ugly, outdated and embarrassing slavery might have appeared to the rest of the country, it was a way of life southerners had practised for generations, and as with anything that becomes comfortable...even normal, they fought to protect it.

The Confederate States had hoped for a peaceful withdrawal from the Union, but what they got was a four-year bloodbath. Under Davis, the southern States fought a fairly successful campaign during the first year or so, but being mostly agricultural based, proved no match for the industrial wealth of the north. Simply and slowly they were starved out, but not before 240,000 lay dead.

I elected to spend my fourth night in Alabama in Brundidge, a picturesque town in the southern part of the state. Seeing no motels while driving the main thoroughfare, I inquired at a small grocery store. Behind the counter, a man in his late 50s sat with a fly swatter. Picking up some groceries at the back of the store, I could hear the fly swatter continually slam onto the counter. As I approached, the proprietor simply brushed the carcasses out of the way with his hand.

As he methodically rang up my order on one of the oldest cash registers I'd seen outside a museum, we talked about the weather and other generalities.

"Where y'all from?" I told him, also that I was heading for Mobile.

"I got a cousin in Mobile but haven't seen him in a while; I don't travel much."

"Well, you have a nice town right here," I replied.

"Yes, it's a good town. Hasn't changed all that much, leastways for appearance...of course there are some things we can't do anything about." The man paused, staring out the window at nothing in particular that I could see.

"I guess things change everywhere," I commented, breaking the silence. He merely nodded. I finally got around to asking about a place to stay. He directed me by name to an address just down the street. "You can't miss it."

I saw no sign of a motel, just houses. Even drove the block twice. I returned to the grocery store. "Is it full up?" the owner asked, continuing his fly crusade. "I must be a little stupid, but I couldn't find it," I admitted.

He put down his swatter and thought for a moment. "I was forgettin', I guess the sign's gone. There used to be a "whites only" sign but after the niggers got desegregation, they made him take it down."

Suddenly I was slapped from my dreamy vision of what I perceived the South to be. The word "nigger" awakened me to the realities of another side of the South I'd conveniently forgotten. It wasn't all oak trees, antebellum homes, Stephen Foster songs, and southern drawls. There was a dark side too: a part of the South that was quite comfortable with segregated schools, churches, libraries, and restaurants; a South that acknowledged and condoned "white" and "coloured" drinking fountains and washrooms...even buses.

It was this policy of bus segregation that prompted a then young Martin Luther King Jr. to boycott Montgomery bus companies. The boycott began simply as a protest against the arrest of a Negro woman who refused to relinquish her seat to a white passenger, and gradually grew into a mass movement. Beginning in the early 1960s, groups, both black and white, conducted "freedom marches" aimed at ending segregation in public facilities in the South.

Alabama's Governor George Wallace made it clear he would tolerate no protests in his state and banned all marches. When 500 blacks set out for Montgomery,

Wallace true to his word sent the state police to stop them, utilizing tear gas, clubs, whips, or whatever it took. Just as clear was his record of refusing entry of Negro students to Alabama universities, forcing President Kennedy to send in the National Guard on several occasions.

Some of these thoughts sifted through my mind as I drove to the motel, realizing what the store owner meant by "changes we can't do anything about." Most notable of this unappetizing period of U.S. history was its recency; in 1977, when I visited, a black man was still unable to get a haircut in some southern towns. It was illegal of course, but that didn't stop the practice.

However I had come for an overall view of the South, so with that in mind, turned into the semi-circular driveway of the large white-framed house. A distinguished gentleman, probably in his seventies and attired in white slacks and matching jacket, was standing on the verandah. I inquired as to the chances of a room and he responded in finest Alabama accent that he did have one available.

"That will be $8, sir." I extracted a $10 bill and while I was returning the two single bills to my wallet, this gent suddenly became quite excited.

"What may I ask kind of money is that sir?" I pulled out one of the Canadian $20 bills in the back of my wallet and showed it to him.

"Never in all my days have I seen money like that!" Like a kid admiring a new toy, he examined the colourful bill. "Is each a different colour?" I then handed him a ten and a five. He was even more amazed. "A number of years back, a Canadian fellow not unlike yourself happened by, but his money bore no resemblance to this."

I explained how this new "colourful" money (I almost said "coloured") hadn't been around long. I made his day when I told him I would trade a Canadian bill for one of his. A few seconds' thought and he chose a $20 bill. At that time there was a large value discrepancy in favour of the U.S. bill but he didn't seem concerned about exchange rates.

Like most Alabamians I'd met on this trip, this gent liked to talk, and while giving me a tour of the grounds, related how he'd run this "guest house," as he referred to it, for forty years and it had been in his family since before the Civil War. He mentioned the time a severe storm sent one of the huge oak trees crashing down on a corner of the house, completely demolishing one room. He proudly showed me two pecan trees he'd planted back in the early 1940s, explaining how he had two different varieties so they would pollinate properly. I noticed these trees were very bushy, with elongated leaves made up of little leaflets measuring some 12 inches long.

Walking back to the house, I told him how impressed I was with his estate and thanked him for his hospitality. "I never would have known you were here if I hadn't asked." As soon as I spoke, I wished I hadn't. The last thing I wanted to hear was how he'd been forced to remove his sign and allow "niggers." However he made no comment other than that he'd never got around to putting up another sign. "People seem to find us anyway."

My initial impression of my room was time had simply stopped some 75 years earlier. The suite was dark in colour; heavy maroon drapes running from ceiling to floor covered the south and west windows. A maroon and black rug containing large patterned violet leaves covered three-quarters of a gorgeously maintained hardwood floor. Even the patterned wallpaper was finished in deep tones. The ceiling in contrast was white. Intricate plaster mouldings along the cornices harmonized with equally interesting designed baseboards. Although made of wood, these baseboards, as was common when many of these fine old houses were built, were painted to resemble marble. "Faux marble" they called it.

No ceiling lights were in evidence, but three wall lamps appeared to be an antique collector's dream. I guessed the units were originally gas and converted to electricity at a later date. The main focus of the room, and what caught my attention initially, was a large four-poster bed, complete with canopy. Only seeing them in movies, I couldn't wait to sleep on it. It was a long way from the firm motel beds to which I'd grown accustomed. Obviously a feather mattress, I disappeared "into" it rather than lying on it.

Two cane-bottomed chairs sat either side of a bay window that faced the front lawn. In addition to closet space, a beautiful three-tiered chest of drawers with intricate hardware graced one section of wall. There was no shower, just a bathtub, one of those gems with the feet and high back. The only item seemingly out of place in this room from another time setting was the television set. But even it was a relic: one of the very early Crosley units with the tiny screen. It didn't work. It would have spoiled the mood anyway.

It was a beautiful evening, so I walked the two blocks to a restaurant for supper. On my return I detoured via a couple of side streets. Walking the streets of a rural town in springtime Ontario, one finds tulips, crocuses, daffodils, and lilacs; In Alabama, azaleas, camellias and honeysuckle thrive in abundance. Although emitting a sweet aroma, the honeysuckle is no match for the magnolia, which dominates everything.

As I entered the driveway, the late April sun was in full decline, casting its last warming rays of the day on the mammoth oak marking the corner boundary of the property. Not clear, but still visible was a small faded section upon the gnarled bark where at one time a flat piece of wood had been tacked. It was a strange feeling realizing what the discarded shingle had read.

As I sat in my room that evening, I couldn't help but wonder if any black person with the exception of servants had ever occupied this room. Obviously none before the mid-1960s, but after that? Once Civil Rights became law, would the owner of this establishment suddenly open his doors and welcome the first blacks into his home? Or would it be more comfortable to simply state, "Sorry, we're full up." As much as I was in love with the "old South" and my perception of what it should be, I had little doubt it would be the latter. At least for a while anyway; there's an old Negro expression that perhaps sums it up.

We ain't what we could be; We ain't what we're
going to be;
But at least we ain't what we was.

Battleships and Bourbon

I AWOKE TO THE SOUND OF A VARIETY OF BIRD SPECIES...SOME familiar, some not...orchestrating a morning concert outside my window. Numerous yellow flickers recognizable by their distinctive dark brown polka dots...here in the South referred to as "yellowhammers"...flitted among the oak and pecan trees that shaded the spacious lawn of the guest house.

I'd spent the night in the distinctly southern town of Brundidge, Alabama, situated roughly halfway between the city of Montgomery and the Alabama-Florida border, and was beginning my fourth day on the road of my tour of the "Deep South."

Weaving southwesterly across some of Alabama's finest agricultural land, I saw foot-high corn thriving in the fertile red soil. I couldn't help but be reminded that back home in Ontario it would be another two or three weeks before our corn crop was even in the ground. As the highway continued westward, the land gradually changed from farmland to forested area and finally into the low swampy region known as the Mobile River Delta.

Traffic arteries are limited from Mobile Bay's east shore into the city of Mobile. It was late afternoon when I entered the six-mile-long causeway, and with three lanes of traffic running at 70 mph, it's not wise to look anywhere but straight ahead, but if one gets the chance, a glance to one's left bears a startling sight. A huge battleship, parked out in the waters of Mobile Bay!

This impressive ship is the U.S.S. *Alabama,* a World War Two veteran that led the U.S. fleet into Tokyo harbour back in 1945. It was my intention to explore this piece of naval history, so I had the foresight to be in the correct lane as I raced over the causeway. I checked into the Quality Motel, then drove the half-mile to where the ship was moored.

Thirty-five thousand tons of armoured steel, 680 feet long from bow to stern, the *Alabama,* built in 1942, earned nine battle stars in its three-year struggle against the Japanese Empire in the Pacific before being decommissioned in 1947. Since then, tourists walk her decks and stare at the then high-tech anti-aircraft and long-range guns that seem to sprout from everywhere.

I had supper in the motel dining room and while waiting for my soup to arrive, noticed a woman probably in her early thirties a couple of tables diagonally from mine. Her hair was sort of a brownish-blonde mixture, rather long, rather unkempt; however on her it looked just right. Everything looked right about this woman, from her captivating wide-set brown eyes that sparkled despite the restaurant's soft light to her low-cut pale green dress that contrasted so beautifully with her suntanned skin. She noticed me staring and looked away; then just as quickly those gorgeous eyes returned the stare. This time it was my turn to divert my eyes, as there was something hauntingly mysterious about her.

While I was trying to figure a casual way to strike up a conversation with this woman who had so captivated me, she picked up her purse and headed for the ladies' room. A few minutes later she reappeared and instead of returning to her table, departed the restaurant by the side entrance, folded her long legs into the bucket seat of a late model Chevrolet Camaro, and sped away. From start to finish the interlude probably hadn't consumed ten minutes but I couldn't get her out of my mind.

I finished my meal, walked into the lounge situated next to the dining room, purchased a *Motor Trend* maga-zine, and tried to catch up on the latest news in the auto-motive world. Secretly I thought that perhaps this mystery woman might reappear…maybe she was staying in this very motel! After nearly two hours I finally convinced myself this evening's event had been nothing more than a "passing ship in the night" scenario…and a fast moving one at that. I nodded goodnight to the hotel desk clerk and headed for my room.

I don't know how many times the phone beside my bed rang before I realized what it was; who in the hell phones you in a motel? I checked my watch; twenty past one. After a couple more rings I picked up the receiver. "This is the front desk…sorry to bother you…" a lengthy pause followed before the voice returned to the line. "Have you got a girl there with you?"

"Pardon me…"

"We're looking for a certain girl and wondering if she might be with you?"

I glanced at the pillow on the other side of the twin bed. "No...not here."

Another long pause followed while in the background I could hear at least two other voices. The desk clerk then came back on the line, apologized for disturbing me, and hung up.

After the call, I began to harbour an unexplained feeling of uneasiness. Was it the "mystery woman" to whom they were referring? But they referred to her as a "girl." But why did they phone me? I then began to imagine what might have happened to this woman. Was she abducted, assaulted? Was I a suspect? But why? Did someone notice me watching her? Okay, I admit I might have briefly fantasized something between us but since when is that a crime ...even in the Alabama Bible Belt?

All these questions raced through the one side of my brain while the other tried to convince me it was someone else they were looking for and not to become paranoid. However I had trouble returning to sleep, as I envisioned being picked up by an Alabama state trooper the next day and thrown into a county jail until I could somehow clear my name.

I must have finally drifted off to sleep, because at 5 o'clock the phone rang again. My heart was beating like jackhammer as I picked up the phone! "Hello...hello..." The phone continued to ring. I realized then it was the fire alarm. As I was on the first floor I wasn't too concerned, but took a look out the door at all the other people looking out their doors. After gawking at each other and with no sign of fire, most returned to bed. I couldn't have gone back to sleep if you'd smothered me, so decided to hit the road.

It was still dark for the most part, with just a faint light in the eastern sky as I loaded up the truck. I elected to have coffee and a biscuit at the all-night cafeteria; while I was sipping my coffee, a state patrolman entered the cafeteria, glanced at me momentarily, but because of events through the night, it seemed like forever. He then turned his attention to the desk clerk. While conversing, the cop again glanced my way...or was it just my imagination? Talk about paranoia!

A couple more minutes passed; then the officer left. At this point the desk clerk came over to my table. "Sorry about disturbing your sleep last night, friend, but the girl we were looking for was under age and...well her parents were freaking out."

I took a deep breath..."So did you find her okay?" He laughed before answering. "Oh, she's fine...well as far as we're concerned she is...let's just say she has a few issues to iron out with her parents!"

I felt as if a Mack truck had been lifted off me. I realize I had let my emotions rule but the entire episode was a good lesson on just how easily a stranger travelling alone could get in a "heap of trouble" to borrow a southern expression.

As I pulled from the parking lot, the eastern horizon was a mixture of soft blues, pinks, and greys. The *Alabama,* silhouetted against this pastel background while shrouded in a veil of mist from the bay, appeared almost ghost-like.

Mobile is very spread-out city, with its waterfront being its most dominant characteristic and home to a large ship-building and repair centre. Pulp and paper was and still is a major industry, and the unmistakable odour of sulphur was quite evident. The numerous billowing smokestacks, back-lit by the rising sun were impressive...at least visually.

Turning west I followed the Gulf coast into Mississippi, through small towns and cities like Pecan, Pascagoula, Biloxi, and Gulfport...all ports alive with local shrimp boats and oceangoing vessels and full of the sights, sounds, and smells only waterfront centres can generate. As well along the Mississippi coast are resorts to no end with pure white sandy beaches that stretch for miles. I had never considered Mississippi a resort centre, but as one native put it..."The crowds may stop here but the sand doesn't."

Another feature of this region...food; on former vacations, I'd eaten most meals at interstate cafeteria-style eating establishments, the type where one sits on a chrome stool at an arbourite (laminate) counter, eating off a plastic plate with plastic utensils. Nearly everything is pre-packaged, pre-frozen or pre-cooked, instantly and attractively presented, but for the most part...tasteless.

On this journey I decided to change this habit and, in a "real" restaurant somewhere in southern Alabama, ordered breaded shrimp and French onion soup, which arrived at my table on fire. Apparently that was the way it was supposed to be.

That episode began an experimentation program of culinary delights that spanned three states. Breaded oysters, catfish, turtle soup, crabmeat salad, blackened redfish... and my favourite, seafood gumbo, which varied widely in texture...sometimes the consistency of soup, other times as thick as stew. The flavour varied as well, through the use of different species of seafood and vegetables and the amount of Tabasco sauce added.

The further I drove along the Gulf, the slower and more congested the traffic. To speed things up, I let Interstate-10 whisk me into Louisiana, and an hour later found me crossing Lake Pontchartrain and heading for the most famous city on the Gulf of Mexico...New Orleans. The sky had blackened considerably as I neared my destination...a condition I hoped wouldn't hamper my visit, as I'd heard the only way to really enjoy the French Quarter was on foot. A large blue sign announced "Vieux Carré: Exit Canal Street.

Just off Canal Street I parked the truck and hadn't walked twenty minutes into this most historic city when the threatening skies turned to steady light rain. I walked the full length of Bourbon Street...or Rue Bourbon as all the street signs are in the French dialect...zigzagging back and forth whenever something interesting caught my attention. Some buildings, with their 200-year old architecture, I couldn't help but admire. Other places looked little more than fire traps and I wondered how they'd ever survived. On a dilapidated structure just off Bourbon, I read the name of one of the best known jazz clubs in New Orleans...Preservation Hall: This historic site as well as other area nightclubs was the birthplace and home of traditional jazz, from which ragtime, rhythm and blues, swing, and rock evolved.

As the rain was falling with more intensity, I slipped into one of the street cafés so prevalent on Bourbon's French Quarter. While listening to the band I enjoyed "café au lait" and a "beignet," which tasted like a doughnut but square and without the hole.

The hub of New Orleans is Jackson Square, dominated by a large statue of the seventh president of the United States, Andrew Jackson. What I'd really come to see, however, was directly behind the square. My first glimpse of that most famous North American river, something I had dreamed of since I was a kid. I rounded the corner and saw...nothing. Just fog and rain; I did hear a foghorn from where I presumed was the river.

At that moment a tour bus pulled up to my left. Through a microphone the tour hostess informed the passengers this was Jackson Square. After a spiel about the history of the Square and the former president, she turned around, motioning through the windshield as she spoke.

"Directly in front of us is the Mississippi River...the largest river in the United States. Stretching more than 2,300 miles long and over a mile wide in some places..." Forty pairs of eyes stared out into the gloom and saw exactly what I saw. The guide continued with her history lesson while I turned and walked back towards the Square. I guess you could say I was a little disappointed.

Despite being soaked, I took my time heading through the grid of streets back to where my truck was parked. At least it was warm, probably 80 degrees. The French Quarter is full of curious little shops; antique, candle, stamp, and coin shops vie for attention and tourist dollars as well as art, dolls, toys, jazz, maritime...even voodoo shops. Voodoo is big business in New Orleans, where potions, medicinal plants, and weird looking – and smelling – herbs are sold.

One of the many interesting characteristics of New Orleans, as well as most of Louisiana, is the cemeteries, where the tombs are situated above ground...a necessity because of the high water table. Most of New Orleans is below the level of the Mississippi River, where an extensive system of levees and spillways is designed to keep the river and city apart. This design worked reasonably well until a hurricane we all know now as Katrina blasted the city on September 5, 2005. By the time Katrina left, the dead numbered in the thousands, and months later they were still finding casualties. The number of homeless was nearly uncountable and property damage incalculable.

A year later it was estimated half the city's population of 450,000 had still not returned. At the time, some analysts claimed New Orleans would never fully recover. During that first year, acres and acres once filled with homes were simply carted away in dump trucks. Although great strides have been made in the last decade, this prognostication proved accurate as some areas, such as the Lower Ninth Ward and sections of New Orleans East near Lake Pontchartrain, remain as of this writing mere ghost towns.

Back in my truck I plotted my next move. As it was nearly six o'clock and the day literally a washout, I decided to find a motel. My plan was to return to the French Quarter the next morning when perhaps the weather would be more accommodating.

I studied my city map as the defogger dispelled the mist from my windshield. I managed to find my way onto Airline Highway, actually Highway 61, the main thoroughfare through New Orleans until Interstate 10 was built. I reasoned this avenue as the logical choice for accommodation. I had no sooner turned onto 61 when the sky opened! I suppose Gulf residents are used to storms like this, but I don't recall ever driving in heavier rain for such a sustained period. Waves of water buffeted the truck as the squall was driven inland by the gusty Gulf winds.

It was probably a good half hour before the rain eased and by this time I was well out of the city. I began searching for a place to lodge, but it was kind of a desolate area, so I drove about twenty miles before a motel came into view. One look told me it lacked class but as it was getting dark and raining steadily again, I decided this refuge would do.

It was a small motel, probably ten units, and stuck on one end was a restaurant that also doubled as the motel office. I sat down at a table, asked the waitress for a hot chicken sandwich and a glass of tomato juice, and while waiting, surveyed my surroundings.

Directly across from me a skinny guy probably in his early twenties with unkempt blond hair halfway down his back was in deep conversation with a woman twice his age. Both were drinking bourbon and appeared to have been doing so for a while. A couple of big dudes attired in black Harley Davidson T-shirts occupied a booth two spaces down, while a guy who spent more time smoking and coughing than eating sat at a corner table.

On the opposite side of the room a man in his 50s, I would guess, was reading a newspaper and every once in a while would blurt..."goddam government!" Next to him, two teenagers who appeared would have been much more comfortable in one of the motel rooms cuddled, cooed, and stared in each other's eyes while eating dessert from each other's spoons. In the booth closest to the counter, a rather pale but nicely featured woman sat reading a newspaper while enjoying a coffee and cigarette. From her conversation with the waitress, I learned she worked there and had just completed her shift.

An interesting mixture of characters...however, the food was tasty and the service friendly, so I ordered a coffee and slice of apple pie for dessert. At that moment, some guy who'd been in the washroom made his way down the aisle where I was sitting and started a rude conversation with the woman at the table by the counter. After a couple more offensive remarks, this woman without any visible sign of emotion, simply told him to...and I'll paraphrase...have intercourse with himself! The guy was obviously caught off guard by the exchange and departed the restaurant quickly, helped along by a chorus of cheers and laughter from restaurant patrons who'd obviously enjoyed the verbal assault.

"Eight dollars," said the lady behind the counter. "Do you want to see the room?"..."No, it'll be fine." I'd regret that decision!

I guess for $8 I shouldn't have expected too much. "Shabby" might be a kind description. A lumpy bed occupied the wall just inside the door. A grubby carpet that I doubt had ever been introduced to either shampoo or a vacuum covered a floor that creaked with every step, while navy blue flowery wallpaper hung loose in several places. I turned on the Marconi television and was greeted by a crackling sound in conjunction with the acrid smell of smoke.

The bathroom was a gem as well; no hot water, dark brown stained toilet bowl, and the bathtub was furnished with...surprise...count them...four cockroaches! As I entered the room they scurried out of sight through a crack in the baseboard. At this point I briefly entertained the thought of complaining, but then beheld a vision of one of those "Harley Hoggers" from the restaurant being sent to resolve my gripe, so changed my mind. After all, I'd been given fair chance to survey the room and passed.

I read and listened to the radio awhile, where I heard about flash flooding in the area west of New Orleans and more rain called for the next day. I switched off the radio and tried to sleep, not easy, with the wind banging something outside my window and the steady sound of water dripping from...well I wasn't sure where.

I must have finally dozed off, because just after midnight a male voice awakened me. "Hey, Brenda! It's me."

"Wrong door!" I hollered back from the darkness.

"Oh...sorry, mate." He then tried his luck at a door further down. About two o'clock according to my watch, I was rudely roused again as if someone fell or was thrown against my door.

"Watch where you're going, you stupid son of a bitch!"

"Sorry...I was looking for Brenda."

"Well keep your eyes open next time you horse-faced bastard!" The guy apologized a couple more times before stumbling away to continue his quest.

Brenda was obviously a popular motel attraction as I recalled her name mentioned in the restaurant earlier; Brenda's claim to fame according to those in attendance was how at some point she'd sexually accommodated four guys simultaneously in one session. I had to admit the overheard conversation piqued my curiosity, imagining how she may have accomplished this feat. Apparently concentration, co-ordination, and bourbon were the key factors.

At the crack of dawn I was more than ready to hit the road. While packing I heard the sound of running water but gave little thought as I'd basically heard that sound all night. One last look in the bathroom to make sure I hadn't forgotten anything discovered the toilet overflowing. The water was simply flowing across the sloped floor and into the crack where the cockroaches had disappeared. I was tempted to simply walk away but noticed a tap on the wall behind the toilet. By stepping into the tub, I was able to turn off the flow without slopping across the soggy floor.

When I left the key at the restaurant desk, I noticed the waitress who'd entertained us the previous evening with her well-timed four-letter remark mopping the floor where

someone had vomited. I had thought of getting some breakfast but decided it could wait.

A few minutes down the road, I passed a beautiful motel
on the fringe of a golf course. A welcoming sign advertised
40 units, colour television, sauna, air conditioning, telephone, and complimentary breakfast for $13.

Power of the Groove

I T'S INTERESTING HOW A CERTAIN SONG CAN PROPEL A PERSON back through the years to a single moment in time. I have a large collection of phonograph records from the mid-20th century that have been transferred to modern CDs, and one that caught my attention today was a particular Gene Autry Christmas song, "When Santa Claus Gets Your Letter."

Immediately I was swept back to the living room of our house in Simcoe County in the mid-1950s, watching the tone-arm of our RCA Victor console move swiftly across the 78 rpm red-labelled Columbia recording. That's the way I always listened to records; chair snugged up close to the player, lid open to observe the intricate mechanism of this most fascinating machine.

As Gene was relaying his musical message through the grooves, the power suddenly failed and his voice came to an unpleasant and grinding halt. It must have been the first time such an incident had interrupted my listening pleasure, because I recall running to the kitchen in tears telling Mom how something dreadful had happened to Gene Autry.

Just hearing a particular melody will spark a personal reminder and take me back to the very first time I heard it, recalling exactly where I was and what I was doing. Music is a powerful force and arguably one of life's most rewarding influences. In the early part of the twentieth century, music transported through the grooves of a flat disc or airwaves to your parlour radio was magical beyond belief.

My great-grandfather Thomas Carruthers' first phonograph was a wax cylinder model. This was later superseded by the more familiar flat wax record, which would dominate recorded music in its various forms practically to the end of the century.

My great-grandfather's favourite musical artist at the time (1920s) was Sir Harry Lauder, a Scottish singer renowned for his trips to the battlefield to entertain troops during World War One. If he could've afforded it, Tom Carruthers would have bought every Lauder record available. Sir Harry's untiring efforts to bring musical enjoyment to a battle-weary European army would provide incentive for others in the entertainment field, like Vera Lynn and Bob Hope, who would carry the torch throughout other world conflicts in decades to come.

Another medium of entertainment gaining momentum at that time was radio. Although few Canadian signals existed, an enjoyable evening could be had listening to programs available from bordering American states. In 1925, a young Toronto electronics engineer, Ted Rogers, had devised a method whereby a radio could be plugged directly into a house electrical system, thus eliminating batteries. The company formed to market his new product was

Rogers-Majestic and the station he founded shortly after, CFRB (Canadian Frequency Rogers Batteryless). CFRB is Toronto's oldest radio station and still broadcasts today.

On the other side of the family tree, the Turners...deep within the rural outreaches of Grey County...didn't have the luxury of hydro and therefore had no choice but to rely on batteries as a power source. My father's introduction to radio began in his late teens. His best friend Lester's father had a side business renting out a couple of cottages that had been part of his farm before the area was flooded to accommodate the newly constructed Eugenia dam. Fishermen from the Toronto area flocked to this new lake each weekend, and the group that rented Lester's father's cottage often left their radio behind when returning to the city Sunday night.

Dad and Lester would break into the building (all you needed was a screwdriver according to my Dad) and spend hours listening to the country music stations that beamed their signals out of the United States. Weather had a lot to do with what you received on any given night. Some nights, nothing but static...others, the airwaves as clear as crystal; generally the later the hour the better the reception.

WLS Chicago was "the" country station of that period, owned by Sears Roebuck...World's Largest Store (WLS). Its 50,000 watts covered a greater area and reached more people than even WSM Nashville, and as long as the reception was clear and the batteries didn't die, the two would sit for hours listening to the fiddle and guitars from the windy city.

It was a momentous day when my father's family received their first radio, powered by B and C batteries, but it could also be operated from a car battery. This was the regular power source during winter when the car was in storage. Occasionally even on a summer's evening the old Ford would be pulled up beside an open window and the radio wired directly to the battery. This would be for a special occasion only, something like the Saturday night Grand Ole Opry from Nashville perhaps.

As hundreds of thousands listened, emcee George D. Hay would announce the beginning of the show by blowing a steamboat whistle. Throughout the evening, Roy Acuff, The Carter Family, Little Jimmy Dickens, Grandpa Jones, Bill Monroe, Uncle Dave Macon, and a host of string bands and fiddlers would take the stage. Interspersed within this entertainment were commercials...everything from home-grown country ham to lye soap and Purina Chow to Prince Albert tobacco, pitched by the performers themselves.

Back in 1975 I took a road trip to Nashville. I was a big fan of country music at the time and it was both an emotional and exciting moment to first set eyes on the city's famous 16th Avenue, "Music Row," which had shaped the careers of so many artists. The country music industry was still vibrant and strong at that time with literally scores of record companies, recording studios, and music publishing firms clamouring for attention along the thoroughfare.

I arrived at the Country Music Hall of Fame just as a busload of tourists from Illinois were disembarking, so simply joined the entourage for a guided tour. The museum showcased rare collections of musical instruments, records, films, photographs, stage costumes, and performers' personal items in conjunction with original recordings of the artists playing in the background.

The building where the museum was housed is gone now, torn down in 2001, and the museum collection moved to a new site eleven blocks away in downtown Nashville.

Next stop was Ernest Tubb's Record Store. For variety of material, this store was beyond anything I'd ever seen. Country albums crammed the store from floor level to eye level, completely surrounding the spacious room. The majority of the three hours spent there was consumed in the "old time" section. In the months preceding this trip, I'd become increasingly intrigued with the southern string bands that were so popular in the 1920s and '30s.

Sylvia Tyson of "Ian and Sylvia" fame hosted a program on CBC radio during the 1970s called *Touch the Earth*, whose feature was the exposure of the Canadian country and folk music scene. However, from time to time Sylvia would highlight the roots of artists from across the border and it was here I learned to appreciate the musical stylings of traditional bands such as the Carter Family and Ernest Stoneman, true pioneers of the recording industry.

The names of some of these old dance bands of which I became enamoured were as interesting as the music they recorded. Many reflected the geography of their origins: Arkansas Travelers, Arkansas Woodchoppers, The Blue-grass Boys, Clinch Mountain Boys, Hoosier Hotshots, Cumberland Ridge Runners, Missouri Mountaineers, and North Carolina Ramblers.

Others adopted more localized titles; Dr. Humphrey Bates and his Possum Hunters, Paul Warmack and his Gully Jumpers, Binkley Brothers' Dixie Clodhoppers and Uncle Dave Macon and his Fruit Jar Drinkers. Ernest Stoneman led two different bands throughout his early career...the Dixie Mountaineers and the Blue Ridge Corn Shuckers, whereas some groups like The Carter Family simply used their family name with no attachments.

Somehow the music of these southern dance bands struck a chord I couldn't explain. It was an almost magical feeling that seem to sweep me away to another world. I think in another life I must have had some connection to this kind of music...maybe I was a member of one of these old-time bands. Even today, some of those old records from the 1920s and '30s leave me with the strangest feeling...

Different bands stand out for different reasons, but a definite favourite centred round a collection of North Georgia musicians...Gid Tanner and the Skillet Lickers. Originally the band consisted of just fiddling chicken farmer Gid Tanner and his blind guitarist friend, Riley Puckett. Soon auto mechanic Clayton McMichen and an excellent banjo player, Fate Norris, joined the group, McMichen and Tanner playing fiddle in unison, along with Norris's lilting banjo and Puckett's superb guitar runs and strong tenor voice, provided the ingredients for a first-class band.

As time passed, the band was augmented by other musicians who came and went with confusing irregularity. Most notable was Lowe Stokes, a fiddler who critics at the time considered to be one of America's truly gifted rural musicians. Later on, Stokes had the misfortune of having his right hand blown off by a shotgun blast during a brawl in a Georgia saloon. He eventually learned to play again with the aid of a prosthetic and can be heard on some later recordings.

The Great Depression of the 1930s caused record sales to tank for many artists, the Skillet Lickers no exception. Tanner went back to chicken farming and both Puckett and McMichen tried to make it as individuals in the new musical world of the 1930s. Neither really caught fire...ah but in their day!

...Back on Nashville's 16th Street, the world within a world hurried on, the sidewalk seemingly alive with people regardless the hour: some gawking around with no particular focus, others bustling by with purpose. To me it seemed there were three distinct classes:

- The tourists, easily recognizable by their cameras, who in this pre-digital era seemed to be continually changing film cartridges.
- The group I guessed to be the aspiring executives. One could tell these men and women weren't the top echelon of the Nashville scene or they wouldn't be walking. They dressed and walked with style, however, and in their minds at least, it was probably just a matter of time before they reached whatever goal they were striving.
- The third group was harder to define. Dress was very casual...jeans and T-shirts usually. Occasionally a guitar slung over the back. Speculation on this cluster of individuals was the most interesting. Were they up and coming musicians waiting for the big break? Or down and out, dejected and disappointed and headed for the Greyhound bus home? Perhaps they worked in the countless behind-the-scenes positions of the recording industry. Or maybe they simply washed dishes, cars, floors, or whatever it took to keep the dream alive.

With darkness settling, I drove north of Nashville and lodged for the night at a motel near the Tennessee-Kentucky border. In the motel restaurant/bar, a fellow probably in his late 30s, struck up a conversation. The general conversation openers – "Where are you headed...where are you from?" – established he lived in Columbus, Ohio.

Lloyd was a truck driver for some company that transported paper products for the printing industry, his route basically covering the states of Kentucky, Indiana, Ohio, West Virginia, and the western portions of Pennsylvania and New York.

When I mentioned that I'd just come from Nashville, Lloyd shrugged and smiled: "Nashville...the city of broken dreams and broken hearts." Lloyd appeared to be the perfect candidate for one of my "character studies" so I asked if he would expand on his comment. Over a toasted corned beef on rye and a couple of Pepsis, I learned Lloyd's story.

If all things in life were fair and progressed as planned, Lloyd would have made his mark in the music business years ago. He and three high school friends had been part of an active country/folk/bluegrass band known as the "Alleycats" or "Hellcats" or some feline derivative, playing in hotels and bars within a roughly hundred mile radius of Columbus, Ohio, during the 1960s. Bluegrass seemed their favourite genre, Lloyd playing both mandolin and fiddle. "We were ten years too soon for the bluegrass revival," Lloyd reflected.

They got a break in the autumn of 1963 when they and a couple of other groups were booked for a five night–five show performance in upper New York State, where a great-uncle of one of the band members had music connections. Opening night was November 22...but was cancelled "out of respect for our fallen president" as the official announcement proclaimed. The show regrouped the following night at the next town on the schedule, but with people still distracted with Kennedy's assassination, the gig just never found its footing let alone an audience and closed after one more night.

It was back to the hotel circuit playing weekend stands for the next two or three years, which appeared to be as far as they'd ever progress. Then a long overdue break surfaced when the band was invited to perform at an outdoor weekend summer concert in Detroit on the last weekend in July 1967. Here they would be playing to an audience the size of which they could only dream. If this event went well the "whatever cats" would be invited to a similar venue in Cleveland the following weekend; there was even talk of a possible recording contract...but this quartet simply couldn't win for losing.

For whatever reason, on July 23, after police raided a black downtown Detroit nightclub, a battle between blacks and whites broke out and within hours swelled to a full-blown racial riot that lasted five days and was only brought under control when President Johnson called in the Army to reinforce the National Guard and restore order.

When it was over, 43 had died, nearly 500 were wounded, 7,000 people had been arrested and an estimated 12,000 buildings lay in various stages or ruin...how be we just say a musical concert wasn't high on the list of priorities the following weekend.

The group disbanded soon after but Lloyd continued on, driving an 18-wheeler Monday to Friday and playing the bar circuit on weekends to people mostly too drunk to care. Occasionally over the years, a hint of an opportunity would present itself, but fade just as quickly for any number of reasons.

I accompanied Lloyd to the parking lot and as I watched the Kenworth disappear into the Tennessee sunset, I was reminded of the song "Sundown in Nashville" recorded by Carl Butler, a popular Nashville music artist of the 1960s. His words describing "discarded love songs and visions of fame on the ground...pieces of dreams that have shattered" and sweeping "broken dreams off the street" seemed to summarize completely all the "Lloyds" in the musical world.

I Do...I Guess

IT WAS AUTUMN 1977 AND I WAS READY – WELL ALMOST – TO venture onto that misty, uncertain, doubtful path of matrimony. My grandfather would have been proud. I was 30 years old, the same age he had been when taking the plunge...and the ideal stage in life in his opinion for marriage.

Mary McKercher was a laboratory technologist at MDS Health Group (now LifeLabs) in Listowel, one of the stops on my courier route. In an earlier account I mentioned how back in the autumn of 1973 after my barn burnt to the ground, I'd undertaken a job as a medical courier "just for the winter." At that point, little did I realize it would become a career.

Well through the courier grapevine I'd heard she liked me...thought I was cute. I was too shy to do much about it for a while but finally raised enough courage to ask her to accompany me on my route the Saturday before Thanksgiving. About a week later Mary invited me to join her for supper at her place and watch the World Series. After a couple of beers to relax I sat down to what should have been a delicious meal. About the third mouthful...guess what? I was heading for the bathroom to throw up! Looking for a memorable date – just ask Dave Turner!

Upon relating that incident to one of the girls on my route many years later, she asked, "Were you sick, nervous, or drunk?" I simply answered..."yeah."

One would think that episode more than enough incentive to ride hard for the hills but for reasons that defy logic and despite my "if you want a party person I'm not your guy" speech...our relationship stumbled along until another Thanksgiving.

Because this weekend was our "unofficial" anniversary, I planned a special surprise. With a few minutes to spare one day I meekly stepped inside the doors of Buzza Brothers Jewellers in Owen Sound, the same store my parents had patronized 40 years earlier for the same reason.

"Are you interested in any particular setting?" asked the salesgirl. My blank stare undoubtedly answered that question. Trying a different tactic she inquired, "Do you have a price range in mind?" I could feel the sweat building beneath my shirt. I mumbled something about not knowing much about this sort of thing, although I had a feeling she'd already figured that out.

Over the years I'd never taken much interest in any diamonds my sister or sisters-in-law had displayed, but here I was standing in front of a display case crammed with dozens of rings that appeared the same. There was obviously a difference...anywhere from $50 to $5,000 difference! I finally settled on a price range I figured I could afford. At least that was a start.

"Have you any idea in what your fiancée-to-be might be interested? Perhaps you would like to bring her in?"

Maybe I was mistaken or just an idiot...but I was under the impression an engagement ring was meant to be a surprise, so how could I "bring her in?" I was sweating clear down to my toenails now, so just pointed to a ring in the middle of the display and blurted out, "that one."

"Do you know your girlfriend's ring size?" She had to have known the answer by this time. By now it must have been obvious to everyone in the store my ignorance factor had disappeared off the scale. Probably so I wouldn't start to cry, the salesgirl suggested I take the ring and then the two of us could come in at a convenient time and they'd size it. Fine...anything to get out of here! I wrote a cheque, pocketed the ring, and left. I swore I heard a chorus of laughter erupt behind me.

The great day arrived. Mary accompanied me on my route and as I exited the car at Wingham Hospital, my first stop, I nonchalantly announced there was something in the glove compartment for her. Pretty cool, eh! When I returned a couple of minutes later it would be understated to say Mary wore a look of surprise. She was even more surprised when she slipped the ring onto her finger and the diamond setting fell off and rolled under the seat. Oh well...can't expect things to last forever I guess! Buzza Brothers were extremely apologetic and offered a choice of an upgrade for our trauma. This time I let Mary make the selection.

As our wedding plans developed, Mom and Dad were also planning for their future. Five years earlier, neither were ready to leave the farm so with that thought in mind, I suggested a couple of ideas. One was buying a trailer and placing it on the property, but no one was very excited about that proposal. How about building a prefabricated Royal Home on the old farm?

By now, however, my parents had decided they were ready for town. I was back on more solid financial footing as I gotten most of my "farming" debts addressed; therefore I was finally in a position to begin repaying what they'd lent over the years.

There was never any doubt as to where Mother wished to retire. Mom had fallen in love with Palmerston upon first sight more than two decades earlier. Dad at one time leaned toward Listowel, but when the time came didn't really care. After looking at three or four possibilities, my parents picked out a house on Boulton Street, a quiet, tree-lined artery just a few minutes from the downtown area and library. Directly across the street was Lawrence Park, where I used to go in my high school days to hide out when skipping Latin.

Mom was head librarian of the Palmerston branch by this time so was especially pleased to be within walking distance of her work and Dad would be 65 in another month and would be retiring from his security position at Campbell's Soups. All that was required now was to wait until Thanksgiving weekend for the big move. Twenty-two years of memories to pack would keep my parents occupied during this period.

There's no doubt they had mixed feelings as they closed the door on that 22-year period. It wasn't as if they'd not see the old farm again as it was still in the family, but it would be our home now. A third of their lives had been spent there and one doesn't simply switch off memories.

That Palmerston farm had touched the lives of many of our urban acquaintances who enjoyed countless vacations and proved to be an integral part of the friendships both received and extended throughout those many years. All had fond memories of blue skies and green fields, cedar rail fences, bountiful gardens, the unmistakeable aroma of curing hay, pastures dotted with Holsteins, fresh breezes, and seemingly endless miles of absolute space.

Even though many, many years have passed, seldom does a family gathering go by that someone, young or old, doesn't convey their sentiments about "the farm." When "the farm" is mentioned...everyone knows what is meant.

Our wedding was slated for September 22, a date that caused me to break out in a sweat at each reminder. Mary wanted a "good-sized" wedding, somewhere in the 100–150 range I think. In her words, "Just enough to get back even a percentage of the money I've doled out in gifts over the years to other people's weddings." My preference next to elopement would have simply been the obligatory four people for the wedding party, no reception, and no expensive professional photographers. My idea...perhaps the minister could take the ceremonial pictures! Mary stated that idea was so ludicrous as to not even be worthy of comment. Fortunately for all concerned, some compromising middle ground was discovered.

Before the actual wedding, Mary and I were subjected to a three-session marathon on marriage counselling as dictated by the Presbyterian Church...at least the Huron County charge where Mary's family worshipped. During our interrogation by Reverend Crook we were asked all sorts of questions.

"What do you like or dislike about each other?...What are your reasons for marrying...especially at your age?" We were both about thirty..."Why don't you just live together?"

Mary answered, "If it wasn't for the fact my dear mother, pillar of the congregation would suffer a heart attack, we would!" Following our trio of sessions, the minister, church elders, Board of Managers, Sunday school teachers, custodian staff, groundskeepers...whoever...handed down a positive verdict.

For some reason Reverend Crook didn't like the music Mary chose for the ceremony. The selection, "Looking through the Eyes of Love" was a personal favourite, but the esteemed Reverend deemed it "unsuitable." Two or three weddings we attended in the following years utilized the song; thus Mary never did forgive him. If that wasn't a sufficient rebuff...when our wedding day actually arrived, the great Reverend opted for another engagement and transferred his duties to an associate from an alternate charge.

(Just for interest's sake...shortly after the alternate minister performed our wedding ceremony she permanently vacated the pulpit of the Presbyterian Church and disappeared with her lesbian lover.)

September 22 dawned clear and bright. Mary and I and our attendants gathered in the park in Listowel. Neither Mary nor I were superstitious about the "not seeing the bride before the actual ceremony" curse and elected to have our pictures shot beforehand. (I had conceded for a professional photographer.) This "pre-ceremony" shoot eliminates that awkward gap between the wedding and reception where everybody stands around and stares at each other. After the photography session, we gathered at Mary's Listowel apartment to await the six o'clock wedding. One of the ushers, a local volunteer fireman, had been fighting a blaze the entire afternoon and, still emitting an acrid aura of wood smoke, appeared just as we were heading for the church.

Following the ceremony, the photographer undertook another round of photos, this time at the front of the church with the candelabra as a backdrop. I'm sure the photos would have been quite beautiful...except for the fact that the apprentice photographer, whose assignment was to perform the inside shots, forgot to remove the lens cap from the camera...Sorry!

We were then relegated to the back of the photography line and had to wait several months before the re-shoot could be re-scheduled. By this time the Maid of Honour was eight months pregnant, so there is certainly a marked difference in our before and after ceremony pictures!

Considering all that transpired...that suggestion concerning the minister taking the wedding pictures doesn't sound so stupid now, does it?

...And the Lucky Number Is...

As well as writing, another hobby of mine is collecting. A building once inhabited by farm machinery over the years has been transformed into an automotive and agricultural museum. The exercise began innocently enough...just a place to display the license plate collection I was beginning to assemble.

License plates progressed to hubcaps, old automobile and newspaper advertisements, antique tools, radios, and records. There are milk bottles, milking machines, a cream separator, and other related dairy products. Old bikes, chrome automotive name plates from cars long gone, oil lamps, small household appliances, a large assortment of oil tins and service station memorabilia, die-cast toys, old calendars, steam-era artifacts including the electric train my brothers and I received for Christmas in 1955...well, you get the idea.

However, the crux of my collection has always been license plates. I have been obsessed with the metal identification numbers from as far back as I can recall. I was only four in 1953 but can remember clearly that white on dark blue plate – 5210 U – that Dad bolted to our 1947 Pontiac. The following year the colours were reversed and 6941 Y became our lucky number. At that point, I secured the expired 1953 plate to my tricycle with a piece of baler twine...my first licensed vehicle. In those early days when a car would pull into our yard, be it a neighbour, relative, or salesman, first thing I'd do was check out the number... and memorize it.

Beginning in 1957 and for nearly 40 years thereafter, I saved a plate from every vehicle our family owned, although I never considered myself a bona fide collector. As I was fascinated with numbers, old license plates were just a natural item to keep. Farmers, never known to throw anything away, often displayed old plates on walls of sheds, barns, and granaries. Some actually became useful...sealing a granary leak for instance. Nailing a license plate over an offending mouse or rat hole was an ideal and simple solution.

My license plate interest was amplified in 1985 when my brother Bill brought to my attention a farm sale in Simcoe County that listed, among hundreds of historical items, a cluster of Ontario license plates dating from the 1930s through 1950s.

I bought roughly three dozen that day and, coincidentally around the same time, a friend who worked in Toronto learned of someone in Peterborough who was moving and needed to get rid of some old plates in the basement that apparently dated back to 1917. Well...she knew just the person on whom to unload them. Long story short...the plates were transferred from Peterborough to Toronto and finally to a shopping centre parking lot in Stratford. To a passer-by it probably appeared a drug deal was going down as I perused the merchandise stashed in her trunk and forfeited a handful of cash.

What I paid for was an assortment of plates from 1912 through the mid-1930s. The quality varied widely from near mint to merely fair, but in conjunction with the plates I bought at the farm sale, I now had a complete run of Ontario plates from 1912 to the mid-1950s. I was now an official collector. A couple of years later I was able to secure a hard-to-find 1911 porcelain plate from a Vermont collector.

As my number of plates increased, so did my interest in the roots of plate collecting. Ontario's first "plates," issued in 1903, were actually not plates at all but leather "shields" with metal numbers attached, manufactured by a Toronto harness maker. Two years later, rubber replaced leather and the shape became what would become standard...roughly rectangular.

That 1911 plate I spoke of was constructed of heavy cast iron coated with porcelain and manufactured by the McClary Stove Company of London, Ontario. Expensive to manufacture and prone to chipping, porcelain plates were made only one year before being replaced by a cheaper flat tin plate.

For the next twenty years, Ontario license plates were made by various manufacturers who had to submit a bid each year to the transportation department. Lowest tender always won, explaining the diversity of plate quality through the years. Beginning in 1931, all plates were made at Guelph Reformatory as part of the provincial prison system. In 1958, Millbrook Correctional Facility near Peterborough took over manufacture of the province's license plates and continues to this day.

In 1921 the first Ontario plate to feature embossed numbers debuted, which also began a trend of varying lengths of plates, depending on number of digits. The "standard" plate was roughly a foot long and contained five numbers. Six-digit plates measured two or three inches longer while "shorties" – about nine inches in length – displayed four numbers.

Most Ontario plates of the 1920s–1930s era were painted with either a cream or black background with contrasting numbers. Starting in 1937, a stab at more vibrant colour was attempted, featuring white on dark red that year and orange on brilliant blue in 1938. Both of these plates are very collectable and in the case of 1938, rare, as quality control was extremely poor, causing the vivid paint scheme to fade badly.

This experiment in colour imagination was short lived as police complained the orange/blue combination in particular limited their ability to decipher numbers. So in 1939 it was a return to black and white or blue and white, a colour combination that would assure Ontario the unheralded distinction of being among the most visually boring license plates in the industry.

Due to measures to conserve metal during World War Two, some unissued 1942 Ontario plates were "over stamped" to become 1943 plates. I have one in my collection, and by close examination, the previous year's stamping is evident beneath the new 1943 numbers. No passenger plates were issued at all in 1944, as a windshield sticker sufficed. Only trailers were fashioned with regular metal plates for the simple reason they had no "windshield" to display a number. I have a rare 1944 trailer plate...found in my next door neighbour's granary after he sold the farm and moved to town, proving you never know where that next collector plate might surface!

Other plates of note...In 1937, as well as the aforementioned bright colour, Ontario applied an embossed "crown" on the plate, a tradition that has continued to this day... with the exception of 1951. For reasons unknown there was no crown that year. Someone in the higher hierarchy of the Ontario's transportation system must have entertained a personal grudge against the Commonwealth that year. That 1951 plate was also noteworthy as it had to endure two years as there were no issues in 1952 due to the Korean conflict.

In 1956 all license plates in North America became standardized in size...six by twelve inches. This change was instituted by the auto manufacturers who complained of the numerous odd-sized, odd-shaped plates being manufactured, necessitating the need to fabricate a variety of bumper brackets.

One day a fellow "tin chaser" was looking over my Ontario collection that spanned ninety years and asked if I was going to branch out to other provinces. I said "no," and he said, "Are you sure?" I answered, "yeah...I'm sure"... until discovering some colourful aluminum Quebec plates of 1950–1970s vintage at an antique shop. Shortly after, I became acquainted with a Manitoba collector and began assembling a collection of that province's plates. Soon, no province was spared in my search...and not just regular passenger vehicle plates: trucks, trailers, motorcycles, bicycles, vendor, snowmobile, boat, RVs, PCVs, taxis...nothing was out of range.

A few years went by and I was asked a similar question: "Have you ever considered collecting American plates?" I said "no"..."Are you sure?"..."yeah...I'm sure"...until Bill gave me a New York plate as well as two sequential numbered Montana plates he'd bought at a sale for $5.

Searching for old plates covering 50 states has been both exciting and rewarding. I've become especially fascinated with the graphics, colours, slogans, and messages gracing U.S. plates for the past century...promoting everything from wheat, corn, pelicans, bluegrass, sunflowers, sunshine, and beef...to mountains, birds, potatoes, peaches, oranges, oceans, and fish.

After years of collecting U.S. plates, I continually come across interesting finds. Illinois 1912–1918 for instance; motorists of that era apparently complained the large license plates (about 7x14 inches) covered their car's radiators, causing them to overheat. The problem was addressed by cutting slots in the plates to increase air flow and aid cooling.

Many Oklahoma plates in the 1920s displayed the letter "F." For many years it was thought this denoted "Farm" vehicle, but a study discovered these plates were issued to "Ford" cars only. The prevalence of Fords in that era was so great they garnered a special low tax rate and their own plate!

For years the state of Montana stamped "Prison Made" on many of their plates and New Hampshire displayed "Live Free or Die," which proved distasteful to many pacifists, causing the slogan to be challenged in court. The Supreme Court ruled, however, that New Hampshire had the right to choose the slogan...but citizens were not compelled to display it. Apparently anyone offended had the option to cover the offensive message, providing the practice didn't obscure the plate number.

Arizona made copper plates in the early 1930s, and in the 1940s Maine manufactured brass plates. Meanwhile Minnesota offered "waffle" aluminum as an alternative. To conserve steel throughout the war years of the 1940s, the state of Louisiana made a fibreboard plate of dried sugarcane pulp, while Illinois utilized a soybean composition for their war effort contribution. Whatever the make-up, license plate legend claims goat farmers in particular had a trying time as the animals would eat the plates right off automobile bumpers!

So as you can see, license plate collecting has been both entertaining and educational...and obviously ingrained in my soul. I never understood as a kid why adults found it so amusing when I explained what I wanted to do when I grew up. The standard answer of my peers in those days ran along the lines of "farmer," "fireman," or "policeman." My ultimate goal was to work in a factory where license plates were manufactured.

In that era, license plates expired at the end of February and Dad usually waited until that very day, necessitating a long, long wait at the license issuing office. Often I'd accompany him, watching closely as each recipient left with his or her new plate. I'd try to catch a glimpse of the number as they walked by...then mentally calculate what number we might receive when we finally got to the counter. I remember once asking Dad if we could move farther back in the line in order to secure a "better" number. Dad didn't seem overly enthused with my suggestion as I recall. I guess he figured an hour and a half in line was more than sufficient.

The moment we finally received our new plate all shiny and dent-free was without a doubt the highlight of my year. Again this annual ritual failed to fuel the same excite-

ment for Dad. Lying in a snow bank beneath the car with a
wrench and pair of pliers, trying to separate corroded nuts
and bolts from rusted brackets...just didn't generate the
same "magic" I was feeling.

In 1962, Dad was deliberating on the purchase of a '59
Chevrolet and I sincerely hoped he'd buy it for no other
reason than it had a "great number"...994 448! However,
license plate fever wasn't something that was just part of
being a kid. I was seventeen when my brother Richard
bought a new Pontiac with the plate number L43 000, and
in my mid-twenties when purchasing a plate for my pickup
and discovered the number E8 888. Both occasions almost
blew my mind!

Even after a quarter century of collecting and trading,
and despite my collection numbering somewhere in the two
thousand vicinity, each new plate generates that same feeling of excitement I felt when attaching that 1953 Ontario
plate to my tricycle six decades ago.

When the metal plates with their annual number
change were phased out in 1973 and replaced by an insipid
paper sticker I was devastated...until I learned trucks would
continue on with the old method. By this time we regularly drove pickups so that took care of that problem...until
1980 when trucks followed suit. After that I'd spend ten or
twenty dollars or whatever and purchase a new plate each
year, thus keeping the previous one for my collection. The
Ministry of Transport insisted the old plate be returned but
that technicality wasn't hard to circumvent. "I'll bring it in
next time in town." I never had any intention of returning
the plate and the Ministry of Transport at that time seemed
to care less.

There was a delightful woman, Wilma, who ran the local issuing office throughout the 1980s and '90s, who understood my addiction to plates and allowed me to pick out my own number, the only stipulation being my choice had to be within that week's allotment.

Now of course with all provincial license offices integrated and connected through a vast, cold network of computers and tracking devices, there's no longer room for the "Wilmas" of this world. There's no room for delinquents uttering empty promises either. These days before a new plate can be issued, the old one must be returned, de-registered, de-certified, and destroyed...no exceptions. Those "next time I'm in town" days are but a warm memory.

A couple of summers ago we hosted a reunion at our place and following the meal several family members wanted a tour of my museum. One of my cousins, after studying wall upon wall featuring plates from 10 Canadian provinces and 50 U.S. states...turned to me. "Have you ever thought of collecting International plates, David?"...I answered "no."..."Are you sure?"..."Yeah...I'm sure."

Steak Salesman

A L SHUFFLED THROUGH THE STACKS OF PAPER LITTERING HIS desk. Reams of brochures promoting rustproofing, extended warranties, security systems, communication systems, global tracking systems, leasing and financing options, life insurance, disability insurance, loss of income insurance, road hazard insurance...

"Selling cars has sure changed," Al peered at me over his glasses. "The only ones making any money are the pulp and paper companies...just look at this mess!"

"I remember the first car you sold my father, Al...a '59 Chev Bel Air...and it took you a week to close the deal."

Al emitted a hearty laugh, tipping his leather upholstered, pneumatically adjustable, chiropractic-approved chair back against a wall practically covered with sales awards he'd accumulated over nearly 50 years. "I probably made more on that sale than I am right now."

Back in the 1950s and '60s there were scores of guys like Al who were part of privately operated used car dealers who would come right to your door to pitch a car. There was one salesman in particular I recall, known simply as Smitty, who was forever trying to update my father into a higher realm of transportation. Smitty was the stereotypical, checkered-jacketed car salesman and he held a strong passion for Fords, showing up at our place with a seemingly endless collection of flashy, dual- and triple-toned hardtops. Smitty liked to sell what he wanted to drive instead of what his customers wanted or needed. Smitty liked to sell sizzle, whereas Dad was looking for steak. He could never seem to figure that out, hence Smitty never sold Dad a car.

Al, on the other hand, sold steak. He'd grown up in the country and was about as honest as anyone in his profession could be. Frankly, that wasn't saying a lot as many used car personnel of that era were basically the bottom rung of the ladder of ethics and fair play.

Rewinding odometers was just the tip of the iceberg; filling the crankcase with heavy duty gear oil would quiet a clattering valve train or slow the flow from a leaking crankshaft bearing. Oatmeal poured into a hot radiator would stop most coolant leaks...at least until the sales contract was signed. The correct amount of Quaker oats could often quiet the gears of a noisy differential as well. Repeat sales were of no concern for these borderline establishments... moving cars off the lot was all that mattered.

But it was different in the country where word travelled fast; buyers were few and so were their dollars and no one understood this scenario better than Al. So when he appeared at our farm that July afternoon in 1962 with the aforementioned Bel Air sedan, he at least had some idea of my father's wants and needs.

Coppertone paint with contrasting ivory trim, whitewall tires and wheel discs, the big Chevrolet made for an impressive display as it sat in our driveway. The one thousand dollar price difference for our six-year-old Ford Customline was too high in my father's opinion, however, so following a lengthy but friendly chat, Al and the Chevrolet disappeared from our midst.

Two days later, Al dropped in for further negotiations. As the previous visit, plenty of time was consumed getting around to the subject at hand. First, world events, especially where the nuclear weapons race between the United States and Soviet Union might end. A discussion on Canadian federal and provincial politics followed, before the agenda shifted to local topics such as crops and weather and the expected army worm infestation.

Al commented positively on our Holstein herd, conversing at length on the healthy fulfilling lifestyle of farming and how he'd certainly be engaged in that occupation today if he hadn't fallen out of that haymow and injured his back.

Even taking 1950s automobile styling excesses into account, there was no denying the 1959 Chevrolet was a flamboyant machine with its batwing tail fins and cat's eye tail lights, so Al cautiously began his routine.

"Well, it's a pretty bold styling statement alright, but it is a Chevy...an honest-to-goodness, downright dependable Chevy."

Dad opened one of the rear doors. Al knew that farmers wanted four doors to provide easy access for kids, dogs, cattle feed, groceries, lumber, hardware, plus a host of other items. "The seats look pretty fancy for a farm car."

"The upholstery is all vinyl," countered Al, "so whether you're going to church or the feed mill it's the best of both worlds, serviceable and attractive."

"What's under the hood?"

"An economical six cylinder that will run forever on regular." Knowing farmers insisted on making maximum use of all that tax-free tractor gas, Al always made sure that point was clear.

"And a standard transmission."

"That's good," Dad replied. "The day I can't shift gears is the day I'll quit driving!"

Assured he at least had my father's attention, Al lopped the ball into Dad's court.

"So what do *you* think it would take to trade, Harold?"

Dad chose his response carefully. "I was thinking about eight hundred."

Al's shoulders sagged. "This is far too much car for that price!" A long dramatic pause followed with no one saying a word. When no move was made on Dad's part, Al somewhat reluctantly resumed bargaining.

"Well...I just might be able to squeeze nine hundred."

Dad simply shook his head.

Three days passed and Al returned again as Dad knew he would. Al had one more swing at the ball. It was sort of like that pivotal third date. Do we get serious?...or do we simply say "Nice knowing you" and move on. There was somewhat less small talk this round, but time was still made available to discuss the Farmer's Almanac weather predictions, the previous night's thunderstorm, and the second cut alfalfa potential.

"I'll drop another 50," relented Al, "but that's it!" Dad, convinced he'd pushed as hard as he could, accepted. The two shook hands and the deal was completed.

"...Yeah, those were the days...$850." Al slowly ran his fingers through what was left of his hair, studying the contract I was about to sign.

"Imagine if I had presented your father with this...he would have told me where to go and what to do when I got there!...Okay, we've got freight, transportation, license, transfer fee, administration fee, federal air conditioning tax, provincial tire tax, fuel conservation tax, plus goods and services and provincial sales tax...and of course the finance charges...oh yes," added Al. "We put some gas in it for you; that's what the twenty dollar charge is for."

"...and that $850.00 you were mentioning," as Al's brain made a 180-degree turn..."that *was* it!"

Al never spoke for a few moments as his mind drifted off to some other era..."Yes, those were good times...okay... so now where were we?"

Musical Magic

Recently I went out to a "pub night"…no it wasn't the local watering hole one would expect down the street; most of the patrons were well past eighty and a couple were probably pushing the century mark. Except for drinks and snacks, the six-piece band worked free of charge as they have once or twice a week for several years; and they weren't some washed up, over-the-hill combo unable to secure a paying gig…rather a dedicated and caring group of individuals, whose enjoyment was bringing a spark of light to a segment that at first glance seemed to have little going for it.

The scene was the dining room of our town's retirement and nursing residence, where my wife worked at the time. I'd volunteered my services to help set up chairs and tables and simply aid in the clean-up afterwards.

My first thought as the band began their set…why are they bothering? Most of the residents of the nursing wing in particular seemed at a loss as to where they were, their empty eyes staring at the floor. But then a unique thing happened...not instantly, but over the course of the evening. Men and women, who seemingly had no recognition of their surroundings, began to respond to the music. A hint of a smile, a flicker of light in an eye, a weathered hand tapping out a weak beat on a wheelchair tray. A husband and wife of sixty years clasped hands, eyes misty as the band sang "When You and I Were Young."

Some of life's greatest memories evolve from music in one form or another. Listening to the band, I was reminded of my mother telling me when she was young, about the enjoyable summer holidays she spent at her aunt and uncle's farm near Kimberley, Ontario, in Grey County.

From her very first visit, Mother had discovered something special about this place. Was it the spectacular view across the breadth of the Beaver Valley? Perhaps it was those marvellous caves that formed part of the Niagara Escarpment, where a child could roam and explore for hours. No doubt these scenes left lasting impressions, but best remembered were the wonderful musical "ceilidhs" regularly staged on summer Saturday nights.

To the accompaniment of a piano, the evening would come alive with the sounds of a fiddle and perhaps a harpsichord. Spirited reels, jigs, ballads, patriotic and gospel songs provided plenty of variety. As the hours clicked by, the music gradually assumed a more nostalgic note, rekindling memories perhaps of the family's bygone days in Scotland, three thousand miles away.

My mother's appreciation of music started early, with her family sitting around their Victrola record player, listening to the popular songs of the day. Their machine wasn't blessed with the modern invention known as electricity; therefore the spring motor had to be regularly wound throughout the course of the evening to keep the record operating at correct speed.

And the music heard wasn't always from the family living room. Their house was a duplex, and occupying the other half was a chap by the name of Bill Charles. Bill was an accomplished violinist who played at some of the nicest concert halls in Toronto. Practice had elevated him to this status and a good deal of this practice was undertaken at home. The sweet strains of Bill's violin easily penetrated the thin walls, granting his neighbours a private concert. Bill played regularly on CBC radio and depending upon audience taste, was introduced as either "William and his Violin" or "Bill the Fiddler."

Music seemed a natural part of Mother's life. Since old enough to hold a hymn book, she was a member of Chalmers Presbyterian church in Toronto, and part of a mammoth chorale gathering that serenaded Great Britain's Prince Edward and Prince George at the grand opening of the Prince's Gates at the Canadian National Exhibition in 1927.

In 1934, in an effort to help Ontario's capital celebrate its centennial, Ernest MacMillan, conductor of the Toronto Symphony Orchestra, called for a special choir at Massey Hall for which Mother was eager to volunteer and thrilled to be chosen. Built 50 years earlier, Massey Hall was considered by experts to be acoustically among the greatest concert halls in the world. For my mother, the grandeur of Massey Hall in conjunction with the overwhelming presence of Ernest MacMillan (a year before he became "Sir" Ernest) was an unparalleled experience.

I would have to retrace my steps back to the late 1950s for a personal musical memory. Mom's sister Jean, an accomplished piano player, and John her Scottish husband, who'd played fiddle since childhood, performed a live concert in our family living room. For more than an hour, with his wife accompanying, my uncle peeled off a steady stream of songs from his homeland. Long after the violin had been returned to its case that evening, the strains of that two-piece band lingered. Now I could more easily appreciate Mom's recollections of the family concerts she enjoyed as a child.

Another personal and fond remembrance was the RCA Victor console record player that my parents purchased in 1949, the year I was born. It measured about four feet wide and almost as high and would stack and play at least ten 78 rpm records at a time. I spent endless hours in front of that grand old machine, listening to the artists of the day and memorizing the lyrics. That music has remained a part of my life, as I presently have the songs recorded on CDs and can listen anytime I choose. Those great songs take me back to an ageless time when life's biggest challenge was how to fill the hours of summer vacation and anything beyond that simply wasn't important.

...As my mind drifted back to the present, I gazed across the crowded floor of the retirement home and into the faces of these men and women from another time. I tried to imagine their thoughts. As the band played, some no doubt were recollecting memories of dances attended in youth, songs that transported them back into the arms of a loved one long since departed. Perhaps recalling how the sweet strains of Glenn Miller and Guy Lombardo made it just a little easier to survive a cruel Depression, as well as songs that gave hope when seemingly no hope existed, through a long and devastating war.

In a setting where the future holds such little promise, it was a memorable experience to witness the rewinding of time for a while. Back to an age when all dreams were possible and limited only by your imagination. Music...its restorative and healing characteristics seem almost magical; containing the power and emotion to compose a smile... a tear...a passing reminder...a gentle thought...a warm memory of friends and loved ones...just for a few moments perhaps...but what a special few moments!

A Very Special Lady

I JUST RETURNED FROM ATTENDING THE FUNERAL OF MY AUNT; kind, generous, compassionate, good-hearted...all these adjectives were thrown around during the eulogies and tributes. But anyone who truly knew my Aunt Alma realized these adjectives were not exaggerations. That's simply the way she was. Alma Carruthers had no children of her own so in effect everyone became her children, hence her family. And family was everything. If you were family you could do no wrong.

Being human, at one time or another we all stumble on life's pathway. That didn't matter to Alma as indiscretions were instantly forgiven and forgotten. And she was so genuine in her character. Show up at her door and she would be beside herself with joy merely because you dropped by. Immediately the kettle would be fired up and tea would be on the way. So whether you were having problems with your kids, parents, husband, job or even your next door neighbour...tea would take care of it. In Alma's world, a cup of tea was the answer to every situation and the solution to every problem.

For 87 years Alma Carruthers called just two places home: No. 8 Hickson Street in the heart of "Old Toronto" and 45 Glenroy Avenue in the west Toronto borough of Etobicoke. As the years advanced and she needed extra help, neighbours and family members alike did their part performing numerous chores, running errands, making sure she made her appointments, and just generally looking out for her. My brother Richard was an immense help to Alma in her later years, both personally and tending to the house. Leaking roofs, aging plumbing, and faulty appliances made 45 Glenroy a routine and regular stop.

When at last alternate living arrangements were a must and close family members a priority, Alma moved to the Royal Terrace Retirement Home in Palmerston, and thus began my weekly Thursday afternoon visits. After she'd told me all that happened the previous week, plus a critique on the week's menu, we'd pick a subject for that day... maybe old records, old movies, old TV shows, old neighbours...Threaded in among these topics, Alma would relate personal glimpses of a lifetime spent in Toronto.

The Canadian National Exhibition...when admission was just a quarter for Toronto's grand two-week extravaganza and you could spend the entire day at the Pure Food Building eating free samples if you wanted.

She recalled the merchants that travelled the streets of Toronto when she was young. The baker, who sometimes had a few broken cookies left in his basket at the end of his route and would dole them out to neighbourhood kids; the iceman, who delivered blocks of ice to your door, this before refrigeration so everyone owned an icebox; you could save 25 cents however if you picked up the ice yourself. Alma and a couple of her sisters would head up to a store on Dundas Street with an old wagon their father had built and haul the 50-pound blocks home. "Now don't dawdle!" their mother would emphasize. The hotter the day the more urgent the warning; Alma related how once a wheel fell off the wagon and what a trauma that time delay caused!

Train rides to visit relatives in Grey County: The family would arrive at Toronto's Union Station with a shoebox stuffed with homemade sandwiches, mostly egg salad and salmon...maybe a couple of peanut butter for her youngest sister Lillian. Evelyn, the oldest, who incidentally hated peanut butter, would forever complain how the peanut butter sandwiches contaminated the "good ones."

"It was such an exciting ride through the Albion Hills," Alma remembered. "Trestles and bridges that towered high above the Credit River and there was one place it was so steep the tracks had to spiral around the hills so the train could make the incline!"

Alma talked of birthdays when she was a little girl. Always, this special day dictated a trip up to the corner of Dundas and Brock for a brick of ice cream. The litre-sized container would be divided among her four sisters, parents, and grandfather who lived with them, so "they were pretty thin slices," Alma recalled.

There was the occasion when all five sisters headed up to the corner store to treat themselves to ice cream. "Lillian was probably two or three at the time," Alma related, and they were supposed to be looking after her but she tripped and fell coming out of the store, splattering her ice cream cone onto the sidewalk. She was bawling her head off and ready to run home and tell their mother, so Alma devised a plan whereby each sister would donate a portion of ice cream from their cones to Lillian's now empty one; not only would that appease Lillian but more importantly their mother who would not have to know of their neglect. But as Alma explained, "It was a hot day and with only fingers for the sticky transfer, that idea turned out to be severely flawed."

Alma recalled when she first entered the job market in the late 1930s. Her first job was working at a dairy washing and disinfecting milk bottles; "I can't begin to describe how I felt upon receiving my first pay cheque. I don't remember how many hours I worked but the weekly pay was $2.80. Two silver dollars, three quarters and a nickel; I didn't spend any of the money for a week or more, but I'd take the envelope from my bureau drawer and count it two or three times a day."

Another job was working at Massey-Harris addressing envelopes for the machinery catalogues the company sent out across Canada. "The position called for neat, clear handwriting straight across the envelope...no slants up or down...and the letters had to be at least an half inch high for maximum legibility." Alma figured there were a thousand names on that mailing list. Her father had worked at Massey-Harris for nearly 30 years by this point, so I would suspect a bit of nepotism might have been involved with this particular placement.

Alma kept her secretarial skills alive during World War Two in a couple of locations: one in Oakville doing government service work, another working in the office at Chorley Park in the heart of the Rosedale District of Toronto. This grand building had formerly been the residence of the Lieutenant-Governor of Ontario but was turned into a military hospital and government services branch during the war. Alma claimed it was the most beautiful place she'd ever seen.

Following the war, Alma secured a position at Allgood's Aluminum Products on Stirling Road just a short streetcar ride from her home on Hickson Street. It was here that Alma cemented friendships that remained for life. Although she enjoyed the people, the building left a lot to be desired.

"The elevator only worked when it felt like it. Sometimes it would leave you stranded between floors and even if it was working, it never seemed to stop level with any particular floor. You either had to jump up or climb down."

The typewriters were pretty rickety too, so it was a grand event when the office staff received new ones. "We even got to pick the colour!" Alma added. "I chose blue of course, my favourite." Later she bought her own typewriter from Eaton's for home use. "Guess what colour it was?" she asked.

A memory that burned bright during her Allgood days was during the summer when my sister Vivien would be visiting. Allgood's had no cafeteria so Alma always came home for lunch. Vivien, who would be 10 or 12 at this point, had gotten this idea that ice cubes would be an ideal way for Alma to battle the summer heat. I guess a cold drink would have been simpler; however, Vivien convinced her grandmother to wrap the cubes in a dish cloth which she'd take up to the intersection of Dundas and Landsdowne and wait for her aunt to get off the streetcar.

As this was a daily ritual, Alma knew what to expect and always made a big fuss over my sister's kindness. She'd rub the frozen cubes over her wrists and arms, refreshing herself from the scorching Toronto heat. "She was such a dear!" Alma recalled.

Allgood's was eventually taken over by the multinational company Alcan and by the mid-1960s, Alma and many of her co-workers ended up on the receiving end of "structural realigning"...I think they called it at the time. Next was a 20-year stint as secretary of the Runnymede Presbyterian Church, a job she kept until retirement.

While working at Runnymede, Alma met a gentleman friend, Alex...a quiet romance that simply simmered on the back burner for a length of time. I never met Alex and Alma kept the circumstances of their relationship low key, but Vivien, who had met Alex a few times, agreed he was a "nice guy." Alex had a winter home in Florida and at some point had even asked Alma to join him there, but apparently she didn't think she was ready for that step. Alex died suddenly while in Florida and Alma only learned of the tragedy when she happened to see his obituary in the paper. A sad ending to what might have been...

So Alma was alone once more...except for Sebastion of course. Anyone who knew Alma throughout the 1970s and '80s was familiar with Sebastion...a Maine Coon cat that must have weighed 40 pounds and controlled the house for some 15 years.

When approaching 50, Alma undertook what was probably her biggest lifestyle change to date. She decided to get her driver's license. She'd never driven a car in her life so enrolled in a special driver's education program where she spent the better part of a year studying written and oral tests on the rules of the road and simulated driving maneuvers.

"You can't imagine how nervous I was the first day I drove a real car on a real street in real traffic!" It certainly didn't help her confidence when during that first lesson she sideswiped an Eaton's department store van.

"It was just a light scrape," Alma recalled, "but I was a mental wreck and it took all the courage I had to return for that second lesson." However it's to her credit she persevered and succeeded.

Then came that special spring day in 1968 when she went with her brother-in-law to pick out her new car. At Bob Bannerman's AMC dealership on Eglington Avenue, Alma fell for a "Saturn Blue" Rambler American parked on the showroom floor. The little Rambler had a lot of features Alma figured she didn't need, so she ordered another with only automatic transmission and deluxe floor mats as options. "The basic mats were just black," Alma recalled "but the deluxe were blue!"

The salesman tried to add a radio to the list but Alma figured that option too distracting. Nearly forty years later, Alma remembered the price to the dollar. "It was $2522. I was so proud of that car, but I didn't put it in the garage for a long time as I was afraid of scraping the wall or something."

Throughout this time period, family remained the priority for Alma, hosting most of the yearly Carruthers' picnics. We'd all be scrunched into her little backyard on the hottest afternoon of the year, with Alma snapping pictures of everyone. No disrespect intended, but no one will disagree that Alma's photography skills were less than ideal. It was a scarce photo where the subject didn't have at least a portion of his or her head missing.

Yes...those afternoon visits at Royal Terrace generated many stories and memories. And the memories continued during her stay at the Terrace. Like her 90th birthday, which my brother and sister-in-law hosted. She talked of that event for weeks after. Seeing her two remaining sisters, old friends and neighbours from Glenroy Avenue, cousins, nephews and nieces, as well as the multitude of cards and letters she received...particularly those from old Alcan associates...made for a memorable day.

As noted, family was everything to Alma...and food. With the exception of pineapple, Alma loved just about anything that was edible. And so appreciative of anything anyone prepared, providing equal enthusiasm whether it was Christmas dinner or Kraft Dinner.

...And on the subject of Christmas...Alma loved buying presents. She always found such unique gifts. Back in the 1950s I remember her giving someone in our family one of those acrylic snowflake things you shake and the snow swirls about inside. At the time I thought it to be the most amazing gadget I'd ever seen.

We always received a second round of presents when we went to our grandparents in Toronto between Christmas and New Year's...although they were all "soft" presents. But without fail for every kid there'd be a surprise gift...a toy, game, book, puzzle or something from Alma. Dad would say..."Oh Alma, they don't need any more toys or things!" Alma would wink at us and answer, "I know the kids like a real present!"

Of all the recollections Alma left me, the one I remember best concerned the winter of 1963 just after her mom had died.

"It was such a lonely time," Alma recalled. "On the streetcar on the way home from work I'd find myself unable to control the tears and I'd turn towards the window so no one would see me. The house seemed so empty. Mother's clothes were still in the hall closet and sometimes I'd take her warm winter coat and just hug it around me. I know it sounds foolish and almost silly now...but my sisters had husbands and children to comfort them. I didn't have anybody...so wrapping that coat around me made me feel like I had someone...it was almost like Mom was hugging me."

Despite a successful operation in Kitchener in early September and a promising recovery back in Palmerston, Alma's 91 years simply caught up with her and she began her decline. But she never lost her sense of humour. Vivien mentioned to her one day that she would be having a male nurse attend her the next day or two. Alma brightened and said. "Maybe I have one last chance for a man yet!"

Each of us spent as much time as we could at Alma's side those last few days...reading, chatting, or just sitting. Especially Vivien, who over the years had gathered such warm memories of her favourite aunt and was Alma's main caregiver for the four years she was a resident at Royal Terrace. Anytime Alma had to go for blood work or x-ray or whatever, it would be my sister who'd accompany her. In many ways, Vivien was closer to Alma than her own mother, so it was especially difficult for her to let go.

One afternoon, although her voice was quite weak by this point, Alma mentioned to me about the dreams she'd been experiencing. "What kind of dreams?" I asked.

"Nice dreams...about family." She then recounted several names...parents, sisters, cousins..."and see that man over there by the elevator, he's always watching."

Where?" I asked.

"There...by the elevator," she repeated. I glanced at the blank wall.

"What does he look like?"..."Well, it's kind of dark but he's wearing a fedora and he looks fairly tall."

Alma's father always wore a fedora...or maybe it was Alex...or perhaps it was her guardian angel. The moment reminded me of a line from a song by Roseanne Cash. "I'll be watching you from above, because long after life there is love."

Then on a Sunday afternoon a couple of days later, the mysterious man emerged from the shadows and said it was time to go. Earlier that week Royal Terrace sent a card to the hospital and on behalf of the entire staff someone had written..."Alma, we miss your soft voice and lovely smile."

Well...I know I certainly do!

Sunday Morning Sunrise

I LIKE SUNDAYS. I ARISE EARLY FOR A MORNING WALK...THE duration depending upon the weather and time of year. Upon return, I enjoy a steaming bowl of oatmeal while the coffee's brewing, then adjourn with a hot cup to the living room, switch on the "easy listening" music channel, and settle back in my preferred chair with a favourite book or magazine.

This morning I mistakenly keyed the three digit number and instead of being soothed with the instrumental styling of Bert Kaempfert or Henri Mancini, was subjected to the fury of some evangelist, intent on saving my soul and at the same time pleading for donations for...whatever the cause that particular day. It reminded me when I visited the U.S. "Bible belt" many years ago. On Sunday mornings the airwaves would be clogged with evangelists promoting their "personal message from God," while continually extracting money from a populace who seemingly could least afford it.

His rant stirred not only thoughts about the powerful effect of religious teachings in general...but more importantly its influence through the years on my own family.

...There was Samuel Carruthers, an uncle of mine from a few generations back who emigrated from Dumfries, Scotland, to Toronto in the 1880s. Samuel was a carpenter, a trade that financed his real passion...the ministry. He must have been a successful orator, outgrowing three churches, although the last expansion was a church on Dovercourt Avenue he didn't live to see. However a bronze plaque dedicated to Samuel Carruthers' memory on behalf of an appreciative congregation was placed in the vestibule of the church when completed.

I have an extensive collection of historical souvenirs pertaining to our family, and included is a Bible presented to my great-grandmother Mary Carruthers (sister-in-law of Samuel) on April 17th, 1905, signed by "The Ladies of the Dovercourt Presbyterian Church." The above mentioned church was completed in 1905, explaining the circumstances for which the book was given. As of this writing well over a century later, the church still stands and is presently used by a Portuguese Presbyterian congregation.

The strong Presbyterian faith of the Carruthers family continued on through the generations. My mother made the trek to church three times each Sunday. Christian Endeavour, an elaborate term for Bible Study, was at 10. She was in the choir for regular church service at 11; taught Sunday school at 3, then joined the choir again for evening services.

There was one notable exception to this Presbyterian lineage...Mom's father, William Carruthers. Occasionally if faced with enough opposition, he'd relent and attend a Christmas or Easter service...but that was the extent.

According to my grandfather, Sunday school sand-wiched between morning and evening church services over a 10-year period was enough to last a lifetime. As far back as William could remember, the Sunday ritual would witness him and his brothers being herded to church in front of their parents, and constantly being nagged not to slouch or scuff their shoes or a dozen other infractions. In between the services of the Sabbath, anything even remotely related to enjoyment was barred. No cards; no board games; no crossword puzzles; and only "appropriate" reading material as defined by parental standards of the day. In summer, activities such as softball, roller skating, or even riding a bike were off limits. Sunday became a day my grandfather simply grew to detest.

The paternal side of my ancestry...the Turners...were Methodists, whose doctrine placed great emphasis on evangelical preaching and necessity for individual conversion. My father had firsthand experience in this department as a five- or six-year-old when he attended a "revival" with his father. A couple of times a year for as long as anyone could remember, some religious organization would appear in the area, camp in a pasture field, erect a tent and immediately begin advertising the fact they were in business to "save souls."

At this gathering, Dad recalled how different members of the sect preached; screaming at the top of their lungs one minute, pleading almost silently the next. Interspersed were fits of feet or even fists pounding the platform as the urgent message of salvation was unleashed; one speaker preached with such intensity that she literally "foamed at the mouth" according to my father.

The hellfire sermon obviously had some effect on my grandfather, joining a large assembly in front of the makeshift pulpit; all were told to pray; nothing specific...just pray. Grandpa prayed for a while then stopped. "Keep praying brother, keep praying!" yelled the one in charge. My grandfather, who perhaps was running out of material, answered, "That's enough for tonight," and returned to his seat.

None too soon as the affair was now bordering on the bizarre, with one of the "messengers" appearing to have gone completely over the edge, his eyes taking on a wide, almost terror-stricken look. During the finale, one of the organization began crawling on hands and knees up and down the aisle "bellowing like a calf" to use my father's words. Little wonder, 70 years later Dad could recall that evening with absolute clarity!

The Methodist congregation of the village of Eugenia, of which my paternal ancestors attended, originally shared the Eugenia Orange Hall with the Presbyterians, one having morning services, the other afternoon. In the 1890s both built their own church, but the Methodists seemed to have chronic financial problems, so in 1925 when a new order, the United Church of Canada, was formed comprised mostly of Methodists and Presbyterians, the former were eager to join.

The Methodists, including our family, adhered well to the change, but the merger never sat well with many of the Presbyterians. The union forced a nasty split in the Presbyterian congregation, many refusing the alliance altogether and taking their chances on their own. It was an unhealthy atmosphere that divided not only the church but the community itself for decades.

By this time my father was a teenager, although admitting enjoying Sunday school, like many his age, he found church to be frightfully dull...fighting drowsiness throughout the sermon, until the minister in a rare display of animation would pound his fist on the pulpit, momentarily waking him up.

When Dad married Mom, there was probably little choice but to follow the teachings of the Presbyterian Church; however, I don't think my father entertained any difficulties with that scenario...he was even on the Board of Managers. He must have had a little push from somewhere as Dad was a quiet, "back of the room" sort of guy and I can't visualize him simply volunteering for the position.

To his credit, Dad remained on the board for several years but gradually became disenchanted with the pettiness, triviality and narrow-mindedness of his fellow members; bickering over the cost of water softener salt or paper for the office copying machine. His associates argued for weeks whether the minister really needed a fan in his study and what the extra hydro would cost if they approved the purchase.

I recall one Presbyterian minister commenting how a certain board member couldn't understand why the minister should have any higher salary than say the church custodian. "They both pay the same for a loaf of bread."

This was in the day when the minister was responsible for most of his family's living expenses, so when a former minister left a partial ton of coal in the basement of the manse, the new minister considered it a bonus... until a member of the Board of Managers learned of it and methodically deducted the estimated value of the fuel from his first cheque.

As had Mom's ancestors, generation after generation, family upon family, we followed the well-worn path of the Church of Scotland. While Dad may have received his religious initiation courtesy of brush arbour evangelists employing scare tactics, at least through Mom's guidance, my sister, brothers and I were immersed into a much gentler system of Bible teachings.

I certainly won't profess that I went willingly to Sunday school each week. There was that age-old ritual of hiding my shoes, but once that was sorted out, there I was... nickel clenched tightly in fist, singing quietly along to "Jesus Loves Me" and "Dare to be a Daniel." On Saturday evenings Mom would review our Bible lessons from the previous week, making certain we could answer any question that might arise the next morning. Each evening ended with us kneeling beside our beds while Mom prompted us through our prayers until finally we were able to remember the words ourselves.

Whether it was our goodnight prayers, or the "Lord's Prayer" that began each school day, I often wondered the meaning of some of the phrases; for instance, what did salad have to do with praying? Yet that's what the grown-ups asked us to repeat. "Lettuce pray."

As a kid himself, Dad pondered why his aunts were always mentioned in his nightly prayers. "Ila and Mamie down to sleep, I pray the Lord my soul to keep."

Reminds me of the story of the little boy who was relating to his mother the Sunday school hymn he'd just learned about the bear; "A bear?...are you sure?"..."Yes," answered the child..."Gladly the cross-eyed bear"!

Like my father, I was reasonably content in the tradition of Sunday school...but also like him...church was a different matter. Not necessarily dull, to me it just seemed the weekly sermons never resonated with the everyday trials and concerns of someone my age, issues seemingly stalled in struggles and programs no longer relevant.

And in the Presbyterian faith at least, I was uncomfortable in the belief whereby everything was pre-ordained and one supposedly had no control over their future. Prayer was the only avenue and God held the final decision. As I was given a mind with which to think and differentiate between right and wrong, I always felt the responsibility lay within my own jurisdiction. However, questioning the Bible in our house...especially when it came to Mom...was a matter best kept to yourself.

To demonstrate what a powerful embrace religious prayer holds in parts of North America, just recently a football player from a southern college was speaking at length of how he prayed before every game that his team would emerge victorious. I remember thinking...With all the floods, earthquakes, landslides, famine, wars and other disasters that God can't seem to get a handle on...why would any intelligent person think He would have the time, let alone care about the outcome of a college football game?

One afternoon, probably three decades back now... Dad and I were strolling among the gravesites of our family cemetery. As we passed the rows of tombstones, Dad would frequently comment about the name of a friend or relative inscribed thereon. We came to a stone bearing the name "Latimer"..."That's my old Sunday school teacher," pointing at the name. "I probably learned more about the Bible from her than anyone else I know."

His statement couldn't help but rekindle recollections of Sunday school teachers I'd known. I recall one who had trouble keeping his facts straight...lecturing at length about Jesus rising from the tomb on Good Friday, and another who veered off track on a discussion about Moses and his multi-coloured coat.

Without a doubt, my most memorable teacher was Aulton Melville. I think I was about thirteen when I came under his guidance. At that point I was in the most senior of the Sunday school classes at our local church. There were advantages to being on this top rung, most apparent the fact we got our own room. "Lesser" students merely gathered at tables strung along the sidewalls of the church basement.

From the solitude of this sanctuary, Mr. Melville relayed the word of God to us each Sunday morning. Whereas other teachers I'd known merely recited dull scripture they expected us to memorize, Mr. Melville spoke from his heart. But he didn't "preach"; he used the Bible as the heart of his weekly text, but applied his own words and style, which consisted of "down home" storytelling mixed with a generous dash of philosophy. By simply helping us better understand and appreciate the gospel, he basically gave us an option he hoped we might accept.

I'm sure Mr. Melville's sermons were enjoyed every bit as much by my classmates, for there was little inattention... a sharp contrast to other classes I'd attended. Mr. Melville had about twenty minutes to get his message across and every week when the time allotment expired, he'd shake his head and make the same comment. "I had so much more I wanted to say." And with Mr. Melville, one almost wished there were more time.

"...so I especially plead with you young people who haven't given your soul to Jesus Christ...do it now! You're living in a world controlled by the devil himself, and you can't see it. But I can see it!...You're wallowing in a cesspool...a sewer of filth, immorality and depravity, consumed by drugs, alcohol, lust and sex. Accept Jesus now. Time is running out. No one except God knows what may happen tomorrow. There's every chance you could be struck down tonight and be damned to the eternal fires of everlasting Hell!..."

I switched the channel tuner, hoping the music of Mantovani would restore serenity to my Sunday morning, but the evangelistic ravings continued in my head. I was under the obviously mistaken impression most of these Sunday morning TV evangelistic extravaganzas had faded away following various scandals of some of their front line personalities. But I guess a timely combination of good script writing, well-rehearsed lines and fake tears...delivered to a susceptible audience...still works.

Through the years there has been only one "real" evangelist in my mind who reigned well above the run-of-the-mill "bottom rung" TV preachers...Reverend Billy Graham, the North Carolina native who preached on radio and television for six decades. Like his lesser peers, Graham learned how to capture an audience...not with tears and rants... but with down to earth sermons, often mixed with humour anyone could appreciate and understand.

While Reverend Graham might be staring into that TV camera that projected his image to millions of people around the world...you knew he was talking only to you! Those steel grey eyes staring through to your very soul, somehow telegraphing the awareness of every sin you had ever committed. But the difference...there was no judgement, only an option to change.

While a significant portion of his associates' evangelistic revenues seem to surface in Hollywood mansions, theme parks, Mercedes Benz cars and Rolex watches, one of Graham's closest friends for forty years, Johnny Cash, claimed "Billy" never wore anything on his wrist but a Timex watch and purchased his suits off the rack at J.C. Penney.

But wherever your thoughts on specific religious personalities might lead...doesn't it raise the question how extreme evangelism has managed to survive for so long in some regions? Why would a congregation in this supposedly enlightened age wish to be berated and shamed and made to feel somehow less than somebody standing at a pulpit thinks they should be?...

How long do you suppose I would have continued to attend Sunday school if Mr. Melville in an effort to relay the teachings of the Bible, had resorted to threats, fear, or other factors of intimidation to justify that end?

Nature's Network

WHEN I WROTE THIS, I WAS SITTING BENEATH THE PROTEC-tive canopy of a large maple tree that grew on our property, my back propped against its weathered trunk, the cooling shade providing welcome relief from the late August sun. If it wasn't for my brother Richard, no tree may have stood there at all. When my parents moved to this farm in 1957, this particular tree hadn't much going for it. With it barely boasting a three-inch circumference, its trunk twisted and bent from too many west winds, Dad's solution was to simply chop it down and replace it with "something worth-while." In my father's defense, it did project little presence for a viable future…but Richard, possessing noteworthy foresight for a 12-year-old, disagreed.

Scavenging a worn-out bicycle tire from the junk pile located behind the implement shed, Richard secured it to the spindly trunk, anchoring it tightly against a thick corner fence post, left when the rest of the fence was removed at an earlier date. It was a remarkable achievement how that maple matured, within three or four years showing no signs of deformity whatsoever...and today stretches 50 feet into the sky, completely dominating its section of the yard.

It was rummaging through old photographs recently and coming upon a photo of our farm taken in the late 1950s that triggered an outpouring of memories. Nothing advertises the passage of time with more clarity than the maturity of trees; the black and white photo rekindled instant memories of seasons past; that home-made swing dangling by a rope from an overhead branch of the russet apple tree. The trio of spruce trees towering above the south lawn perfectly spaced to allow the installation of a hammock, and whose lower branches were the perfect height for teenage boys to "skin the cat" or perform other gymnastic maneuvers.

I remember that all too short timespan each summer when the lilacs were in full bloom, their indescribable fragrance saturating the June air. Or summer afternoon get-togethers with relatives and neighbours, sipping a cool drink in the comforting shade of the maples. And not just summer; who couldn't appreciate the hushed beauty a line of evergreens projects, as the heavily laden branches bend beneath a thick layer of new snow...likewise, who could not be mesmerized by the glistening rime coating of a silver birch, backlit by a frosty February sunrise?

Trees are far more than simple landscape. Like family members, they become part of our lives and eventually our history. If a row of trees must be removed to widen a highway, or a century-old maple succumbs to lightning, windstorm, or some other whim of nature, the loss is no less similar than the passing of an old friend.

I'm reminded of travels through the southern United States many years ago, and being absolutely overwhelmed by gigantic oak trees that once lined laneways leading to magnificent plantations. Although many of these plantations along with their mansions were long gone, these stately oaks continued to govern their piece of earth as they had for 250 years in some cases.

Sometimes just a recollection of a single tree can ignite everlasting memories. I recall my mother reminiscing about summer vacations spent at her aunt and uncle's farm in Grey County. In their orchard grew an ancient apple tree ideally suited for a young girl to climb. The gnarled old trunk with its spreading limbs created a natural seating position for a city kid to dream away the hours. With only the sound of rustling leaves to interrupt the solitude, a delicious apple within easy grasp, and a book to read, it was heaven on earth. It's said for everyone there's a place in life where he or she wishes time could stand still...Mom always claimed this was hers.

Continuing to study the faded photograph...I observed how the two large maples that provided an archway to the farm's entrance 50 years ago still do so today. However, little else in this photo of yesteryear remains; the russet apple tree, the lilac bushes, the aforementioned spruce trees...all departed with the progression of time.

If a person were to glance across the driveway today, attention would focus on a forested chain of Colorado blue spruce that provide seasonal refuge for blue jays, finch, robins, chickadees, sparrows, and woodpeckers. Planted in the mid-1980s, these eight trees grew to a stage where they completely blocked our westerly vision of the highway... and frustratingly, what our neighbours were doing. They did however afford an excellent windbreak from prevailing winds, as well as provide a natural snow barrier.

This now 30-foot high column of blue spruce have replaced the orchard I knew as a kid. At one point this seemingly exclusive area abounded with pear and cherry trees, bushes of gooseberries, red currants, and raspberries. As well, four apple trees provided shade for cattle and a playground for growing boys. While I was still a teenager, a severe windstorm uprooted a couple of trees while time simply took care of the rest.

East of the house where our Holsteins once grazed is now lawn and serves purpose to a new generation of forested growth. Ash, locust, and spruce all exist in harmony...as well as a weeping birch under which our faithful dog for 14 years, "Happy," rests and a sugar maple, a final resting place for "Shrub" " the cat. In December of each year, this variety of foliage furnished an added dimension to the property when accented with the brilliance of the Christmas season.

A creek meanders through the property as restful as five decades ago. Brown and speckled trout, minnows, muskrats, scores of frogs, ducks, herons, and even the occasional turtle claimed title on that creek when I was young. On the creek bank, a large willow spread its branches across the narrow waterway offering an excellent fishing perch, or simply a vantage point to observe nature's inhabitants. We even had a swimming hole of sorts and a small waterfall built of field stone. During the late 1960s, the waterway was "upgraded" by the township, and we had no choice but to stand by and watch our special tree topple into the creek as the dredging destroyed its fragile footing.

Something that hasn't changed: the six-acre woodlot dominated by sugar maples at the extreme northern tip of the property. I recall as the crisp days of early October descended no sight more resplendent than those maples in their varying degrees of coloured splendour. Hardly an autumn passed that I wasn't reminded of that old poem by Wilfred Campbell we studied in public school.

Along the line of smoky hills the crimson forest
*   stands,*
And all the day the blue jay calls throughout this
*   autumn land.*
Now by the brook the maple leans with all its glory
*   spread*
And all the sumacs on the hill have turned their
*   green to red.*

Although not in recent memory, these trees were once tapped; as a small "sugar shanty," although severely dilapidated, stood at the entrance of the bush. Inside, the rusting remains of an oven were just barely evident. Little effort was involved, however, for the senses to recall a smoking wood fire and the sweet smell of sap boiling in the cast iron furnace.

When our family moved to this farm, the eastern and western boundaries were as variable as night and day. While the western perimeter was basically clear and open, the eastern property line consisted of a mixed wall of hawthorn, chokecherry, crabapple, and various other tree species, all jostling for position along a combination rail and barbed wire fence stretching the length of the farm. While a few maples provided a splash of colour in autumn, the most striking feature of this assortment of vegetation was the dozen or so elm trees that dominated the boundary's entirety from front to back.

When I was a kid, these beautiful tall trees with their straight soaring trunks were as familiar to rural Ontario as rail fences, bank barns, and gravel side roads. So familiar, we took them for granted...until the Dutch elm beetle invaded the province in the early 1960s...and within a span of a few years hardly a live specimen was left standing. These once stately trees with their umbrella-like canopies were relegated to no more than barren skeletons silhouetted against the eastern horizon. In their decayed state, the falling limbs became a hazard to cattle and machinery, and one by one ceded to the ripping teeth of local chainsaws.

Today, no evidence whatsoever remains of those glorious elms, as huge tractors pulling eight-furrow plows and 50-foot cultivators till the earth above that old fence line. Along with my own memories, only the occasional chunk of rotted wood that periodically surfaces...indicates it was ever anything else.

Harold Turner, security guard, 1970.

Woodington House resort, Muskoka.

Surge tanks at Eugenia Power Plant.

David and Mary, September 1979.

Doug Hamilton's '85 Pontiac Fiero.

Mom and Dad with Peggy and Hugh Hayes.

Doug Watt and David, New Year's Eve, 1989

Glen and Viv, 2002.

The Turner brothers, 2007.

Life and Laughter

I RECALL IT WAS A SATURDAY NIGHT IN LATE JANUARY WHEN MY neighbour David Hamilton phoned to tell me his mom had passed away. Marilyn was just 73...not very old these days. My first thought following the news was...I've lost a great friend. But I suppose countless people when learning of Marilyn's departure, lost something...be it a friend, mother, grandmother, mother-in-law, aunt, sister, cousin, neighbour, or fellow church parishioner. Marilyn's colourful life touched a lot of people.

My first introduction to Marilyn Hamilton dated back to a day in 1958, the year she and her husband Doug were married, and I along with my Dad and a couple of brothers was baling straw at their farm, which was located about a mile from ours. I believe my job was driving the loaded wagons to the barn. That particular job that particular day was significant as it began a life-long association with the Hamilton family. And the meal I enjoyed would only be the first of hundreds I'd spend at their table in the years to come.

Both Doug and Marilyn's families attended the same church and by 1953 the couple had been together for five years...ever since Doug was 19 and Marilyn 14. Their age differential caused such an upheaval among the conservative congregation a special meeting was convened to discuss the situation.

Part of the problem was Doug was already into the livestock trucking business and a dealer of anything else that might turn a dollar...so his character was in question from the outset. Marilyn, in their opinion, was simply too young. However the church consultation resolved nothing and they continued to date, although Marilyn stated from that point onward when Doug came courting, her father sat between them on the parlour couch.

I began working at the Hamilton farm in a semi-regular capacity when barely a teenager and what I remember most about Marilyn is how hard she worked and how much she contributed to the ultimate success of their farming and trucking operation. In the early stages of their farming career there were few automated conveniences, and when Doug was out in the fields or away with the truck, it was Marilyn who fed the cattle, forking corn silage into a galvanized wash tub and carrying it to the feed manger. It sometimes took a dozen trips to supply the amount needed.

Feeding cattle, sorting cattle, loading cattle, hauling grain, unloading hay, fixing fence, answering phones, taking messages, bookkeeping, cooking, washing, scrubbing, delivering lunches and refreshment to the men in the fields... were just a few of the tasks on Marilyn's job description.

In the house Marilyn was forced to do without a lot of conveniences most took for granted...like water. Because of the low position of the barn and well in relation to the house, it was "first come, first served," thus the cattle received first dibs on the water supply and during periods of high usage, often there was nothing left for the house. Marilyn simply kept the faucet turned on in the kitchen sink throughout the day in order to catch what she could when she could.

While writing this I tried to imagine how many meals Marilyn must have served in her 45 years on the farm. And how many trips did she make to the local John Deere dealer, hardware store, or welding shop to retrieve parts or repair something that had busted? Or how many cattle do you suppose she chased over the years? More times than we cared to count, we'd get a call that the cattle had broken out and my brothers and I would race to the scene, trying to head off the stampede before it reached the road.

Marilyn learned early in her married life that if she wanted something done around the house, especially in the busy planting and harvest seasons...she had to be creative and find a way to do it herself. I arrived one day to see a ladder leaned against the tractor loader and Marilyn standing in the manure bucket fifteen feet above the ground painting a second storey window.

When she had free moments, Marilyn made the most from it. Reading was her favourite pastime, especially if it pertained to British Monarchy, although she was fascinated with the history of most any country around the globe. But she also admitted enjoying "lighter" reading...books that perhaps fell short on literary substance...but countered with a "bit of steam," as she referred to them. My mother was the librarian in Palmerston for 20 years and Marilyn was one of the library's most prolific customers. Utilizing that dry sense of humour she employed so well, Marilyn would often say, "So, Mrs. Turner...what under the counter specials are you featuring today?

It's my belief most people missed the subtleties of Marilyn's humour. I don't think she herself had any idea how funny she could be. Most of her stories you couldn't repeat...and I don't mean that in a derogatory context... it's just that trying to repeat or re-create one of her yarns seemed impossible. What seemed hilariously funny when initially heard was simply lost in the interpretation.

I'd known Marilyn 45 years...or at least thought I did... when Doug passed away in 2003; but it was actually only a beginning. Doug and I had been very close and she realized that, but requested that we not lose touch as so often happens under these circumstances. Well, over the next few months, since I was co-executor of an estate that consisted of a dozen farms, an extensive line of machinery, livestock trucks, and hundreds of cattle, Marilyn and I would spend a lot of time together sorting out the details of his far-reaching estate.

I lost count how many trips we made to the lawyer's office in Elmira that winter, and after each session we'd have supper at the Crossroads Restaurant, just down the road. During one meal, Marilyn said, "Doesn't it seem strange to you that this restaurant serves only chicken 'legs'...nothing else? There must be a lot of legless chickens roaming around Elmira!"

It was once the estate was finally settled and the legal formalities addressed that Marilyn again stressed how important it was that we stay in touch. Thus began our "every other Friday" visits, where over a glass of Pepsi or some flavour of juice, Marilyn would share captions of her life.

How she moved with her parents and sisters and brother from the small town of Gormley, northeast of Toronto, to a farm in Howick Township near the village of Fordwich in 1950, and the chores she performed before going to school. "I grew up with manure on my boots." She talked about driving their McCormick International tractor or her father teaching her the mechanics of shooting a rifle..."a talent I got to be pretty good at," she boasted.

Groundhogs, squirrels, raccoons, weasels...it didn't matter...if they trespassed or in any way interfered with the day-to-day operation of the farm, they were extinguished. Noting my look of surprise upon hearing of these unfamiliar characteristics, Marilyn said, "You had no idea I was such a hillbilly did you! That was one distinct advantage I had over Doug. He was scared to death of guns but knew I knew how to use one!"

When Marilyn married and moved a few miles east to Wallace Township, her marksmanship continued the tradition of eradicating nuisance wildlife. If these creatures minded their own business they were safe...if not...they learned their lesson the hard way.

One particular raccoon had been harassing the Hamilton homestead for some time, clambering across the roof... "I swear it was wearing steel-toed shoes"; trying to force its way through windows, attic vents, and cellar openings was all part of the animal's nighttime adventures...until it got caught in Marilyn's sights. It wasn't long after that episode that the tenants who lived in the house across the driveway inquired if anyone had seen "Voizie," as they hadn't seen their pet for a few days.

Marilyn would expound at length on the many trips she and Doug took to Hawaii as well as a couple of tours to England and Scotland. Visiting century-old castles she'd read about in books and travel magazines was the ultimate high. Another benchmark was the excursions undertaken with her sister to foreign lands scattered throughout the world.

Marilyn always took great interest in observing the customs and traditions of these foreign countries...how the Chinese for instance served soup at the end of the meal and breakfast often consisted of fish and vegetables. Or how the Chinese administered population control: "You're allowed one child without penalty. Any more, the parents are punished by progressively reducing their wages with each child born."

Of course her humour was never far below the surface, recounting aspects of world travel not mentioned in the brochures, like using the so-called "washrooms" in some countries: "Toilet tissue is a valuable commodity and strictly rationed," Marilyn began..."so there's this lady standing at the entranceway of the washroom handing out toilet tissue the size of a post card. What did she expect a person to do with a little scrap like that?...especially if perhaps that fish you consumed at breakfast didn't sit too well. "

A majority of my visits with Marilyn were spent talking about her family or other people's families. Marilyn was visibly worried about her youngest son Dale and how he was faring while on a 10-week vacation in Thailand and Cambodia in 2012. But she was also fascinated and even a bit envious, as that part of Southeast Asia she had hoped at one point to visit herself.

Church – and religion in general – was a subject that surfaced frequently in our Friday afternoon visits. Marilyn was finding it difficult adapting to some of the more progressive changes in church music and dress code. "Paint me old-fashioned...but I believe we lost something special when we strayed from Sunday dresses, suits and ties...to shorts and 'flip flops.'"

An important part of Marilyn's life was collecting, specifically bears and dolls. She had scores of beautifully attired dolls representing nations from around the world, and bears of every size colour and shape. Some were highly collectable and obviously expensive, others "common" bears she may have picked up at Zellers because "they spoke to her."

If you were sitting in her living room, dolls and bears stared from every shelf at every level while dogs and other stuffed animals peered at you from the floor. Nestled among the dolls and bears were stacks of books, CDs, magazines, and photos pertaining to travel and Royalty.

When I think of my friend Marilyn, it will always be in a light-hearted vein. It was her sense of humour I will remember best and miss the most. The laughs we enjoyed over the years are infinite. "There's no better medicine than laughter," Marilyn once commented, "...unless you happen to be suffering from diarrhea."

Marilyn had always been a strong supporter of my writings, being as enthusiastic as I, if one of my stories appeared in some magazine. She was aware I was working on a book of short stories but familiar with the timeline of such projects, asked if she could read a few examples in advance. Whether she entertained some projection she might not be around...I don't know, but thus began a routine of taking five or six of my stories with me upon each visit and Marilyn would give her review. As her comments were always favourable I told her she wasn't a very sincere critic. I probably offered about twenty-five for her to critique.

The last words Marilyn said to me were, "I enjoy your stories so much...I read them all as soon as you're gone... usually twice." Next evening I received the call from David.

Marilyn stipulated in her will years ago she wanted me to write her eulogy and just recently said, "You know it's too bad I couldn't read my eulogy beforehand instead of waiting until I depart. I'd like to see what you have to say about me."

My answer was I actually knew very little about her before she was married and that she should write her own story in her own words. I remember her laughing and saying, "Oh I don't think so, David. All the things I've seen and heard and describing them in my words...it probably wouldn't get past the censor board!"

"All my life I've had this habit," she continued, "of saying exactly what comes into my mind and sometimes that doesn't go over too well in this world...in fact I wouldn't be too surprised if when I get to the Pearly Gates I find them locked!"

Well...I doubt that. I'm willing to bet even Saint Peter himself would say, "Oh, come on in...we could use a good laugh around here!"

And on a personal note...I hope there are copies of my books somewhere on the shelves of the Heavenly library.

Our Neighbours
Across the Road

B EN NELSON, WHO LIVES ACROSS THE ROAD FROM OUR PLACE, is a handy guy to have around. As the seasons pass and jobs aren't as easy as they once were, Ben, who's a young and healthy 20-year-old came to my aid last fall to help hang some sliding doors on my shed. The year before when I injured my shoulder, I hired Ben to pound in some 50 steel posts for installation of snow fence.

This spring, Ben was the man asked to help my brother and me carry a desk from my upstairs office down to ground level. The solid steel desk once resided in a Royal Bank from a nearby town and must have weighed 500 pounds. Somehow the desk made it downstairs without anyone being crushed to death. While I was working with the young lad,, it occurred to me the heritage our particular property holds for him.

In 1931, when the Great Depression was gradually but steadily securing its grip on the economic climate of North America, Ben's great-grandparents Wesley and Ruby Nelson purchased the farm and moved into the house where I lived for 57 years and where my wife and I have resided for 35 years, a house now well into its second century.

To this 100-acre farm in 1931, the Nelsons brought a son, Murray, Ben's grandfather. The Nelson family had a strong legacy in township affairs, Wes's father being the Wallace Township treasurer for many years. When he passed away in 1936 his son acquired the position and in 1952 secured the job of Tax Collector. A year earlier, Wes Nelson purchased a 100-acre lot directly across the road from their property where Ben's newly married grandparents Murray and Elsie Nelson moved two years later. It was here that Ben's father, Tim, was born.

Murray and Elsie lived in that house until 1966, when they purchased and relocated to the farm next door. In addition to a succession of renters, Elsie's sister and her husband lived there for many years, subsequently severing the house and a one-acre parcel from the agricultural property. In 1990, Tim and his wife Geraldine purchased the property, added an addition to the house, and built a workshop/garage. This is where Ben was born and lives today.

There are few dull moments next door as Tim Nelson is a helicopter pilot, a partner in an aerial crop spraying business based in Chatham, Ontario. Tim also teaches student pilots at an airfield in St. Thomas. At certain times of the year, company helicopters are almost as common as vehicular traffic across the road, Tim often bringing home a "chopper" when spraying in the immediate area or commuting to a new site. A couple of times a year he treats me to a bird's eye view of the surrounding countryside...an exercise that never loses its appeal.

On the last Saturday in March 1957, when I was eight years old, our family moved from Simcoe to Perth County, and that's when I first met Ben's grandparents. Murray and his father helped unload our household belongings, providing countless trips lugging furniture into the house. The milk cooler proved the biggest challenge due to its sheer weight and awkwardness but Murray was a big man and we quickly learned to appreciate his strength and stamina in such situations. Late in the afternoon when everything had been moved in, Murray and Elsie invited our family (seven of us) over for supper. "It's no trouble," Elsie insisted, adding, "it's so difficult to find everything needed to make a meal that first day."

When Murray's parents first listed the farm for sale, Murray didn't hide his disfavour. He simply wasn't comfortable with the idea of "strangers" living on the family homestead as this had been the only home he'd known in his 28 years.

While my parents were still negotiating a deal with the elder Nelsons, Murray always made a point of showing up during the proceedings. He'd offer subtle comments about the terrible winters they endured in this part of the country, or the year of the ice storm when they were without hydro for three days. Or he'd make indirect remarks such as "Are you still having problems with foxes killing the little pigs, Dad?" The day we unloaded our little Allis Chalmers from the truck, Murray commented, "So this is the tractor I'll be pulling out of the mud holes this spring!"

However, once Murray realized the farm was indeed going to be sold and we would be living across the road, he and Elsie couldn't have been better neighbours. Murray would lend anything he had and give a hand for whatever we might need. Murray and Elsie didn't have a television set, and as we'd just purchased one, my parents would often invite them over on a Saturday night. Dad and Murray would talk crops, weather, and associated farm topics as they cheered for the Maple Leafs, while in the kitchen, Mom and Elsie would discuss their lives and those of their neighbours around them. I remember my mother, an outspoken woman in her own right, saying, "I like Elsie Nelson...you never have to guess what she's thinking."

On so many farms of that era, ours included, times weren't easy. While Dad worked the graveyard shift one winter at the local textile factory to earn a few extra dollars, Murray similarly was forced to take part-time work in Kitchener driving a taxicab. My brother Bill would milk Murray's cows and haul the milk to the local cheese factory with a home-made trailer hooked behind whatever old car or truck Murray happened to be driving at the time.

Murray bought his vehicles at Shoemaker Auto Wreckers on the Perth/Wellington County line, about five miles from our place. For about $100 he could ultimately find one that would last a year or so. Some of the vehicles I recall were a 1941 Studebaker, a 1946 Chevrolet, and a 1948 Ford pickup. Those were the days before safety inspections so one just bolted on a new license plate and one was in business.

Insurance?...who needed it! Never mind that one could often see through the floorboards to the road below on many of these vehicles, or maybe you couldn't always count on the brakes to operate sufficiently all the time, but these cars were operated on back roads for the most part anyway. Knowing our love for old metal, Murray would sometimes take me and my brothers with him to the wrecking yard where we'd climb in and out of every discarded wreck we could find while he was searching out some part to keep his "$100 special" intact.

Of course Murray always had a "good" car too, a "Sunday car" we used to call them. At this time it was a '51 Chevrolet. Elsie worked at an insurance office in Kitchener and commuted back and forth, so through the week the Chevy was essentially hers. Murray and Elsie had one child at that time, Janey, whom my sister Vivien often babysat while Elsie was away. In fact Vivien was there the day Murray and Elsie received word from the hospital confirming that Janey had been diagnosed with leukemia. It was a tragedy felt by the entire community when she died later that year. She was but three years old.

The months following were especially challenging as our closest neighbours tried to adjust to life without their daughter. Trading the seven-year-old family Chevrolet on a nearly new Nash Rambler and taking a trip to visit relatives in the States proved to be only distractions. Returning to an empty house and a long winter only amplified their grief.

As difficult as it must have been, life moves on...with or without you. Murray engrossed himself in the operation of their farm and Elsie went back to work as well. Ever since she had been a teenager, "working out" had been part of life. Domestic help, clerical duties with an insurance company, secretary at Palmerston's only doctor's office, and chief bookkeeper at the local Case/New Holland machinery dealership kept Elsie occupied until retirement.

After Janey was gone, a steady job and time itself were probably the best, if not only therapy available. Although Elsie worked out continually over the years, her business career never took precedence over friends, neighbours and church affairs. If one were to define the character of Elsie Nelson...sacrifice...hard work...and faith would be the appropriate ingredients.

Meanwhile, Murray and Elsie continued to be the ideal neighbours. From each other's vantage point, we kept track of one another and what each was doing. If the car, tractor, whatever, slid off our slippery wintry laneway, Murray was there to pull us out. If the cows escaped from their pasture, Murray was the first to help corral them. If you were wheeling cement and needed an able body for an hour or two, Murray was your man. If we updated a car, tractor, or piece of farm machinery, Murray would be the first one there to provide a complimentary assessment.

But it worked both ways. If Murray needed help... maybe someone to drive the baler for a load of hay before it rained, or assist in picking a few stones or rid a field of mustard, there were plenty of "Turner boys" to offer a hand. In later years when I was farming on my own, Murray, while swathing grain, mentioned that some of my fields were kind of rough. "They could use a good once over with a heavy cultivator, Dave...at the end of the season you can use my outfit." So after the crop was harvested, I borrowed his 1070 Case and eighteen-foot cultivator and levelled the fields in question. Of course he wouldn't take anything... "Just put some fuel in it."

Even when Murray wasn't around, his presence was felt. Stretched across the full width of one of the sliding doors of our old implement shed, Murray, many years before, had painted in red letters a foot high: **DODGE, BEST CAR MADE, MURRAY NELSON, JULY 31, 1950.** That message remained as clear and legible as the day it was written, only disappearing when the building was demolished in the 1980s.

I often wished I'd salvaged that door, or at the very least cut out the printed section and gave it to Tim Nelson as a rustic memento of his family's heritage.

Of all the deeds of neighbourliness over the years, in my memory, December 1958 stands above all. Mom's family lived in Toronto and it was an implied tradition we hold a "second" Christmas somewhere within the Christmas season. This particular day, gifts were packed for Mom's parents and sisters while we kids geared ourselves for a bonus round of presents.

It was a bitterly cold morning however, and our eight-year-old Pontiac was entertaining severe issues about starting. So Dad and my brother Bill hooked a chain to the bumper (bumpers were tough back then) and towed the car out the laneway while the rest of us watched from the living room window. The Pontiac showed no indication of life, thus Dad and Bill pulled the stubborn vehicle all the way to the next block and back, a two-mile trek...with no luck.

Dad was ready to cancel the trip when the phone rang. It was Elsie Nelson. No doubt she and Murray had noticed the tiresome procession up and down the sideroad. They somehow knew of our destination that day and suggested we take their car. Dad refused the kind offer but Elsie insisted. "The car's warming up right now...and besides we'd hate to see the kids disappointed."

Murray brought the car over...the aforementioned Nash Rambler...familiarized my father with a couple of its features, wished us a good day, and walked home. It was a beautiful car... red and black and white exterior and a complementing plaid interior; did we think we were in style! Once home,

Dad filled the gas tank to the brim and returned the car. Dad tried to offer Murray some sort of monetary thanks but to no avail…"We were just glad to help."

The generosity extended by the Nelsons towards our Christmas so long ago was even more significant when reminded theirs was one of sorrow. One can hardly imagine the sadness of their Christmas that particular year with the loss of their daughter just three months earlier.

The kindness and sincerity of the Nelson family has carried on through the years; Tim and Geraldine seldom miss an opportunity to lend a helping hand or do a simple favour for the "old couple" across the road. And we always tried to reciprocate; I was honoured when Tim asked me to be a pallbearer at his mother's funeral a few years ago.

Geraldine has become one of my biggest fans when it comes to my writing endeavours, never missing a chance for book promotion to anyone willing to listen. During the summer of 2013, she and her sister posed on Facebook in their swimsuits to celebrate the introduction of my first book, lounging by our pool, each with a copy of my book in their hands.

The tradition of "neighbour watching" continues as it has for decades and from our verandah vantage point, we've watched Tim and Geraldine's children Ben and Holly grow from babies to teenagers and beyond, Mary never letting a single birthday of either pass unnoticed since the day they were born.

I guess it should come as no surprise, when Mary and I moved from the neighbourhood this past spring, that it would be Tim and Geraldine Nelson who'd host a farewell party. We had a vague idea the invite was more than just a "barbecue" but upon arrival were pleasantly surprised to discover in attendance close to three dozen neighbours as well as my sister and brothers. An enjoyable evening of food, refreshment, and conversation in the company of friends and family, a generous cash donation, kind words from well-wishers...all hosted by a great couple.

...But what else would a person expect from a family who'd reached out to offer a welcoming hand to another family that long-ago March day? Obviously the tradition of simply being good neighbours continues 57 years later.

More Than a Friend

I WAS WAITING AT A RED LIGHT ONE DAY WHEN I NOTICED SOME kids rolling tires around a vacant parking lot behind a gas station. These days when most every kid...and seemingly adult as well...have their eyes glued to their blackberry, blueberry, apple (some kind of fruit) computer phone, these kids caught my attention. A closer glance showed three kids standing in a circle 120 degrees apart, seemingly rolling their tires toward the centre of this imaginary circle. The nature of the game I deduced was directing your particular tire to the person opposite, without colliding with your opponent's tire when it passed through the circle's centre.

The scene reminded me of summer vacations when my brother Brian and cousin Doug Watt chased our own rubber tires down a gravelled laneway. A time in life when our greatest worry was that our chosen tire would veer off into the ditch, and in our short pants we would have to wade into the thistles and burdocks that lined the driveway to retrieve it; an ageless period of time dominated by automobiles and trains...and as far as the future...well it never crossed our minds.

> *Doug's father had a Plymouth, a dark blue forty-six, to start in misty weather often would resist.*
> *Take off the distributor cap prop up the hood then pray for sunshine...he'd done all that he could.*
> *Those were the years of the great "tire rolls," started by accident and just continued to grow.*
> *The rules were simple as the trio lined up, Brian clinging tightly to his big "Dunlop."*
> *Doug liked his "Goodyear" it was small and fast, but my "Firestone" and I often got the last laugh.*
> *The steel rails would beckon us a dozen times a day to come and watch the trains that passed our way.*
> *Black smoke and cinders sprouting from their stacks and us waving wildly as the crew waved back.*
> *If things got quiet we'd indulge in some sports then cool off with ice cream and "Freshie" by the quart.*
> *Underneath the spruce trees our conversation filled with dreams and plans of "go-cars" still yet to build.*
> *But everything cycles, revolves and turns, vacations are no different it's just something that we learn.*
> *The Plymouth's loaded and she's running fine, "Everybody ready?" it's leaving time.*
> *Jean and Johnny in the front seat, Doug in the back, surrounded by everything the trunk*

wouldn't pack.
One last wave and John puts it in gear...
"Goodbye...safe trip...see you next year!"

I looked forward to those two weeks more than anything else the entire year. I missed Doug when he worked a few summers in Muskoka, but thereafter began a series of regular visits with no boundary of season. When weather was fair, Doug would arrive by motorcycle. During winter months, visits were by rail courtesy of Canadian National. Throughout the 1980s, Doug and I relied upon Bell Canada to keep in touch as other commitments kept personal visits to three or four times a year, as by this time Doug and his wife Judy had moved from the town of Orangeville back to the city of Toronto.

I'd enjoyed those Orangeville years...less than an hour's drive away...as some great times were had. However I could see clearly their reasons for returning to the city. Judy worked at the Kodak plant in Brampton just 20 minutes down the highway from Orangeville, so her commute was reasonable.

Doug on the other hand was still working for the Department of Sanitation down on Toronto's southern lakeshore, a job he thoroughly enjoyed, although Judy believed he should be doing something more within his educational capabilities. This included a couple of years at University of Toronto immersed in subjects such as anthropology and environmental studies. Judy had a lot of friends at Kodak and she sometimes felt uncomfortable, even jealous, when her girlfriends would be boasting of the great jobs their husbands had and the successful lives they were leading and making it all sound so true.

Doug tried a stint at Kodak, working four to midnight in the darkroom. During those short days of winter it was dark when he arrived at work, then, after labouring in blackness for eight hours, he drove home in darkness. After a couple of drinks, he'd eat supper...it would be about 1 a.m. by then...watch television for an hour or two, then retire. Up at ten, do a few odd jobs, eat a late lunch, then in his words, "leave for the coal mine."

A regular feature of those difficult days was the constant arguments between Doug and Judy. There was no malice in their feuding, but rather a constant irritation brought on by an unhappy situation. Judy would yell at Doug for forgetting to bring salad dressing from the downstairs refrigerator. Likewise Judy would be reminded...loudly...she had neglected to refill the ice cube trays. I recall looking at my watch one time soon after arrival and saying, "Boy, that's pretty good...fifteen minutes before anybody got yelled at!" I said it lightly so it would be construed in similar vein, but hoping they'd notice what I and everyone else was seeing all too clearly.

It was finally decided that perhaps commuting wasn't their thing and a decision was reached to return to Toronto. By this time Doug had secured a position with the Toronto Board of Education doing something he always wanted... driving buses. If they hadn't undertaken that move, there's no doubt in my mind Doug would have become an alcoholic and their marriage would have dissolved. Back in the Orangeville days it wasn't uncommon for Doug to have a partially filled glass of some alcoholic beverage in every room of the house. There was no one happier than I when events began a decided turnaround for my best friend.

Beginning in 1979 when Mary and I married, a tradition of spending New Year's Eve in each other's company was initiated. Our 11th New Year's was ushered in with a great meal only Judy could prepare. Along with some fine wine we played "Win, Lose or Draw," laughed at old photographs ferreted from dresser drawers, and told and retold old stories. We discussed the plastic cars of the automotive industry, the airlines' poor safety record, the pathetic state of Canadian passenger rail service, our embarrassingly underfunded Canadian Armed Forces, the colossal mess of Toronto's traffic, and one of Doug's favourite topics...one we discussed and debated upon every visit..."the goddam gravel trucks on Highway 10."

We attempted to solve the problems of the Middle East and Ireland and other hot spots at that time as well as the dismantling of the Berlin Wall. We hoped that the U.S.A. would soon come to its senses and elect a Democratic president to office and Canada would likewise elect a Liberal prime minister. Closer to home we discussed what our friends, neighbours, and relatives were doing wrong with their lives and how much simpler the whole process could have been if they'd only thought to consult us. We talked about upcoming marriages as well as those already on the rocks, who had a new car, a new house, or a new job.

We reminisced about departed relatives and how their spouses had coped, pondering how our parents would handle similar circumstances when affected. Doug reminded us of the plans for his mother's upcoming 75th birthday; we watched a new year as well as a new decade ushered in from Times Square and agreed with our elders that New Year's without Guy Lombardo just wasn't the same.

Doug and I talked on the phone a few times following, and barring a terrible snowstorm promised to see each other on February 17th for his Mom's birthday celebration. Weather presented no such problems however as the day dawned clear and bright. It was one of those gorgeous mid-winter mornings of which poets write and artists paint. A frosty tingle highlighted the morning air, introducing a cloudless blue sky.

Around nine o'clock the phone rang. "That'll be Doug," I said to Mary. Doug had a habit in these instances to check on rural weather or confirm some last minute detail. Instead it was Mom. I commented on the beautiful morning but her mind seemed far away.

"I've got some bad news from Toronto," she began. My mind changed gears as the names of various elderly aunts and uncles surfaced...who would have guessed in a hundred years it was Doug of which she spoke?

Mom briefly explained how Doug and Judy had come home around 9:30 the previous evening. Judy went to bed an hour or so thereafter and Doug, as he often did, chose to watch TV.

About five in the morning Judy awoke, noticed Doug had never come to bed, and received the shock of her life when she discovered Doug lifeless in the same chair in the same position she had left him in a few hours earlier. While Mom informed me of all of this, I just sat on the sofa, my mind numb!...Doug was like my own brothers...possibly closer in some respects.

That third weekend in February was a difficult one. I took a couple of long walks with just my own thoughts for company, trying to get this tragedy into perspective. How could a 43-year-old person die of a heart attack? What sustained that weekend and the days and weeks following were the memories. They were countless. Even through tears I'd discover myself smiling when reminded of something we'd done or perhaps Doug had said. In the days after as old friends reunited, this seemed to be the underlying theme. Everyone had a "remember the time" story. It appeared only by grabbing onto a piece of the past did we feel we could face what lay ahead. .

My greatest feelings of inadequacy during that period were for Judy, feeling helpless in words or actions. As I was struggling to comfort her, she was worrying about me, knowing how close we were. Judy also had to deal with informing her mother, who was on vacation in New Zealand. She thought the world of Doug, and the sorrow endured on that long flight home is almost unimaginable.

Also I wished I could say or do something for Doug's parents. Aunt Jean appeared so fragile and vulnerable as if her entire world had collapsed...and I guess it had. The day she was supposed to be celebrating her birthday, she'd lost her only son. And Uncle John?...the day of the funeral was his 73rd birthday.

About the only positive aspect of those few days was renewing old friendships, mostly from those years when Doug and Judy lived in Orangeville. There was Brian and Phyllis, who lived directly across the street; "crazy Frank" and his wife Elizabeth. How Frank could make me laugh! They'd moved back to Toronto as well by this time.

...and Trish...a very special person I'd met through Doug and Judy nearly two decades earlier; what memories were rekindled when I saw her! In my eyes she hadn't changed...just as beautiful as I remembered. Neither of us probably expected to see one another again, and never under such circumstances.

However time passes and things change...and not always for the better; Scott and Mavis, who I always thought the perfect couple, were now divorced. John and Buffy, next door neighbours in Orangeville for several years, were killed in a car accident a few years back. Rudy Hoffman, next door neighbour on the other side, had gone on ahead, a heart attack victim. Readers familiar with my earlier writings will remember "Ed who wired the stove." Well he was gone too; dropped dead of a heart attack while barbecuing pork chops in the back yard. Less than a year after Doug's death, "crazy Frank" suffered a severe coronary. He survived but just barely.

During the reception following the funeral, one of my cousins said he felt he was at a family reunion, except the one person who hardly missed a gathering...wasn't there. "It seems very strange without him," he added. It sure did...and would for many family gatherings to come. Of all the epitaphs offered that week, none rang truer than that spoken by Judy's mother. "We have a lot of great memories," she said..."there just should have been a lot more."

I had a dream about Doug a few months later. Doug and I never talked much about an afterlife or what might be waiting out there for us...but sometimes without getting too deep and profound we would let our imaginations wander. We had this idea that we'd sort of float around in outer space for a while until another lifetime presented itself. I believe Doug had found that "next life" and through my dream was extending his final farewell from this one.

Our shared vision was that our next life would be a chance to correct the mistakes and disappointments of the previous one. Or maybe fulfil a dream that had been impossible for whatever reason the first time around. Learn to play the guitar or piano for instance, or drive a race car. Maybe swap stories with Tom T. Hall, sing harmony with Merle Haggard, or join the Tennessee Three behind Johnny Cash. Perhaps write a book or float over the Rocky Mountains in a hot air balloon. Maybe simply relive a great moment or period of childhood.

A great period of time in Doug's mind...was to be a kid again when life's greatest challenge was building model cars and airplanes and collecting Dinky toys and comic books.

A period of time I'd like to relive...maybe just once more to chase a rubber tire down a gravelled driveway with both my brother and best friend at my side...only this time maybe we could do without those burdocks and thistles!